THE LAST HURRAH

Stephen Cole is a freelance writer who recently returned to Canada after spending five
years in Brooklyn, New York. He lives
with his wife and son in Toronto. He is the
author of *Slapshots* and *More Slapshots*.

THE LAST HURRAH

A Celebration of Hockey's Greatest Season '66-'67

STEPHEN COLE

Penguin Books

PENGUIN BOOKS

Published by the Penguin Group

Penguin Books Canada Ltd, 10 Alcorn Avenue, Toronto, Ontario, Canada
M4V 3B2

Penguin Books Ltd, 27 Wrights Lane, London W8 5TZ, England

Penguin Books USA Inc., 375 Hudson Street, New York, New York 10014,
U.S.A.

Penguin Books Australia Ltd, Ringwood, Victoria, Australia

Penguin Books (NZ) Ltd, 182–190 Wairau Road, Auckland 10, New
Zealand

Penguin Books Ltd, Registered Offices: Harmondsworth, Middlesex,
England

First published in Viking by Penguin Books Canada Limited, 1995
Published in Penguin Books, 1996

10 9 8 7 6 5 4 3 2 1

Manufactured in Canada

Canadian Cataloguing in Publication Data

Cole, Stephen
The last hurrah

Includes index.
ISBN 0-14-023808-5

1. National Hockey League - History.   2. Hockey - Canada - History.
I. Title.

GV847.8.N3C65 1996   796.962'64'09046   C95-933111-5

Visit Penguin Canada's web site at **www.penguin.ca**

I'd like to dedicate this book to my father,
Frank Cole,
who drove me to the rink,
encouraged me to play,
and tied up my laces just right.

Contents

THE LAST
HURRAH

"Oh, I loved going in there to play against Toronto. Those games were wars. They hated us. We hated them. Did you ever hear the story about Toe [Blake] in Maple Leaf Gardens? Well, one night we were in there, Toe was changing after a game, it was winter, he couldn't find anything to wear on his feet. It was cold out, so he says, 'Bring me a pair of socks.' Someone brings him back a pair of white socks with blue leafs up the side. Toe, he just flipped. 'I'd rather freeze,' he says, then turns away. Then he goes outside in the freezing winter with no socks. That's the kind of rivalry it was."

—Montreal Canadiens forward, John Ferguson

Red Sweaters, Pink Bellies

I figured it would be easy to return home to Canada and hockey in 1966. All I had to do was leave my Brooklyn apartment, drop anchor in a good Canadian library, pore through some old newspapers, and...Mikita-to-Wharram-to-Mohns, I'd be there.

It didn't work—not right away, anyway. At best, newspapers function as road maps to their time and place, and you don't get anywhere just staring at maps. Finger-drumming bored one long library afternoon, I decided it was time to really go back home, and so fled Ottawa's Public Archives and an unspooling reel of microfilm from 1966 ("Cat Has Hot Rangers Skating on NHL Roof!" shouted a sports headline), then crossed the Chaudière Bridge into Hull to visit the old neighbourhood, Lakeview Terrace, a mostly English suburb that beards the French village of Deschênes.

It was an empty weekday afternoon, with everyone somewhere else. Soon I was gone too, transported back thirty years. In those days, if a lady on my street, Lakeview Drive, staring from a window, saw a solitary man on the road, she'd duck behind the drapes. Could be Father Ducelle. If it was the little priest, she'd hurry to the phone to warn ladies down the road. This moment of self-sacrifice often meant Father Ducelle was at the door before she could steal down to the basement.

"More coffee, Father?"

"No thank you, Madame."

"Fruit cake? I just ma—"

"Madame, how are things in the home?"

"Oh…fine, the boys are in grade school now. St. Médard."

"There are problems of a med-ee-cal nature?"

"Father?"

"Well, you have been in a marriage now sixteen year," the priest would say, smoothing his robe, "only two children."

Yes, 1966 was a long time ago. Quebec had two school systems: Protestant and Catholic. English were supposed to be Protestants; Catholics had to be French. As an English-Irish Catholic going to a French school, I enjoyed a special perspective on the province's ancient battle of cultures.

"What'd you do-oo," the old French nuns would ask in Religion, "if a Pro-test'nt came to you on a street and ask to give up your fate ["faith," I think] upon fear of the tor-ture?"

This I came to understand, after years of safe passage among Anglican neighbours, was a rhetorical question. There existed in my village, however, a very real religious war; one fought between followers of two hockey clubs: les Canadiens de Montréal and the Maple Leafs of Toronto.

I was a Leaf fan. Stretched out on the rug in front of the old black-and-white, watching Punch's boys win, I was happy as the last day of school. After a Leaf loss, however, I was inconsolable. The rug got kicked. Pillows tossed.

"Tch! Now, now," Mom would say, peering over Ross Macdonald's latest.

"Bloody refs! Vern Buffy hates the Leafs."

"Ah geez, someone's tired," Dad would groan, folding away the Ottawa *Citizen*.

I spent third period of most Leaf losses in my room, staring at the ceiling, the taste of defeat bitter as copper at the back of my throat. A loss to the Canadiens was really "the torture," for next day at recess I'd have to suffer a legion of red-toqued René Lecavelier impersonators (Quebec's Foster Hewitt), reliving every goal by kicking ice chunks into the schoolyard fence:

"Béliveau à Talbot, à Rousseau—Il lance, il compte!—Ah, bravo, Monsieur Rousseau!"

The morning after the Habs retired the Leafs in the 1965 semi-finals, I couldn't face the happy crowing in enemy camp, so faked sick, holding my breath every other minute to encourage a mottled sweat. ("Well, you're definitely clammy," Mom said, feeling my forehead.)

Years later, crossing Deschênes (now Vanier) Road, I remembered it was no easier being a Leaf fan here when my guys won. Standing at the edge of a wide, swaying field across from St. Médard, I remembered one of Toronto's Cup-winning springs—it must've been 1963 or 64—when I treated pals to an impression of my hero, Leaf star Frank Mahovlich.

"The Big M grabs the puck behind his net," I sang, sailing past crumbling, mud-crusted snowbanks. "Past Provost at centre—around Tremblay at the blueline—"

Before I could put the moves on Charlie Hodge, two older French boys, out for du Maurier in the field behind us, hopped the snowbank and grabbed me. Seconds later I was sitting in a swelling ditch, sobbing, my nicely fringed Davy Crockett jacket ruined.

It worked the other way too, of course. I remember a fall weekend, hanging with the Doran boys up in our neighbourhood, when we were surprised by a French kid from the village, wearing a crimson Canadien sweater, picking through a ditch (our ditch!) in search of two-cent empties.

"He-hey, what've we got here?"

"Ribbit. Ribbit."

We swiped his bottles, gave him a pink belly, then sent him packing to his own solitude.

What was a pink belly? Well, two guys held a prisoner down, while a third lifted his shirt and beat out a furious tattoo on his stomach. Couple minutes, his skin started to burn...presto! you had a pink belly. A pink belly was worse than a purple nurple (a hard tweak of the nipple), but not as bad as an Indian rubber burn: a slow, evil, two-handed twist of the wrist. Kid sisters passed out thirty seconds into an Indian rubber burn. It was believed the Iroquois gave Father Brébeuf a twenty-minute Indian rubber burn before the heathens tore into his heart. (And yet, nuns assured us, he never renounced his "fate.")

Myles Evely and I once gave Larry Pilon an Indian rubber burn for getting too cocky after Montreal won the Stanley Cup. Not a Father Brébeuf job. Just enough of a burn for him to shout, "Oiii, yoiii!" which is what French kids yelled instead of "uncle!"

Larry never got out to play much. He was mostly home studying. He received good, but never outstanding, grades. We called him Provost, after the diligent, sad-looking plodder on the Canadiens.

Other than the odd intermission interview with Ward Cornell on Hockey Night In Canada, or an Andy O'Brien profile in Weekend Magazine, we never encountered players off-ice. Still, we knew exactly who they were. Action is character, after all, and twice a week on TV, through a childhood of winters, we stared into the souls of these men. They were as real to us as the kids who pushed us off monkey bars or borrowed our yellow-and-orange Beatle 45s.

Maybe more real. As I progressed through school I recognized Canadien and Leaf archtypes everywhere. The kid who wore a tie to photo day and sponsored a foster child in India was Jean Béliveau. An Henri Richard character was quiet, dependable—married his first girlfriend. Ron Ellis types pitched in to help with props on school plays. The class clown who collapsed an EAT MORE candy wrapper to read EAT ME, then slipped it into Miss Krause's desk? Eddie Shack.

I know I wasn't the only one who played this game. As an eleven-year-old, I played defense like an old man. Not a twenty-five-year-old, unfortunately…no, a real old man. Although slow, I liked to think I had moxie. Was always headed in the right direction. One day I was in the change shack with the best player on our team, Charlie DesGagnes. ("Skates like the wind," Dad always said.) Charlie was French. We never really talked. Just nodded, said hello.

Except this particular afternoon.

"Stanley, got some tape?"

God, he didn't even know my name. I handed him a roll of electrician's tape. He did up his stick and pads.

"Thanks, Stanley."

"Stephen," I said, grinning foolishly.

"No. Stanley. Like for Leafs."

Of course. Allan Stanley, number 26. Stanley was slow as molasses in January, but a good player. An All Star, in fact. Well, good enough. At least he didn't say Duane Rupp.

Charlie went to St. Médard, too. But we never acknowledged one another in the schoolyard. Too complicated. And we were on opposite sides during the epic French-English snowball wars. Now don't go smiling and think, "Ah, snowball fights! High-spirited chums engaged in reckless fun." I was scared for my life during those battles. I saw a friend, Barney O'Neil, fall at The Battle of Lower Road late one Friday afternoon. Monday morning, he told us the Frenchies washed his face in dog shit. We believed him. (Mind you, we also believed Barney when he told us he had an uncle in Australia with a TV so big you could see "everything" on the actresses in the shower in Lifebuoy commercials.)

No, there was an edge of malice in these battles as hard as the grapeshot—gravel, chunks of ice—that the dirty-fighting French kids put in snowballs (we did likewise, reluctantly, to protect ourselves). It was the same with the Leafs-Habs' rivalry. "You know," a French Quebecer who now lives in New York told me, "we hated those Maple Leafs. And we hated anybody who liked them. We wanted to kill them!" I said nothing (but to myself thought, *oh, what I wouldn't do for a snowball right now*).

Anyone under thirty-five reading this must be confused: Montreal and Toronto hockey fans fighting; whatever for? To them, the rivalry must seem as remote as the nineteenth-century competition between the Hudson's Bay and North West Companies. Today, the teams play twice a season, and have met in the play-offs once in twenty-eight years. But if you came of age in Canada in the 1960s, or 50s, 40s or 30s…well, I think you understand.

"The thing you have to appreciate," Montreal defenseman Terry Harper told me, "is that all the players were Montreal and Toronto fans growing up. You listened to your team on the radio; they were your heroes. And if you were a Montreal fan, you fought with the kids who liked Toronto. Then you got signed up to play for the Canadiens or Leafs when you were a teenager, and you fought against each other's junior teams. Then, oh geez, you made the NHL, well, no one had to prepare you for a game against Toronto. Any time we played the Leafs was a special game. Everybody got all pumped up…. You could never get hockey that good anymore as far as I'm concerned. Never."

Agreed. But before lapsing into the kind of old poopism that would've had me running for cover back then, I should come clean and say that hockey wasn't perfect in the old days. For one thing, you never got to see the first period of a game. Telecasts began at eight-thirty, half an hour into the contest. (Official explanation: Teams feared ticket sales would suffer if whole games were televised, though we kids suspected it was all a CBC plot to force us to watch "Country Hoedown" at eight.) Also, four clubs made it to the post season, and Boston and New York were pretty crummy, so playoff races were over by Christmas. Finally, well, maybe rules weren't exactly fair. Prior to the draft, Toronto and Montreal staked out the richest talent pools in the world. (Until 1969, Montreal claimed the two best French-Canadian players every graduating junior class.)

"Lemme tell you something about your so-called 'great rivalry,'" Boston GM Harry Sinden told me. "Back then, the league was rigged to benefit Canadian teams. I get just a little sick to my stomach whenever I hear about the good old days. My God, those teams should be ashamed to take credit for their success back then. You know, the NHL used to have this regulation where teams could protect any player within a fifty-mile radius. Well, that was dandy for Montreal and Toronto, sure. But what about New York? What about Chicago? Christ, who did they ever get to protect? No, don't talk to me about dynasties."

But to us growing up it seemed reasonable that, from 1945 to 1969, Canadian teams won twenty Stanley Cups

(Montreal eleven, Toronto nine). Hey, hockey was our game. During the 1966–67 season, only one non-Canadian played in the NHL: Boston forward (and Duluth native) Tommy Williams. Maybe the sport wasn't fair to New York or Boston, but...well, who knew or cared? Where I grew up, Bruin and Ranger fans were as rare as albinos.

No, there were only two real hockey clubs, which made the rivalry more absolute. In choosing one team you made two decisions—the "agin" was implicit in the "fer." Not that you even made the choice. You rooted for the team your father and grandfather did. I dimly recall a living room conversation between my father and uncle back in the late 50s, the heyday of the Rocket Richard-era Canadiens:

"Geez, Frank, how you ever gonna beat 'em in Montreal?" my uncle moaned, emptying a foaming Dow into a huge beer glass. "Every Canadien player's got a hundred bloody cousins sitting up in the stands, ready to come down after the referee if a call doesn't go their way. Know what I mean?"

"Well, I suppose there's some truth in what you say," my father said, nodding gravely.

Dad got me a Leaf sweater for Christmas when I was seven or eight. That would've been 1961 or 62. In some ways I've never taken it off. I'll always be a Leaf fan (Lord knows, if I got through Harold Ballard I can get through anything). But I don't hate the Canadiens any more. Now, I pull for them every time out—except maybe when they play Toronto.

And I really wish the two teams played more. I miss the rivalry. I miss the sweet suffering of the annual play-off battles. From 1959 to 1967, Montreal and Toronto met in the playoffs seven times. Perhaps because the teams changed little from year to year (Toe Blake took centres Béliveau, Richard, and Backstrom into both the 1959 and 67 finals), these playoff encounters seemed to escalate in drama with every installment. By overtime of the third game in the 1967 finals, I for one couldn't take it anymore.

"Where you going?" Dad asked as I left the TV room.

"Bed. Listen to it on the radio."

I couldn't even manage that. Fluish with excitement, I'd turn on my pocket transistor every five minutes, bracing myself for the worst. Incredibly, the game would still be going. Finally, I snapped on the radio to hear the surf's roar of a crowd cheering.

Toronto won!

I raced back to the TV room to catch the replay of Pulford's goal. Had Béliveau scored, I would've stayed in bed. Maybe for a whole week.

I don't feel like that anymore about hockey. And I miss it. The Toronto *Star*'s Milt Dunnell told me that just prior to expansion, he'd get tangled in midnight conversations with drunks on the phone at work. "They're gonna ruin hockey, they're gonna ruin everything," callers would blubber. Occasionally, I've felt like blubbering, too. Then I slap myself and say, *c'mon, it's your childhood, not hockey you really miss.* There's a little of that, I know. But only a little.

"To me the Leafs and Canadiens were more than just two hockey teams," Terry Harper told me. "It was a way of life, you could say. The Canadiens and Leafs were all that you cared about in the winter.... I remember when I got traded to [Los Angeles] after being in the [Montreal] organization since I was a kid. What a shock to look down the jersey and there was no CH there." He laughed. "I thought it was permanent."

Just as we all thought the Leaf-Canadien rivalry would last forever. It didn't. The 1966–67 season was the last hurrah for a rivalry that sustained Canada through more than forty winters. The last time that hockey seemed securely, yes, perhaps even smugly ours. Those who were there will never forget. Those who weren't will never understand. There's not much the former can say to the latter, except to explain that for four decades there were two professional hockey teams in Canada. One of two hockey sweaters was passed out under the tree at Christmas. Somewhere along the way the dye from those scratchy wool sweaters must've seeped into our skins.

Crowd noise
Montreal mini-skirts

It was rush hour on St. Catherine Street. Stop-honk!-
and-go for blocks. Nervy cabbies lurched from stalled
lanes, insinuating mud-crusted Biscaynes into the
smallest cracks in traffic. Then, five o'clock sharp,
brakes squealed, windows flew down, and everyone
started honking, like when the film breaks at a drive-
in movie. Soon cars were backed up forever. Police
arrived and arrested a nineteen-year-old woman out strolling
St. Catherine near St. Elizabeth. "But I haven't done
anything," she protested. Police charged her with
disturbing the peace. Her thigh-high mini-skirt, they
would later tell the judge, had stopped traffic.

—Incident reported in Montreal newspapers,
October, 1966

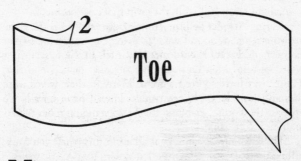

2

Toe

Making conversation with a cabbie on the way to the
Forum on Saturday, October 22, 1966 for the
Canadiens' home opener against the Bruins, you
might've made the mistake, perhaps as you saw a smart crowd
emerge from the Métro at St. Catherine and St. Laurent for a
show at Place des Arts, of remarking on how fast the city was
growing. Montreal's subway had opened the week before. And
the gleaming arts showcase was just two years old.

If so, you probably would've got back an earful: "Sure,
growing fast. Too fast! Place Ville Marie...the Autostade...
the big new Radio Canada office they're making on Notre
Dame—where's the money coming from? Right here, my
friend," the cabbie would say, lifting a hip and slapping his
wallet. "Traffic? Forget about it. Concordia Bridge, Lafontaine
Tunnel, just new. Still, Drapeau don't stop. Eye-ways going up
everywhere. [The Bonaventure and Decarie were under con-
struction.] And this new Métro? My God, what happens they
get a accident under there?"

Figuring it'd be a mistake bringing up tomorrow's civic
election, where Mayor Drapeau's powerful Civic Party was

STEPHEN COLE   12

going up against a chiropractor (Gilbert Croteau), or the
Bernie Faloney-George Bork Alouette quarterback controver-
sy, you'd move to a safe topic.

"So who's gonna win tonight?"

"Who they playing?"

"Boston."

A slight chuckle. "Well, they win that one for sure."

Nearing Atwater and the Forum, traffic slowed as the game
crowd streamed around cars, crossing St. Catherine Street
everywhere. It had been a nice day, high in the 60s. Still, it
was cool now. Men had on top coats over jackets and ties.
Those over forty sported fedoras. Many of their wives wore
furs and jewellery. No teenagers. They'd have long since
entered the Forum, grabbing the $1.25 standing room tickets
an hour before game.

"Think Montreal can take it all again this year?" you'd ask,
killing time.

After dressing down the team—Toe should get rid of
Harper, J.C. Tremblay made him nervous—the cabbie would
turn grave as he considered the question.

"Sure, who else? Black Hawk? Maple Leaf? Forget about it.
Only one team beat the Montreal Canadiens of 1966—"

"Un-huh?"

"The Canadiens of 1956. My God, what a bunch. I tell
you—the Rocket, Béliveau, Boom Boom..."

Even Montreal's vinegary cab drivers believed the Habs would
win their third straight Stanley Cup this season. Everybody
did. Dink Carroll in the *Gazette* had the NHL race handi-
capped: Montreal, Chicago, Detroit, Toronto, Boston, and
New York, with Montreal winning it all in May. In Montreal
Matin, Jacques Beauchamp figured it much the same, with
Toronto finishing third and Detroit fourth. The Montreal
Star's Red Fisher wrote that the only race would be for second
place:

"Canadiens, even at this early date, must be considered as
men with a lock on everything that will be rich and reward-
ing in the National Hockey League during the forthcoming
season," Fisher predicted. "Barring key injuries [Montreal]

should run away and hide from the rest of the league this season. The only way they can be stopped is to author a law against them."

The reporters weren't homers. Even NHL coaches believed the Canadiens would take first place. Some made concession speeches before the season started.

"Montreal's third centre [Ralph Backstrom] would be the number one guy on a lot of the other teams in the league," said Ranger coach Emile Francis. Chicago's Billy Reay elaborated, "Montreal is the only real sound club in the league. It has no problems. Toronto has an age problem. Boston has youngsters. New York has a problem in the nets, and Detroit on defense. [His own team was starting the season without Glenn Hall, who'd retired.] The Canadiens should run away from the rest of the league. With the centres they've got, they're too strong for the rest of us. They shouldn't lose five games all year."

Even Punch Imlach ceded Montreal the regular season.

"Montreal, Toronto, Chicago, Detroit, Boston, and New York," was how the Toronto coach called it. "But we'll take the Canadiens in the finals," he promised.

He was the only one who thought so.

Montreal's strength, as Reay and Francis suggested, started at centre. The season previous, Backstrom, Jean Béliveau and Henri Richard had all scored more than twenty goals (big Jean had twenty-nine, Henri and Ralph, twenty-two); this in an era when twenty goals was held to be the standard by which stars were measured. That one team should have three twenty-goal centres was extraordinary. (Boston, for instance, hadn't a single twenty-goal pivot.)

Rhyming off the Montreal centres' offensive totals only began to explain their importance to the team. The trio were the club's veterans; all had contributed to the great Canadien dynasty of the 50s. More important, their style—swift, effortless skating and constant motion—defined what was wonderful (and for other teams, frightening) about les Canadiens. The team went as its centres went, and its centres were always going. In flight, Béliveau seemed to enjoy one more forward gear than other big men. Dipping, darting Henri was harder to nail than a blob of mercury. Backstrom was faster still, with fewer moves maybe. The Canadiens came at you in ever-accelerating waves.

Toe Blake did his coaching by tinkering with linemates for his team's great middlemen. Béliveau normally played with butter-smooth Gilles Tremblay on his left. But in a rowdy contest up the 401 in Toronto, hatchet-faced tough guy John Ferguson might line up there. Then again, down a goal late, Toe could toss out a clutch scorer like Dick Duff on Béliveau's port side.

Right wing Bobby Rousseau, the NHL's number two scorer the previous season, with thirty goals and forty-eight assists, might be double-shifted on the Richard and Béliveau lines at home in a shoot-out against the Wings. But the feint-hipped winger was, alas, sometimes only faint of heart on the road. Next night in Detroit, Bobby might get only a few shifts, with scrappy Jimmy Roberts picking up extra time. Streaky Claude Larose patrolled Backstrom's right side when hot and sat next to back-up goalie Charlie Hodge during inexplicable dry spells. Against Chicago, Claude (players called him "Joe") Provost, the team's best checker, would spend thirty game minutes honed in on Bobby Hull's cologne. Left winger Dave Balon usually played with Richard. Pinball blur Yvan Cournoyer, the league's fastest skater, was trusted only on the power play, while Jean-Guy Talbot killed penalties and took an occasional blueline shift.

On defense, the number one pairing was Jacques Laperrière and J.C. Tremblay. The stork-like Laperrière had an odd, egg-beater skating style and an erratic shot, but when in synch, as he had been the previous season in winning the Norris Trophy, he was a superb two-way defenseman—a nifty passer who could lug the puck out, and a peerless defender who neatly broke up rushes with his extension-ladder reach. Although J.C. played as if hockey was a non-contact sport, he was, after the Hawks' Pierre Pilote, the league's best blueline playmaker.

The second defense tandem consisted of Prairie boys Terry Harper and Ted Harris. Hockey Night in Canada's Danny Gallivan inevitably referred to Harris as "Montreal's big and

burly policeman." Harper was one of the team's more intrigu-
ing players. Though not a good fighter, he was a fearless
brawler. An ungainly skater, he frequently took out-of-control
solo dashes up the boards, trying the boundaries of his skill
(and the crowd's patience). While he sometimes looked bad
in 6–3 wins over New York or Boston, number 19 was very
often Montreal's best defender in a tight contest with
Chicago or Toronto.

Gump Worsley, a Montreal boy from Point St. Charles,
was good in the clubhouse, and better in nets. The only shots
the squat, loosely packed goaltender couldn't stop came from
the press box. "Gump looks like a pound of butter that had
been left out of the fridge overnight," Dick Beddoes once
wrote.

With great goaltending, an efficient defense, and a smart
offense led by the team's superior centres, Canadiens were the
class of the NHL. Certainly, the team did nothing to discourage admirers during the exhibition season, winning eight of
ten. (One loss, a 4–2 defeat to Houston, Montreal's farm
team, must've intrigued Blake and GM Sam Pollock—rookie
Houston goalie Rogatien Vachon was the first star, and
youngsters Serge Savard and Jacques Lemaire looked good
scoring against the parent club.)

Unlike Toronto, where five regulars threatened to sit out
the home opener over contract disputes, Montreal experienced no labour problems over the summer. But then the
Habs never seemed to have labour problems. In his rookie
season a decade earlier, Henri's contract talks consisted of
brother Maurice imploring GM Frank Selke to let the kid
play on the big club. Selke relented and the contract was
signed without the Richards discussing salary.

Asked this fall if he was happy with his contract, J.C.
Tremblay replied, "It's enough that I get to play for the
Canadiens. I never thought as a child it would come true."

The allure of playing for the bleu-blanc-rouge extended to
more than the team's French players. As a member of the
AHL Clevelend Barons in the early 60s, Ferguson was scouted
by New York and Boston. But the Vancouver native, a life-
long Canadiens fan, waited for a call from Montreal.

"I had a chance to make it with another team, but Montreal is where I dreamed of playing," Fergie says. "Growing up you either wanted to play for Montreal or Toronto. And I aimed for the top, Montreal; the best team in the world as far as I was concerned. I figured if I didn't make it there, I could always try out somewhere else."

Fourteen Stanley Cups into its remarkable fifty-five-year history, the Canadiens had long ago cultivated the ideological fervour that distinguishes empires. Players were believers. In 1962, *Maclean's* polled NHL players to determine an all-star team. The magazine had to scrap the survey, however, when the Montreal ballots arrived. The team had filled every position on both the first and second team with Hab players.

Corporate culture only goes so far, however, in explaining success. The Canadiens' dressing-room slogan—"TO YOU FROM FAILING HANDS WE THROW THE TORCH, BE YOURS TO HOLD IT HIGH!"—and the championship banners that hung from Forum rafters never won a faceoff or killed a penalty late in a tight game. Banners don't make championship teams, championship teams make banners. According to Béliveau and Red Fisher, the individual most responsible for the banners Montreal accumulated in the 50s and 60s was coach Hector (Toe) Blake.

"Toe did not like to lose," Fisher says. "And, as it happens, he did not lose. He did not lose on the ice. He did not lose playing cards afterwards on the train. He simply did not lose. His energy and focus in competition was complete."

"Toe always knew the potential of a player," Béliveau recalls, "and he would never let you give less than your ability. This is very difficult over a long season. Very difficult. But he would never let you drag your feet. He was very good at motivating a hockey player. And even more important, I think, he was good at motivating a team—Toe could fire the team up."

Although brilliant organizational men, Selke (1946–64) and Pollock were reclusive by nature—grey, hand-wringing technocrats. (Here's Trent Frayne's sketch of Selke in "The Mad Men of Hockey": "A trim gloomy man of perhaps five foot three, with a funereal mien, and a soft high voice...

[Selke] sounded like a pastor visiting a covey of spinsters.") So it was left to Blake to breathe fire into the ranks. A complex man, who in Fisher's words "could be intelligent, thoughtful, funny, and cruel—sometimes in the same afternoon," Blake spent all of himself in pursuit of victory. "We saw him cry when we won and cry when we lost," Béliveau says. "He gave a lot to the Montreal Canadiens."

Toe could excite greater effort from his charges with a blistering dressing-room scolding.

"He had a volcanic temper, the likes of which I have not seen anywhere in sports," Fisher remembers. "The temper was always there and Toe would often be mad about something or other. But three or four times a season he would simply explode. And his anger then would be literally chilling. He would start yelling, at the top of his lungs now, and he would continue yelling for three or four minutes. During that time, his points would be made with brutal clarity. And the object of his displeasure would sit there and take it because he would have no choice... Toe's anger was a physical force."

Any kid who had to hand over a failing report card to a dramatically concerned father knows what it was like to be called into Blake's train car after a rough loss.

"I saw guys crying come out," J.C. says. "I'm not saying who. No, I'm not saying." He laughs. "Yes, me sometimes when I wasn't playing well, I cry going in. Toe was tough."

"You know, Toe was like a father to me, and I always respect him," Cournoyer says. "But I didn't understand him until I got older. You get older, you have your own children, you yell at them, sure. But why? You yell at them because you love them. Because you're afraid for them if they don't do what you want them to do."

Blake could also make his point with humour.

"Fascinating man," Harper says. "If we were lousy, most times he'd come in and kill us. But, God, I remember times we had a bad period, he'd come in and you'd go, 'Uh-oh, here it comes.' And you'd sit there watching him pace back and forth in the dressing room, staring at the floor. You'd be waiting for the explosion, and then suddenly he'd go into this act: 'Red Fisher is right,' he'd say with this sad voice. 'You guys look tired.' Then he'd fake like he was going to collapse and let his arms fall down to the floor. 'Oh, we're so ver-r-r-y tired. I think we'll just go to sleep now and let the other team do whatever the hell it wants. Because we're sleepy, sleepy.' Then he'd yawn. 'A-n-n-n-h-h.' Man, the players, we'd be rolling on the floor, crying, we'd be laughing so hard. Then we'd go out there and score three or four goals next period."

Harper's laugh trails off. "Man-oh-man, how did he know when to give it to us and when to let up? I'll never know. But he did. He was a great coach."

"Toe could play a team like a violin," Ferguson says. "Sensitive guys he would never yell at in the dressing-room. It might hurt their game. The only guys he ever yelled at in front of everyone else were Talbot, Backstrom, and me. Why? because he knew he could give us shit and it wouldn't matter. Also, he trusted us to make sure the other guys stayed in line. [Ferguson once dumped a pitcher of beer on J.C. in a bar when the defenseman groused about playing time.]

"But Toe also knew how to keep the game fun," Ferguson continues. "Say we looked a little flat; he might call me aside and say, 'You know what, I think Mickey Redmond has made this team, what do you think?' What he was doing was giving me the OK to give him the team initiation [a very, very bad haircut], so we'd go catch the guy, give him the business in the corner of the dressing-room, everybody would be hootin' and hollerin'. Then you'd look back at the doorway and there was Toe lookin on with a little smile on his face."

"When people ask about Toe," Béliveau says, "I say, 'Toe was so good because he was a players' coach.' I think it is important to have a players' coach in Montreal because of all the pressure. He knew how to coach in Montreal. Maybe because he played here in his younger days."

Blake arrived in Montreal in 1932. He'd grown up in a small Northern Ontario town, Victoria Mines, in a bilingual household. (The nickname "Toe" came from a baby sister who couldn't pronounce "Hector.") After playing a handful of games with the Montreal Maroons, he joined the Canadiens in 1935. In thirteen years with the Habs, he won a scoring championship and league MVP trophy (in 1939) and captained two

Cup teams while playing on the Punch Line with Elmer Lach and Maurice Richard. After a broken leg ended his playing career, he turned to coaching, eventually taking over the Habs in 1955.

"Yes, I think it help him a lot playing here," Béliveau says. "Toe, he knew about all the media and fan pressure. He kept the pressure on us, sure. But the fans, the media, he took care of all that. If you work hard and never embarrass him, he would never embarrass you."

Blake never criticized a player in the paper, Béliveau says. With the arrival of television, he was careful not to be seen berating a player on the bench.

"If something was wrong on the ice, Toe would have to change something, say something to a player," the captain recalls. "But he knew that maybe the television was watching. So he would look up and he would start yelling at the clock. Well, he was not mad at the time, or talking to the clock. He was talking to a player. He wouldn't say a name, but the player would know. But the fans at the Forum, and the television, they would not know."

Blake protected players until the last reporter left the dressing room, Harper remembers. "You'd be sitting there after a game, listening to Toe go on about referees. 'They stole the game from us,' he'd scream. 'See that play where Hull scored? Well, Harper was being held.' That'd get written up in the paper. You'd see it next morning at breakfast and say to yourself, 'Geez, Toe's right; wasn't my fault at all.' Then you'd show up for practice, Toe sees you, he'd scream, 'How the hell did you let Hull get past you?'"

Finally, players worked hard for Blake because he was an honourable man who respected the game.

"One story tells you what a fair hockey man Toe was," Béliveau says. "Before I play for Toe, I play against him, remember. In the early 50s, he was coach for Valleyfield in Quebec. Isn't it funny that my coach at the time [on the Quebec Aces] was Punch Imlach? One year I can remember I was going for the scoring championship with André Pronovost. It was the last game in Valleyfield and we were neck and neck. Toe put Pronovost out against me every shift and said, 'Here, it's up to you guys to decide who wins.' He could've put two checkers on me and made sure his guy won. But no, that wasn't Toe. He was a very fair hockey man."

Toe was outwardly in good spirits during training camp this fall. When physical fitness guru Lloyd Percival criticised what he called the Canadiens' lax training program by suggesting hockey players should run more, Toe shrugged and said, "OK with me. And next time [Olympian] Bill Crothers is training to run a mile, he can come skating with us for a few hours."

After camp scrimmages, Toe golfed with cronies like Danny Gallivan. During one match, Gallivan put his arm around Blake and said, 'Toe, the other day Beth [Blake's wife] told me that if you don't give up golf, she's going to leave you.' Without breaking stride, Blake took a fat cigar from his mouth and replied, 'Danny, I'll sure miss her.'"

In truth, Blake was in some distress. Betty had been fighting a losing battle with cancer for years. Because of the strain at home, and the relentless pressures at the rink, Toe sometimes felt his nerves shrink taut. Before, he'd always been able to control the wide play of his emotions. Now he wasn't sure.

"Toe started to think about retiring about this time," Béliveau says. "His nerves started to go. I can't remember which spring it was, but once in the 60s, we were in the playoffs, something happened I will never forget. We used to go up north [to the Laurentians] to a resort between games. One night Toe, he calls me into his room. And when I came in he was walking in that room back and forth like a bear in a cage. And I said, 'Toe, what's wrong?' And he said, 'Jean, I don't know, I feel like something is going to snap.'"

"The players, yes, we knew about Toe's problem at home," Cournoyer says uneasily. "We could see sometimes the struggle with him. But we didn't know. We were young. We didn't know about those things yet."

And the players figured Toe could handle anything.

"I don't know how many times I saw Toe swap two guys on a line in the third period and then have both of them score or make a big play," Harper says. "Or take someone off the bench who hadn't played in a week, stick him in and he'd score. He was incredible. And what a dominating personality!

Think of the guys who played for him—Rocket, Geoffrion, Harvey, Plante, Dickie Moore. Brilliant players, but guys with egos and agendas. But Toe, he kept them all in line. He kept everyone in line."

Fans attending Montreal's opener sensed something happening inside the Forum before making their seats. In the shuffling queues that squeezed through the narrow red and blue corridors, you heard an excited rumbling spilling up from the rink. (Maybe Fergy and "Terrible" Teddy Green were going at it before the game!) Finally, you passed through a smoky, basement-dank stairwell and saw for yourself. The lights, my God, spaceships must be landing! You had to screen your eyes. And the ice wasn't white, it was the colour of a cloudless fall sky in the Laurentians. Then you remembered the Molson's ads in the paper that week:

> Here it comes! Hockey in colour on TV!
> This Saturday and throughout the whole year!
> Brought to you by the Big Ale in the Big Land.

In September, Canada became the third country (after the U.S. and Japan) to introduce colour TV. Although only 60,000 homes had sets, the technology changed TV production. Without proper lighting, subjects took on the colour of parrots (viewers complained Juliette's blonde hair was green). At first, players grumbled, too. With fifty-four new 50,000 watt bulbs in the Forum's heavens, players looked like cadavers, they said. In Toronto, Johnny Bower complained he received flash-bulb blindness when looking at the clock. Until Punch ordered him to stop with the raccoon make-up, Kent Douglas applied burnt cork under his eyes. A week into the season, however, the whining stopped. "To tell the truth," Béliveau says, "it didn't take long before we ask ourselves how we manage to play so long in the dark."

Canadiens played the first period of tonight's game as if without instructive light. As the crowd took their seats after the playing of "God Save The Queen," Bruin forward Wayne

Connelly, an old Habs farmhand, found himself in alone. Gump threw out a pad to make the save. Seconds later, Pit Martin set up rookie Ross Lonsberry in the Montreal crease. Again Gump sprawled, turning the shot wide.

At the bench, Toe screamed at the clock. Why aren't we banging their little forwards? Put pressure on their youngsters on defense, for Chrissake. Half of them were kids—Bobby Orr, Gilles Marotte, Joey Watson, and Dallas Smith. The Stanley Cup champs were getting beaten by teenagers and rookies!

Midway through the period, Danny Gallivan might've tartly observed that the Zamboni would have little work in Boston's end, first intermission. Fans who had come to see the Hab centres whirl and gavotte sat with folded arms and watched Martin, Murray Oliver, and Ron Schock dance with the puck. The number 4 who yanked them to their feet was not Le Gros Bill, but a bean-shaved youngster who resembled a Steinberg's bag boy. Twice in the first, Orr, Boston's scrawny eighteen-year-old rookie, dazzled the crowd with slalom runs through the Montreal team.

Late in the period, Rousseau and Béliveau combined on a nice rush. The tricky Rousseau threw a shiver on Marotte, then slipped into the clear, until a scrambling Marotte either pushed or hauled him down. In some rinks, it might've been a push—no penalty. But the old Forum was a special place. Squat outside, cramped inside, the fifty-five-year-old barn wasn't much to look at. Aisles were narrow. Seats jammed together. But the closeness produced a real intimacy. Fifteen thousand saw the game with the same partisan eyes. And when a Montreal player was tampered with, the crowd stood and shouted with the same injured voice:

"HEYYYYYYYY!"

And so at 19:21, Marotte was sent off. Early in the second, the Habs finally tested Eddie Johnston (like Gump, a Montreal boy). Point men Rousseau and J.C. worked the periphery, setting up Béliveau and Cournoyer in close. Johnston was resilient, however. Boston seemed to have killed the penalty. The crowd settled back as Toe threw out Harris and Harper, a sure sign Montreal was falling back (the pair had scored two goals between them in as many seasons).

Then Béliveau intercepted a clearing attempt, slipped a pass to Cournoyer, and rushed the goal. Yvan fed the puck to Harris, who skipped a shot at net. Johnston crouched, found the puck, and moved left, but the shot glanced off the skate of Watson, Béliveau's dance partner in the slot, shooting into a naked corner.

"CCCCCCCHHHHHHHHH!"

The crowd ignited a second time when the goal was announced:

"Le but de Montréal, son premier de la saison, compté par numéro quatre, JEAN BÉL-I-VEAU!...avec l'aide de TED 'ARR-IS!...et Y-VAN COURN-OYER!"

Béliveau skated to the timekeeper and shook his head. "Change the goal to Harris. The puck did not hit me. It hit Watson," the former altar boy dutifully informed the official.

The Forum sagged when it was announced that Harris had scored. Little matter, Montreal was flying now. The Balon-Richard-Provost line swirled the Boston net a full minute. When Johnston finally jumped on the puck, Orr and Marotte staggered off as if they'd spent the shift in a revolving door. Then J.C. feathered an outlet pass to Rousseau, who flew down the right side, turned Marotte inside out, and golfed a shot over Johnston's shoulder. (When the goal was announced it wasn't credited to Bobby Rousseau, but to "numéro quinze, R-R-ROBER-R-R-RT R-R-ROUSSEAU!")

Montreal controlled the rest of the period, outshooting Boston 14–9. While Watson scored with five minutes left to ruin Worsley's shut-out, the Canadiens seemed to have the game in hand, were finally playing like—well, like the Canadiens.

Second intermission, a young fan with a few Royal Crown colas under his belt might feel the need to seek out the facilities. Leaving his two-dollar terrace seat above the Montreal net (the whites), he'd reluctantly head for a lobby washroom. In describing the old Forum, writers inevitably talk about the building's great history—the banners hanging from the rafters—or the ambience, the sweet tension that gripped the place game night. But a kid making his first visit to the Forum remembered the washrooms. The ammonia reek had you blinking before you hit the door. By the time the crushing mob swept you inside that industrial aroma was spiced by crosscurrents of Export A and Brylcreem. There was no good air to breath. You couldn't think either. Voices echoed off sweating cement walls in every direction until it seemed there were 500, not fifty men in with you.

Where were the urinals? Why was the tide pulling you to the middle of the room? At the end of the line was a spectacle twelve years on Montreal's West Island couldn't have prepared you for: a grey fountain two-and-a-half feet high and eighteen, maybe twenty feet in circumference, into which a wide circle of maybe forty loudly chattering men were peeing, crossing swords in fact, as they discussed the fine points of Rousseau's brilliant scoring dash. In the fifty-five-year history of the Forum, not one kid ever washed his hands afterwards. He was in too big a rush to leave.

Bruins enjoyed a territorial advantage in the third. Orr made some nice rushes. The Lonsberry-Martin-Westfall line played with speed and imagination. But Montreal's defense, particularly Harris and Harper, kept attackers outside. And Joe Provost, with his funny sitting-down skating style, blanketed Bruins' only sniper, Johnny Bucyk. After utility forward, Léon Rochefort (playing tonight with Backstrom and Ferguson), deflected a Harper shot past Johnston, Canadiens turned turtle and coasted to a 3–1 win.

In some ways, Montreal's competent final twenty minutes were more distressing to fans than the team's careless first period. Sure, the defense looked good. Worsley was solid. But where was the offense? Big Jean mishandled the puck a few times. (In Monday's paper we'd learn he had a bad thumb.) Henri and Backstrom seemed content to cover their men. Where was the passion? Other than Rousseau, nobody was flying. Habs played professional, "no mistakes" hockey. Yes, they'd won. But in guarding the lead in the third the team didn't look like itself. In fact, it looked a lot like—ugh! Toronto. A quarter of the opening night crowd were out the door before the siren sounded to end the game.

MONTREAL
Goal—Worsley, Hodge
Defense—J.C. Tremblay, Harris, Laperrière, Talbot, Harper
Forwards—Béliveau, Cournoyer, Provost, Richard, Rousseau,
Balon, Backstrom, Larose, Ferguson, Rochefort, Roberts

BOSTON
Goal—Johnston, Parent
Defense—Orr, Marotte, Green, Smith, Woytowich, Watson
Forwards—Oliver, McKenzie, Bucyk, Martin, Westfall, Lonsberry,
Schock, Connelly, Murphy, Dillabough, Hodgson

FIRST PERIOD
No scoring
Penalties—Harper 7:47; Marotte 19:21

SECOND PERIOD
1. Montreal, Harris 1st (Cournoyer, Béliveau) 1:11
2. Montreal, Rousseau 1st (J.C. Tremblay) 8:18
3. Boston, Watson 1st (Connelly) 14:30
Penalties—Orr 7:43, Harper 18:49

THIRD PERIOD
4. Montreal, Rochefort 1st (Harper) 5:25
Penalties—Worsley (served by Larose) 14:52

Shots on goal
Boston	12	9	12 —	33
Montreal	8	14	7 —	29

In the six-team NHL, clubs played weekend home-and-home
series. Because the league stretched no further west than
Chicago, rail travel was possible. After the game, teams
dragged themselves onto a train at Queen Elizabeth Station
for Boston. In the first hours of a trip, players talked over the
game while gargling smuggled beer. Sometimes there was
horseplay. Talbot, Ferguson, Provost, and Backstrom once tip-
toed onto the baggage car and liberated a prize rooster GM
Selke was importing for use on his chicken ranch.

Toe played cards in the front car with reporters Fisher and Beauchamp. He looked the other way at shenanigans. After all, he'd fooled around in his playing days. One night in the 30s, he surprised a squeamish roomie by tucking a few live eels under the covers of his bed.

Only Ferguson ever had the nerve to play pranks on Blake.

"What I'd do was let him get all caught up in a card game," Fergy remembers. "Then I'd start turning up the heat in the car a little. Toe would start getting a little uncomfortable, take off his hat and loosen his tie. Then I'd turn it up full blast. He'd take off his coat. 'Boy, it's hot in here,' he'd say. After a while, he'd really start boiling. Finally, he'd figure it out.

"'FERGUSON!' he'd scream."

There were, however, no monkeyshines after a Hab loss.

"Oh, Christ, no," Ferguson laughs. "You didn't even want to look at Toe after a loss, let alone talk to him. A prank? Never."

The Sunday game in these weekend home-and-home series often produced exciting, play-off calibre hockey. Feuds escalated from one match to the other. Also, two losses in a row to the same team was somehow worse than consecutive losses to different teams. The latter meant you were in a slump. To be swept, however, was a humiliation, indication the team lacked character. Maybe changes had to be made.

One Bruin rookie in particular worried about being sent down.

"That season was my first year coaching Boston," Harry Sinden once said. "And I figured if I didn't get the team into the playoffs I might be out. Back then the Bruins had spent four or five years in last place. Then the year before, they finished fifth, and it was considered a real accomplishment. Now people expected us to make the playoffs because we finally had our saviour…"

Boston had been waiting for this saviour since 1960. That's when Bruin boss Lynn Patrick and junior team GM Hap Emms happened upon a tiny eleven-year-old flying circles around boys three years his senior in a minor hockey tournament in Gananoque, Ontario.

"See what I see?" Emms asked Patrick.

"I see what you see. Who is he?"

Emms inquired after the little Parry Sound defenseman, then reported back to Patrick.

"That number two is Bobby Orr. Nobody's sponsoring him."

Two years later, Orr was with Emms' Oshawa Generals. In 1964, while Boston was in the midst of a five-year slide that saw the team win 104 of 420 games, the saviour scored his twenty-eighth, twenty-ninth, and thirtieth goals on the last game of the schedule to break Laperrière's junior record for goals in a season by a defenseman.

He was fifteen years old.

While Orr was a General, Emms told reporters, "I wouldn't trade him for the whole Maple Leaf team. He's worth a million dollars." Three summers later, as the new GM of the Bruins, he cruised down Lake Huron into Sarnia in a forty-two-foot cabin cruiser to meet with Orr, his parents, and the player's agent, Alan Eagleson.

Emms welcomed the Orr contingent onto his boat, made sure everyone had drinks, then opened negotiations by offering the rookie an $8,000 first year salary, plus a $5,000 signing bonus.

"Thought you said he was worth a million dollars?" Eagleson snorted. The agent wanted a $30,000 first-year deal.

"That's impossible," Emms countered. "Hull, Howe and Béliveau are only getting $40,000, and they've all been stars in the league for years."

"Hockey players are underpaid," Eagleson snapped. "How about all the $100,000 bonus babies in other sports: Gail Goodrich, Cazzie Russell, Nate Thurmond in basketball; Joe Namath, Tucker Frederickson, Craig Morton, Jack Snow, and Tommy Nobis in football." The Eagle peeled off a hundred names of youngsters who'd emerged from colleges and minor leagues to command six-figure deals. By the time he got to Rick Reichardt's big contract with the Los Angeles Angels, Emms knew he was sunk. Six hours later the GM finally wobbled down the plank off his boat looking for a phone to call Boston to OK a two-year $70,000 contract.

Orr proved he was worth it the moment he took the ice.

"I guess I was a little nervous his first game in the exhibition season," remembers Sinden. "Geez, you'd heard so much about him, and everyone in Boston had such high hopes, you just prayed he'd be as good as everyone said. But I knew right away, that first exhibition game against the Leafs, in London, Ontario. I think the score was one-all, and Bobby skated circles around everyone, and was far and away the best player on the ice."

"First time I saw Orr, I was coming down the wing on him," Geoffrion recalled. "He was skating faster than me backward. I see I can't get around him so I wind and shoot. He falls and blocks the shot. I stop then turn to chase him. I look up, he's twenty yards the other way. I been playing hockey a long time, but I never saw anyone move like that."

As usual, the back-end of the weekend series was the better contest. Bruins, wearing their hornet-coloured home uniforms, played with speed and determination. Oliver and Martin were flying. Little Pie McKenzie delighted the crowd with reckless hunting trips into corners after Montreal's big defensemen. Green and the cement-hipped Marotte threw punishing checks. And in a brilliant first period rush, the saviour drew astonished gasps with hummingbird dekes around Backstrom and Harper.

Montreal was better, too. Henri and Backstrom found their legs. The defense coolly managed the furious Boston onslaught. And Gump erased whatever mistakes teammates made. The goalie with the bowling-ball waistline looked particularly good turning aside early chances by Bucyk and Marotte. A tip-in off a rebound by Martin was the only shot to elude him in the first forty minutes.

Blake also enjoyed a good night. Seeing his guys outskated, he juggled players, replacing the lumbering Rochefort with a frisky Larose. Seconds into his first shift of the season, number 11 collected a Ferguson pass and drilled a thirty-five-footer between Johnston's legs.

Another Blake move led to a second-period goal. To further increase speed, Toe gave Cournoyer a regular turn with Béliveau and Rousseau. First shift, the trio blitzed Green and Smith, forcing a fumble. Rousseau stepped between the defenseman and fired a low hard shot past Johnston.

"Blake was head and shoulders the best coach in the league when I got here," Sinden says today. "Just to watch him run a team was beautiful. He saw everything. As an opposition coach if you saw one of their defensemen looked weak, you'd say something to your guys. Next shift, he wasn't there. If anybody on that ice made a mistake, didn't matter if it cost the Canadiens or not, he was on the bench to think about it a while. And the way he played his bench was wonderful to watch. So fluid. And you never caught him out. He always had the right match out there."

Down 2–1 going into the third, the Bruins redoubled their efforts. With the drop of the puck, they were all over the Canadiens, forcing Montreal to circle the wagons.

Significantly, Orr was getting more ice time.

"What Bobby brought to the team was something it never had. Something only the superstar can bring—an ability to change the course of a game by himself," Sinden says. "If we were down a goal or two, we figured he could get us back. It's a lot easier playing the game when you've got the best player on the ice."

At four minutes, Ferguson tried to relieve pressure by dumping the puck. Orr saw what number 22 was thinking (something only saviours can do) and moved in. After snaring the clearing pass at the blueline, he turned and threw his hands in a furious downward arc, bringing his stick down like a scythe. No one saw the puck until, eighty feet later, it bulged the twine over Worsley's left shoulder.

The first goal of Orr's career tied the game. It also delayed action for three minutes as the 13,909 in attendance hopped around, cheered, threw things, and generally deported themselves like happy fools in love.

"Well, people in Boston had been waiting a long time for Bobby to get there," Sinden remembers. "And I think everyone felt that that goal was maybe the start of something pretty special."

The Canadiens regained their poise after Orr's goal, and for ten minutes the teams traded frantic rushes. Then, with time running out, Bruins got a break: Roberts was tossed for hauling down Bucyk. The crowd moved to the edge of their seats as Orr and the Bruin power play took the ice.

Backstrom won a face-off in Montreal's end. The puck was cleared. Boston regrouped at centre. Oliver grabbed a pass and circled behind the red line. Moving into the Montreal zone he threw a blind pass in Orr's direction.

But Orr wasn't there. Jean-Guy Talbot was. As the sellout crowd swallowed its scream, the veteran penalty killer put his head down and raced in on Johnston. Thirty feet from the net, he looked up and buried a low shot in off the post.

Montreal won 3–2.

In the Boston dressing room after the game, thirty-three-year-old Harry Sinden tried to make sense of his team's weekend. "I thought we played really well tonight," he said, shaking his head. "I thought we weren't too bad last night either. But what do we have at the end of it all?"

Nothing, Blake knew. As the Canadien train rocketed toward Montreal and into Monday morning, Toe had all four points in his back pocket. Neither win had been great. But they were wins. What else mattered?

FIRST PERIOD
1. Montreal, Larose 1st (Ferguson, Backstrom) 11:23
2. Boston, Martin 2nd (Murphy) 14:02
Penalties—Westfall 7:06; Marotte 10:06; Richard 15:06; Ferguson 17:01

SECOND PERIOD
3. Montreal, Rousseau 2nd, 8:16
Penalties—Harris 3:40; Béliveau, Marotte 19:13

THIRD PERIOD
4. Boston, Orr 1st 4:13
5. Montreal, Talbot 1st 17:55
Penalties—Rochefort 6:31; Roberts 17:21

Shots on goal
Montreal: 6   11   6 — 23
Boston: 8   13   10 — 31

Crowd noise
Toronto principles

Howard Szafer, a fifteen-year-old grade eleven student at Bathurst Heights, was banished to a hallway desk for the first weeks of classes. His father, Samuel, a Polish immigrant working in a clothing factory, threatened to whip him. Betty, his mother, tried bribing him with money and tears. Still, Howard refused to trim his collar-length hair. Principal J. Wilkie Davey defended Howard's expulsion by saying, "Education must develop a followership as well as leadership…the very qualities insisted upon by business and industry."

—October item in Toronto newspapers.

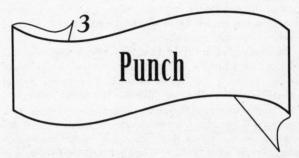

3

Punch

On the evening of October 27, 1966, more than 10,000 Torontonians gathered at Nathan Phillips Square. It took an hour to get to the front of line, but no one complained; it was a nice night—windbreaker chilly with a three-quarter moon. Besides, the city was handing out free hot dogs. As you got closer you could hear kids squeal, "It's terrific"…"it looks like a propeller"…"It looks like a sick mushroom."

"It" was "Three Way Piece No. 2—Archer," a bronze sculpture by British artist Henry Moore. Mayor Philip Givens committed civic funds to obtaining the piece in the spring, but after council rejected the $140,000 price tag, Givens raised money privately. Still, the Archer remained controversial. "Masterpiece? Mushroom?" The Toronto *Star* asked in a banner front-page headline. Givens' rival, controller William Dennison promised to make the "abomination" an election issue.

For Dennison, the Archer represented all that was distressing about modernization. "A $140,000 piece of sculpture— and even the man who made it didn't understand it!" he moaned. In his mayoralty campaign, Dennison attacked both the Archer and Mayor "Go Go" Givens' declared intention to make Toronto a "booming, dynamic, pulsating city." Warned Dennison, "Toronto may be growing too large for its own good."

The sixty-one-year-old speech therapist's words stirred the fears of the electorate. Two months later, Go Go was gone. Dennison was mayor. Once again, Toronto, a city of round holes, had rejected a square peg.

Months earlier, art dealer Dorothy Cameron had exhibited a series called Eros 65, featuring drawings by Harold Town, among others, in her Yonge Street gallery. Pierre Berton hailed the exhibit, declaring "Toronto has finally grown up." Days later cops raided the joint. Cameron was charged with obscenity. "Most of the drawings...depict scenes of pre- and post-intercourse," prosecution charged in court. Defense suggested, "every adult could be described as being in a state of pre- or post-intercourse." The judge was not amused. Cameron was convicted and fined.

Despite public censure, the square pegs seemed to be gaining. On weekends, thousands of hippies and day trippers crowded the boutiques and coffee houses of Yorkville, the candy-coloured youth village north of Bloor and Yonge. Late at night, the honeyed reek of marijuana wafted from washrooms of folk clubs like The Penny Farthing, Seven of Clubs, and The Riverboat. Two, three o'clock, Sunday mornings, teenagers with Rubber Soul haircuts were still out roaming the corner of Bloor and Yonge.

While most kids evaded police, they didn't escape the disapproving eye of the Toronto media. The fall of 1966 saw an anti-drug crusade in city papers, particularly the Star. There, respected drama critic Nathan Cohen made an unhappy "Visit to [LSD guru] Timothy Leary's 'church,'" while staff writer Peter Gzowski conducted an investigative series on "young people with long hair and short morals." In the Globe, Allen Spraggett answered the question: "LSD (MESSIAH OR MENACE?)" Maybe the most frightening report on the drug peril came from a rare pro-dope article in Maclean's from actress Pam Hyatt, entitled "How LSD Saved My Marriage":

> ...The walls took on many colours. Then pictures—
> of spires, birds' plumage, feathery trees—came with
> incredible swiftness.... I had reached the very depth,
> engulfed in hatred. Now I was killing my own father,
> plunging a knife.... Now a tremendous love came over
> me, and I felt a whole woman, understanding the dig-
> nity of my role as woman, wife and mother.

Reading Hyatt's testimonial, Punch Imlach might've been tempted to drop acid in water coolers all over Maple Leaf Gardens. I need something to get people in line, the GM-coach must've figured on the eve of his team's opener. Carl Brewer was playing for Canada's national team. Defenseman Bob Baun and half the offense, Frank Mahovlich, Bob Pulford, Dave Keon, and Eddie Shack were unsigned. Owner Stafford Smythe was meddling again, pushing for the promotion of green tomatoes like Mike Walton. Everyone wanted Punch to employ more kids. With nine players over thirty, Leafs were on the other side of the mountain, experts said. Jim Coleman at the *Telegram* had them finishing fifth. Same with Dick Beddoes at the *Globe and Mail*.

But even the youngsters were griping. Walton refused to report to Rochester. Wayne Carleton complained the exhibition season was too demanding. Brian Conacher waltzed into Imlach's office and calm as you please demanded a two-year, $30,000 contract or else he was going to school. None of them with their skates wet and they were telling Imlach, coach of three Cup winners, how to run things. Well, they could all go peel an eel as far as Punch was concerned—rookies, unsigned veterans, reporters, ownership...all of 'em.

Punch's problem this autumn was simple yet profound: He was a fierce round holer, an up-from-the-bootstraps guy whose only jobs had been coaching and bossing soldiers. (He'd also dabbled in banking before and after his years as a second lieutenant in His Majesty's service.) In his employ were a growing number of square pegs—free-thinking professional men. Many had attended university. Most had careers, were themselves bosses outside hockey.

"Lot of the guys on the team [in the 60s] were making

more money on the stock market than playing hockey," Baun says today.

Red Kelly had served as a Liberal M.P. for York West under Lester Pearson. Mahovlich just started a travel agency. Tim Horton had his donut chain. Baun was a cordon bleu chef and wine connoisseur. "Players usually let me order when we're in the sophisticated French restaurants," he told *Hockey Illustrated*. "I've often been asked which wines I prefer. My favourite Bordeaux is Château Pontet Canet, 1961. However, if you like a white Burgundy, as I do, I prefer Meursault, 1947. A red Burgundy I highly recommend is Beaune Clos des Moches, 1949."

Imlach made a show of being unimpressed by his players' diverse interests. "Treat 'em all the same—badly," he said. When asked his coaching philosophy, Punch liked to tell the following story:

"Long time ago there was this fella who raised mules. Guy was the best in the business. People from all around came to him. 'How come your mules are so good?' they asked. 'Simple,' he says, 'I treat every mule with the milk of human kindness. Want something done, I whisper sweetly in their ears. Afterwards, always give 'em a carrot. That's why they're so faithful.' Guy out shopping for a mule, he hears this, he says, 'Terrific, I'll take two.' He takes the team to his farm, goes to plow a field or something…animals won't budge. Back he goes to the mule salesman to complain. 'Whisper in their ears?' salesman asks. 'Unhunh.' 'Give 'em carrots?' 'Yeah, tried that too.' 'Geez, better have a look,' salesman says. So off he goes to the guy's farm. Sure enough, he whispers in the lead mule's ear, gives him a carrot, then he reaches back and smack! wallops it with a plank right across the forehead. Guy who just bought the mules is stunned. 'What about the milk of human kindness?' he asks. 'Oh that stuff works fine,' salesman says, 'but first you gotta get their fuckin' attention.'"

When Imlach's mules arrived in Peterborough for training camp they found the following schedule chalked out on the blackboard in the lobby of the Empress Hotel:

> 6:30 am reveille
> 6:50 breakfast for first shift
> 7:15 breakfast for second shift
> 8:00 first shift on ice
> 9:30 flood ice
> 9:50 second shift

First problem was getting from breakfast to the Memorial Centre rink, a mile away. Punch fined players for taking cars—sidekick King Clancy was dispatched with a notebook to search for familiar license plates—so the team walked or hitchhiked. Upon arriving at the unheated rink, athletes were met by Karl Elieff, team physiotherapist, who put the men through a brisk RCAF fighter pilot warm-up: 15 minutes of push-ups, knee bends, and stretches. Then Punch took over. The *Telegram*'s George Gross described what happened next:

"Being musically inclined, Mr. Imlach likes to play the whistle. So he hauls out one of those short, shrilling instruments for the next exercise. On E flat you have to sprint from blueline to redline and—stop. Then on D minor you sprint from redline to blueline and—stop. Finally on C sharp, you have to make it [back] to the other blueline and—stop. [Then you] repeat the manoeuvre again [and again]…"

This could go on for an hour. If Punch had a thorn in his paw that morning, much longer. First work-out this fall, Marcel Pronovost lost seven pounds. While early practices were draining, at least they weren't dangerous. That wasn't true of afternoon scrimmages. Louis Cauz, who covered the Leafs for the *Globe*, recalls those inter-squad matches:

"I was with a guy from Detroit once, watching a Leaf practice. He sees Baun take a run at someone. Then Shack fires one past Bower's ear. There's a couple of fights. Vicious body checks all over the place. He turns to me and says, 'Jesus, these guys practice harder than the Red Wings play in a real game.'"

As long as no one was killed, Imlach enjoyed these battles, Cauz says.

"Punch acted tough, and he liked tough players. I think being in the military...really had a lasting impression [on him]. He was big on discipline. And he didn't mind people going out there and pounding each other. If anything, he encouraged it."

This pre-season, fifteen Leafs were racked up with injuries. Most came in inter-squad games. Carleton beaned Terry Sawchuk with a slapshot, ripping him for eleven stitches. Baun took Pulford's knee apart with a hip. Kelly tore a leg muscle one scrimmage. Other injuries included Baun (broken nose and thumb); Kent Douglas (separated shoulder); Johnny Bower (dislocated finger, strained back); Mahovlich (broken rib); Pronovost (knee ligament damage); Conacher (sprained wrist); Jim Pappin (bad back); George Armstrong (stiff back); Shack (badly bruised ribs); Larry Jeffrey (broken jaw); Carleton (sore knees); and John Brenneman and Brit Selby (pulled groins).

Training camp survivors were thrown into the exhibition season treadmill: fifteen games in thirty days (five more matches than other NHL teams played). Unlike the Canadiens, who performed mostly in Montreal or Quebec City, the Leafs were never home. Toronto did the mining-town circuit in northern Ontario, and there would be a trip to Quebec City, plus a long hop to Victoria. Imlach also loaned players to Rochester or Tulsa for more game time. Carleton, who had bad knees, ripped Imlach after playing five games in six days.

"I don't care what I say," the winger declared, wobbling into the dressing room at the end of his sentence, "just ask the vets what they think about all these exhibitions. I don't care if they send me down to Charlottetown." (Actually, Carleton didn't know how lucky he was. In 1964, Leafs played eighteen exhibition games in a month, including eight matches in fourteen days.)

Imlach squelched complaints about overwork with a fallacious remark calculated to infuriate players while ingratiating himself with fans. "They're [the Leafs] lucky if they play twenty minutes in a game," Punch said. "What working man wouldn't like a job where he only has to work twenty minutes a day?"

Unfortunately, Punch was getting off his best hockey lines at press conferences. With injuries and salary squabbles, the forward lines he was looking at starting against the Rangers included: Brenneman, Kelly, Armstrong; Selby, Conacher, Pappin; and Carleton, Stemkowski, Ellis. Good enough to beat New York, maybe, but Imlach knew he could have this lot memorize Norman Vincent Peale's *The Power of Positive Thinking** backwards and they still wouldn't win the Stanley Cup…maybe not even the Allan Cup.

So he backed down. Friday practice prior to Saturday's opener was declared a light work-out—no skating, just a short shooting drill. Punch had a line painted from centre to the blueline, parallel to the boards. At the blueline, this marker refracted to the nearest goalpost. Players were told to follow the line in on goal then fire away.

Leafs couldn't believe it. Except for Shack, who needed a line to lead him down the wing? When the exercise got off slowly, Punch started with the wisecracks. Players answered with harder shots. Then goalies Bower and Bruce Gamble started complaining.

"Don't you fuckin' know how to shoot?" Punch screamed whenever a skater broke a stick. "Fire the thing right, stick doesn't break!"

Hearing this, grumbling players skated to the bench, firing broken sticks into the runway. Which made Punch madder still. So the short shooting drill stretched from forty to ninety minutes. When the Leafs finally stomped off, the *Globe*'s Cauz counted seventeen splintered sticks heaped in a sloppy camp-fire near the bench.

Another fence-mending move that day was more success-ful. Imlach gave Clancy ("Vice President in charge of Vice Presidents," Trent Frayne once called him) the OK to open the wallet a little wider in an effort to ink the team's missing forwards. King, who could talk the ears off a field of corn, reported back with good news: He'd signed Shack, Keon, and Pulford "easy as eight goes into sixteen." No luck with

---

* *The self-help manual was Imlach's bible. During a slump in 1964, he passed out paperback editions to the entire team.*

Mahovlich, however. Frank was holding to his demand for $40,000. (The others signed for contracts ranging from $20,000 to 30,000.)

Punch was happy to hear about Pulford and Shack. Although he respected Pulford as a player, Imlach had problems with the fiercely independent centre off ice. Reporter Gross had a fly-on-the-wall perspective on the previous Pulford-Imlach negotiations:

"Leafs were playing an exhibition game in L.A. It was a hot night and the hotel the team stayed in had no air conditioning. I had a corner room next to Punch. I get in my room, lie down. It's too hot. I get out, walk over and throw open the window. Punch must've done the same. I say that because later, as I'm falling asleep, Pulford comes into Punch's room, and I can hear them like they're sitting right across from me. Anyway, they start contract negotiations. I'm just about asleep again when I hear Punch yell, 'No fuckin' way!' Then Pulford yells back. Then they start to go at it. For three hours, until three in the morning they screamed at each other.... The language? Well, it's nothing you hear in church, I tell you."

Another time, Gross stumbled upon Punch and Shack in the steam room of the Empress Hotel in Peterborough. Imlach was diapered in a towel; Shack, naked as a tomato.

"I walk in, they're going at it—contract talks. Punch doesn't look at all happy and Eddie, well, you know Eddie, he has the big grin on his face. It was awkward, I tell you. I didn't know what to do. Finally I just said, 'How's it going?' Punch yells back, 'None of your fuckin' business!'"

As Imlach wrestled his pillow for sleep on the eve of his team's home opener, he must've wondered how it ever got this bad. Once upon a time players loved him. In 1959, he was a saviour. The season before, Leafs had finished last, missing the play-offs again. Owner Stafford Smythe hired Imlach, a career minor-league executive, as the team's GM—co-assistant GM, actually, as Clancy also held that title. Billy Reay was coach. Imlach watched with growing impatience as Leafs won five of twenty games. We're better than this, he figured, so he fired Reay and took over as coach and GM. It was an astonishing move for someone with a few months' desk time in the NHL. But Imlach had confidence in the team and himself. Especially himself.

"Rather be shot for a lion than a lamb," he told the *Globe*'s Rex MacLeod hours after taking over.

Under Imlach, Leafs played like lions, grabbing fourth place on the last night of the season. In the play-offs, they defeated Boston in the semis before losing a competitive five-game Cup final to the fabulous Rocket Richard-era Canadiens. While Montreal took the Cup, Imlach won the country's imagination. Short, horseshoe bald, with pork chop ears, the brazen forty-year-old had hockey fans slapping their knees all spring. To publicise his prediction Toronto would defeat Boston in six, Punch posed for a photo with Clancy, who was wearing a swami's turban, gazing into Punch's naked crown (see photo insert). After the Leafs finally took the Bruins in a seventh game, co-owner Harold Ballard strode into the dressing-room and hollered, "Boys, you played well tonight and I feel this is an appropriate time to introduce you to your new coach for next season!" Then Punch strolled in wearing a beatnik toupee, convulsing the room.

After disappointing play-off losses in 1960 and 61, Imlach and the Leafs knit together three Cup wins in a row (1962–63–64). They fought like lions again the spring of 1965, losing in seven to the Cup-winning Canadiens, but went out like lambs, bowing four straight to the Habs early in 1966. "Team's too old, game has passed Imlach by," experts now said. To critics, Punch responded, "Yeah, they may be bums, but they're my bums, so that's the end of that."

And they were his players. In 1958, he convinced Bower to leave Cleveland to give the NHL another try. Sawchuk he grabbed from Detroit in 1964, when the Wings failed to protect him in the draft. The mule salesman was at his slippery best picking up back-up goalie Bruce Gamble from Eddie Shore in Springfield.

"We've got some good young minor-league goalies—Gary and Al Smith, but I need an experienced back-up. Tell you what, I'll trade one of my Smiths for Gamble," Punch told Shore.

"All right," Shore replied, relieved to unload a goalie who'd vowed never to play for him. "Gimme whichever Smith you want, I don't give a shit."

Springfield Indian captain Brian Kilrea was with Shore when Smith joined the team.

"This little guy shows up at the rink," Kilrea remembers. "Eddie takes a hard look at him. 'Who're you?' he asks. 'Guy you traded for,' he says. Eddie, he looks skeptical. 'Kinda small,' he says. Then he sees the kid's skates, which are regular, not a goalie's. 'Where's your goalie equipment?' He's getting suspicious now, eh? 'What? I'm a forward,' little guy says. Now Eddie, he's starting to go red. 'What's your name?' Shore asks. 'Billy Smith,' kid says. Eddie just closed his eyes. 'Fucked again,' he says."

In another manoeuvre, Punch traded Jim Morrison to Boston for the wily Stanley, in 1958. Sam, as players called him, was slower than church, but as Scott Young observed "played defense as if he had oncoming forwards on a string, drawn to him." Imlach paired Stanley with the speedy Horton, who was encouraged to carry the puck more; this matched set became the heart of the Leaf defense for a decade.

The third defense veteran was Baun, the team's best hitter and a junkyard dog in front of the net. He and the stylish (though sometimes dotty) Carl Brewer* were once as effective as Horton-Stanley. Brewer quit because he couldn't abide Imlach. Baun, who didn't get along with Punch either, hadn't been as effective since. Everybody was now waiting for the other skate to drop.

Rounding out the defense was the usually dependable Pronovost (another veteran lifted from Detroit in the draft); the occasionally reliable Douglas, here as the result of a five-for-one deal with Shore; and Larry Hillman, the team's extra

---

* Upon joining the Canadian national hockey team, Brewer was given a player form. Under nickname, he wrote "Skitz." Coach Jackie McLeod discovered why during an exhibition match against the New York, when Brewer, who had not yet been cleared to play, raced up and down the boards, heckling Rangers and shouting instructions to teammates. McLeod banished him to the stands next game. After witnessing Brewer's antics, one teammate said, "Geez, maybe it wasn't Imlach's fault at all. This one is different."

rearguard. (Unfortunately for Larry, in the era of eighteen-player teams, the sixth defenseman sat not on the edge of the bench, but at the end of a long train ride in from a minor-league city; in his case, Rochester.)

Up front, except for Mahovlich and Shack, the forwards practiced Imlach hockey. Centres Pulford and Keon were good offensively, but superb defensively. In need of a third good two-way pivot in 1960, Imlach traded journeyman Marc Reaume to Detroit for Kelly, an all star defenseman whose career had stalled. Imlach then converted Kelly to centre, announcing, "he's the only guy in the league who can stop Béliveau." The fourth pivot was Pete Stemkowski, a big kid who wasn't fancy, but could hit and check.

On right wing, Ellis was a prototypical Imlach winger—twenty goals a season, and he moved up and down like a toy player trapped in the furrowed grooves of a table-hockey game. At this point in his career, captain Armstrong played some nights as if he'd forgotten to take off his skate guards, but no one could get the puck away from him in the corner. More important, without Army, the only player who could deal with Imlach, there might be a mutiny in the dressing-room.

The Leafs' third right winger, Jim Pappin, could skate and had a great shot, but relied too much on the stick when checking to suit Imlach. Still, the team needed more goals, maybe he could help. Finally there was Shack. The Leafs' conservative play inevitably led to draggy stretches. That's when Punch pointed to Eddie. With his astronaut haircut, shark nose, and deflating-balloon skating style, the right winger jolted the Leafs awake like a second cup of coffee.

Left wing was the team's weakness. After Mahovlich, there were four guys who reminded Punch he made a mistake trading Dick Duff—Carleton could score but not check; Jeffrey and Brenneman could skate but not score; and Selby showed up to camp twelve pounds overweight. Conacher looked good, could play a couple of positions, he'd help some—but only some. All summer, Imlach tried to swing a trade with Detroit for a left winger. Once he had a deal sending Brewer to the Wings for Paul Henderson. But Detroit figured it'd have trouble signing Brewer, so pulled out. Punch also tried to get Vic Hadfield from New York. Ranger GM-coach Emile Francis told Punch he was rebuilding, Hadfield was a kid he had to hang onto, but hey, how about a deal involving Donnie Marshall? A solid twenty-goal veteran for…oh, say Sawchuk? Punch never got back to him.

Although these men were Imlach's players, hand picked and polished, they weren't his team. At least not the way the Habs were Blake's club. Like all coaches, Punch spoke a there's-no-I-in-team philosophy, but in practice he often put himself first, a hypocrisy that cost him his players' allegiance. The first person is everywhere in his books with Scott Young:

"Early on, during the honeymoon years when Imlach of the Leafs and the Leafs of Imlach were the world's best-known, and best, hockey team, I had total control…. When I was winning Stanley Cups…when I'd stand down there behind the bench and hear the roars of Go-Leafs-Go…" (from *Heaven and Hell in the NHL*).

While Punch took credit for wins, losses were the team's fault.

"Maybe it was his military background, but Punch believed in disciplinary action when we weren't doing well," recalls Ellis. "If we had a bad game we paid…. Coming in from Detroit, we might get home at two in the morning. Guys in Mississauga might not get home for another hour. Practice would be at nine. Why nine? Well, that meant you'd have to drive at rush hour. You'd have to leave the house at seven. You might get three hours sleep. And Punch would call another practice for three that afternoon. Why not twelve o'clock? Punch wanted to make you hang around all day. That meant you were getting rush hour going home, too. Punch didn't miss many tricks."

Imlach's tricks helped send Mahovlich to the hospital with a nervous breakdown. "[My doctor] told me to pull an imaginary curtain around myself whenever Punch was around," he told writer Paul Rimstead.

Even some of his cherished veterans had doubts about Punch's tactics.

"In 1964, Mr. Pearson asked me to represent Canada in

Tokyo for the Olympics," remembers Kelly. "It was quite an honour, so of course I wanted to go. Problem was the trip would take me away from training camp. Punch said OK, but wanted me in Detroit first game of the season, just to sit on the bench. I brought skates over, and my wife, Andra, who was a world-class figure skater, we went skating in Osaka. Boy, that was something; when got on the rink, all the skaters left the ice and watched us. In Tokyo, I worked out, too, renting a rink at five in the morning for an hour to do stops and starts. Worked pretty hard when I was there; still, I was worried about my condition when I got back.

"I remember sitting at the end of the bench that first Detroit game, thinking, good thing Punch told me I didn't have to play tonight, because, y'know, I'd missed so many practices. Then Detroit scores early. It's 1–0. Minute later, they score again, 2–0. Out the corner of my eye I see Punch looking at me like it's my fault." Kelly chuckles. "Couple of minutes later, they score again. Now it's 3–0. Punch yells, 'Kelly, get the heck out there!' I go uh-oh and hop to it. Rest of the way I take a regular shift. Things went OK that first period, and I say to myself, boy, I hope I can last through the third on account of I haven't had the benefit of a training camp.

"Funny thing is, come the third, I'm skating around fresh as a daisy, and all the guys who'd been through training camp with Punch looked awful. They could hardly move. Well, I learned a lesson about Punch's practices that night."

Kelly remembers Imlach as an engaging character. Most players liked him at first. In the gag photo of swami Clancy reading Punch's bald head, we see the team gathered behind him, indulging their new skipper in affectionate laughter. As long as they stayed in the background, everything was fine. But when someone else got the laughs, Punch's sense of humour shrivelled.

In the 1963 semi-finals against Montreal, someone stole Imlach's shoes one practice. It was the kind of prank players pull to relieve tension before a big game. Punch acted as if someone swiped his car.

"I don't have time to play games, which one of you fuckers took my shoes?" he thundered. When players collapsed giggling, Imlach fined each of them, including the trainer, ten dollars on the spot.

Punch was an only child. Like many in that situation, he grew to be a man who craved fellowship, who loved the the-atre of good friendship, and yet—and here is the paradox of the species—he remained forever unwilling to cede the spot-light. Eventually, players turned against him. Imlach couldn't have cared less, those who knew him insist.

"I don't think Punch regretted a thing in his life," the *Star*'s Milt Dunnell says. "He did what he wanted, the way he wanted. And if someone disagreed, it just wasn't their opin-ion—they were wrong." George Gross adds, "Punch was a tough man…who accomplished a lot in his career. If someone had a problem with the way he did things, believe me, he could take the heat."

But there is evidence Punch regretted how his players drifted. When asked to name his favourite season, Punch never mentioned the times he won the Cup, but rather 1959—the year he won his team's respect. "That season was the greatest thrill of my life," he told Scott Young. "Truth is I could talk to them [the players] that year better than I ever have been able to since."

Curiously, for a man consumed with winning, Imlach achieved little lasting satisfaction from even his greatest vic-tories. Here, from *Hockey Is a Battle* again, is Punch's response to finally winning a championship, Easter weekend, 1962:

"When we flew into Toronto a few hours later there were a lot of people to meet us at the airport…. City Hall called to say [it wanted] to give us a parade, if we wanted one. Ballard took the call and came to me about it. But after I've won something like that, after being 'up' for so long, I sometimes feel depressed. I said, 'Hell, we won it—anything more would be an anticlimax.'"

Hockey writer Stan Fischler remembers Imlach in the dressing room the night the club won its first Stanley Cup for him.

"Toronto hadn't won since [1951] so there was a lot of cele-brating. I remember Carl Brewer on his hands and knees run-ning around like a dog, and Billy Harris taking photographs of everyone, which I thought was touching. Anyway, here the Leafs were having a good time, hugging and kidding; it was quite a warm scene. Then Imlach storms into the dressing room. 'Cut out the bullshit, we've got a fuckin' plane to catch,' he screams. He was absolutely livid. Boy, I remember thinking, this guy is something else."

Even standing in the centre of a crowd of 15,000 cheering fans sometimes failed to satisfy Punch's need for attention.

"I remember after one game, we get back to the hotel," Gross recalls. "Three-thirty in the morning, phone rings. It's Punch. 'C'mon over,' he says. I race over, thinking, what's going on? Punch lets me in the room, puts a bottle of scotch on the table and we both sit down.

'What is it Punch, you going to make a trade?' I say.

'I'm not going to make a goddamn trade,' he says. 'Sit down, have a drink.'

'Anybody injured?'

'Nobody's injured.'

"So we sit there talking for a while. I figure any minute now, he's going to break the news to me and I'll know why I'm here in the middle of the night. He's called somebody up from the minors, maybe. There's got to be some kind of story here. After a few drinks, I realize, Jesus, Punch is just lonely."

A fan falling into his old seat for the Leaf opener with New York must've figured he'd put on weight. His knees gouged the seat below. An elbow spilled into a neighbour's lap. But no, he hadn't grown, the seat had shrunk. After Smythe, Ballard, and John Bassett bought out Conn Smythe in 1962, the Gardens was reconfigured every other summer. In 1961, the rink seated 12,583; by 1964, room was found for 14,038; in 1966, seating was expanded to 15,461. Prices kept pace. A seat in the reds that went for $2.00 in 1960 now cost $6.00.

To squeeze in more fans, builders ripped out the huge por- trait of the Queen on the south wall, wedging in a mezzanine. By tucking leg room here and there, space was invented for more rows in the pricey reds. In return for increased prices and decreased comfort, patrons got an ugly battleship-grey time clock, hobbled together by Gardens staff. The rink also received a splash of paint. Under the glaring new TV lights, the Gardens gave off a phosphorescent glow. "Looks like somebody painted a house and forgot to put back the drapes," groaned a woman next to the Globe's Jim Vipond before opening face-off.

First period, opening night, the famous blue team on Maple Leaf ice was nearly unrecognizable. "If my youngsters perform, who knows, veterans might have trouble getting jobs back," Imlach had warned, hoping to scare Pulford, Mahovlich, Keon, Shack, and Baun into signing. Determined to make his point, Punch gave his young players lots of ice time early on against Rangers. Sometimes it seemed he picked line combinations out of his fedora. In the first minute of the new season, he had Selby, Conacher, and Shack out together.

"I used to cover horse racing so I got to know Conn Smythe [who owned a stable]," says the Globe's Louis Cauz. "Smythe thought Punch was the best coach in the world, but a bad GM. Jesus, I thought just the opposite. He knew talent better than anyone, but some of his on-ice moves were crazy."

"You never looked away when Punch was coaching," recalls the Telly's George Gross. "Say it's the beginning of a game; you've seen a thousand games, you're not paying attention. Then you look, my God, he's started five defensemen." (Stanley was one of five defenders Imlach started one night against Montreal. "I was left wing across from the Rocket," he recalls. "Richard skates to opening face off, then breaks into a smile. 'Hey Alain,' he says, 'Punch got a new play?'")

"Maybe he was a great motivator, but I never thought much of Imlach as a strategist," Harry Sinden says. "He wasn't in the same class as Blake. You could beat him with the same line match-up all game. And he was always making showboat moves. He was a showboat."

But even his fiercest critics had to admit that Punch's showboat moves often worked. Before this game was a minute old, Shack gamboled down the right boards, his mouth set in a kamikaze scream. From the corner, he slapped a too-hard pass into the slot that Conacher redirected past Cesare Maniago. Four minutes later rookie Carleton got his Troy Donahue pompadour tousled after scoring on a power play. For both young-sters, it was their first NHL goal. Midway through the first, Leafs employed a more familiar combination to beat Maniago, with Kelly converting an Ellis pass out to make it three-zip.

This wasn't a good night for Cesare. After Kelly's goal, he dropped to block a puck and took a home-run swing to the face. Soon he was on his knees, spitting out $500 dentures in fifty-buck chunks. Second period, after Shack fed Conacher for Toronto's fourth goal, an errant Leaf stick carved a second mouth in the goalie's face. Maniago staggered to the boards and signalled he was calling it quits by firing his equipment to the floor of the Ranger bench.

As Eddie Giacomin took his turn in the barrel, Emile Francis searched the Leaf bench for Sawchuk. Francis loved Giacomin's tools. He'd given up four farmhands to get him in a 1965 trade with Providence. "Best reflexes in the league," Emile told everyone. But Francis, an old netminder himself, knew Eddie's form was bad. ("Giacomin is too inexperienced an acrobat to work without a net," tsk-tsked George Gross upon seeing the netminder give up two bad goals one night wandering from his crease.) Now if Giacomin served as Sawchuk's understudy, he'd learn the position, Francis figured. With experience, he wouldn't get rattled after a quick goal. (On opening night this year, against Chicago, he fanned on long blasts by Bobby Hull and Stan Mikita after giving up an early goal to Pierre Pilote.)

The Leafs never got that first one past Eddie this night. Imlach continued mixing and matching, but with Maniago gone, nothing seemed to work. Worse still, Rangers Phil Goyette and Rod Gilbert began to expose Toronto's weak left side. After scoring late in the first, Gilbert found himself alone in front of Bower twice in the second, beating him both times to register his first hat trick. In the dying moments of the middle frame, the right winger drew a crowd, then dropped a pass to Wayne Hillman, who fired a low screen shot past Bower to tie the game at four.

"After the eight-goal scoring spree of the first two periods," wrote Jim Vipond, "the game slowed. The terrible condition of the ice [from the new colour TV lights], which had the

puck bouncing like one of those new-fangled rubber balls,*
was probably the reason."

Imlach changed strategy in the third, benching his rookies.
Kelly hounded Goyette, and Stanley was on every time
Gilbert appeared. While the Leafs looked better defensively,
their dump-and-chase offense was all dump, no chase. Other
than Kelly, no one was skating. And not even Fast Eddie was
hitting. (Leafs received two minor penalties all game.)
Sensing they might grab a rare point on the road, Rangers fell
back. And so the contest turned into a baseline tennis game
between old men. With a few minutes to go in a tie game that
no one deserved to win, more than a few of the freshly painted seats in the reds were empty, twinkling brighter than rubies
under the glare of the new colour TV lights.

TORONTO
Goal—Bower, Sawchuk
Defense—Larry Hillman, Horton, Douglas, Stanley, Pronovost
Forwards—Keon, Pappin, Carleton, Kelly, Jeffrey, Brenneman,
Conacher, Shack, Armstrong, Selby, Stemkowski

NEW YORK
Goal—Maniago, Giacomin
Defense—Howell, Brown, Neilson, Wayne Hillman, MacNeil
Forwards—Gilbert, Marshall, Goyette, Hicke, Fleming, Hadfield,
Berenson, Ingarfield, Seiling, Robinson, Mickey

FIRST PERIOD
1. Toronto, Conacher 1st (Selby, Shack) 0:58
2. Toronto, Carleton 1st (Keon, Douglas) 5:10
3. Toronto, Kelly 1st (Ellis, Stanley) 11:15
4. New York, Gilbert 1st (Goyette, W. Hillman) 14:47
Penalties—Neilson (elbowing) 3:47; Brown (cross-checking) 8:34

---

* Ah, superballs, a dense golf-ball sized orb made of demon rubber. Superballs
took schoolyards by storm in September. Properly fired against pavement, a
superball would expode forty feet into the air. That was thirty-six feet higher
than kids' heads, figured vice principals everywhere. Invoking the powerful "it
could poke your eye out!" anti-toy law, school officials had superballs banned
by Thanksgiving.

SECOND PERIOD
5. New York, Gilbert 2nd (Goyette, Marshall) 4:10
6. Toronto, Conacher 2nd (Shack) 6:08
7. New York, Gilbert 3rd (Goyette) 12:52
8. New York, Wayne Hillman 1st (Gilbert, Goyette) 16:49
Penalties—Stanley (high-sticking) 6:53

THIRD PERIOD
No scoring
Penalties—Douglas (cross-checking) 6:27

Shots on goal
New York   10   14   12 — 36
Toronto   12   9   15 — 36

From 1951 to 1966, the Rangers never won a playoff series. Red Foley of the New York *Daily News* summed up fifteen years of blueshirt blundering in the lead of his story on the team's 1966–67 opener, a 6–3 loss to Chicago: "Rangers last night opened the hockey season in the same old way—trying to sit on a lead they never held."

"We were bad," recalls Emile "The Cat" Francis. "No farm system, eh? Cripes, we had two junior teams: Guelph and Winnipeg. Montreal had eighteen. End of story. First thing I did when I become assistant GM in 1962 was hit the road. Two years, I wore out ten suitcases. By 66 we had affiliations with eighteen teams, that's junior A, B, C. We lifted Brad Park out of Toronto. Punch bet [Leaf head scout] Jim Gregory fifty bucks he'd never make it. Hope Jim got his money... heh, heh. And we got Walt Tkaczuk when he was fourteen."

Confident he had "some for-sure dandies coming up," Francis turned his attention to the parent club.

"I got Reggie [Fleming] in a trade, the year before. And I drafted Orland Kurtenbach,* a big guy who wouldn't back down from anyone, from Toronto in the off season. I figured we finally had a team that wouldn't get pushed around; some-

---

* Imlach agonized over letting Kurtenbach go. He loved the big centre, but the day before the draft he decided to keep Stemkowski instead.

thing Rangers hadn't had in geez, I don't know..." (Indeed, even when New York was competitive in the 50s, the team was composed of nervous forwards with nicknames like Camille "The Eel" Henry, and Larry "The Pope" Popein.)

Francis knew, however, that the Rangers needed more than improved goaltending and a few tough forwards. "Truth is, we'd become losers," he says. "We'd got used to losing. And once you've accepted losing, believe me, you're gonna lose." Which is why he grabbed Boom Boom Geoffrion when the thirty-five-year-old came out of retirement.

"Oh-h-h, I dunno, Emile," Geoffrion told Francis. "My back is sore and the legs, they're shot."

Geoffrion was trying to tip-toe past New York, Boston and Detroit—the sixth, fifth and fourth-place finishers (in 65–66)—to sign with third-place Toronto. In fact, he'd already worked out a deal with Imlach. But The Cat wouldn't let him get away.

"We were last, so we had first shot at him. Bernie had won all those Cups, and he was the best scorer in the league a coupla times," Francis says. More important, the charismatic winger always led the league in hollering. "Bernie was a leader," Francis says. "A coach doesn't want to spend all his time in the dressing room. With Bernie, I always knew the right message was being put out."

At the first day of camp, Boom Boom's one-man marching band stirred the team out of its fifteen-year coma. "Say, friend, everybody knows you're a good player, how many goals you score last year?" Geoffrion asked Hadfield after the team's first practice.

"Ah, sixteen."

"Sixteen?" Geoffrion feigned astonishment. "You're big and strong and you're twenty-six years old. You should score thirty. What are you doing, dogging it?"

Days later, Boomer chewed out a rookie who complained after a hard work-out. "Twenty-two goddamn years old and you feel bad? How the hell you think I feel? ...You ought to be ashamed! You think you're going to win while you're feeling sorry for yourself?"

Soon, Francis began to notice a different atmosphere

around the locker room and hotel lobbies.

"Hey Boomer," Gilbert called across the dressing room to Geoffrion the last day of the exhibition season, "I read where you were supposed to be my idol when I was a kid. Well, I got news for you. From now on, I'm going to be your idol."

New York's newfound swagger was evident in the opening moments of Sunday's Leaf–Ranger return match in Madison Square Garden. Four minutes in, Stanley circled his net and slipped past Fleming. Just as the defensemen was escaping, Reggie drove a stick into his spokes. Number 26 got up and took off after Earl Ingarfield, pitchforking him into his bench. Seconds later, Fleming crashed the boards, spilling Stanley into the Ranger nest. When the Leaf rearguard's stick came down on Francis, Emile grabbed a club from Hadfield and began whittling away on Allan's skull.

It was like that all night, as the invigorated Rangers hit back twice for every knock taken. First period was all shoulders and hips, with teams managing four shots each. The second twenty minutes saw the weekend's best hockey. New York controlled play early, with Bower making big saves on Ingarfield and speedball Billy Hickie. But the Leaf defense steered away rebounds. Only once, midway in the period, did Gilbert shake free. Tonight, however, Bower won the duel, snaring a bullet drive with the ratty black dish towel he called a glove.

Late in the second, Leafs took to offense. This was their game: cautious, tight-checking hockey—let the other guys become frustrated and over-extend themselves, then counter-attack, capitalizing on mistakes. With Seiling off, Leaf forwards Carleton, Keon, and Pappin stormed the net. Twice Giacomin made lightning kick saves. At one point, the puck squirted between his pads, trickling toward the goal line. The crowd's scream alerted Giacomin, who turned and pounced on the puck. When Carleton tried to snowplow the goalie into the net, he was flattened by Jim Neilson.

The third period saw the teams revert to the conservative tactics of Saturday's final frame. It was how Imlach played tight games. We've got better goaltending, a more disciplined

team, if a mistake or long shot settles it, chances are we'll finish on top, he figured. It was how the team won three Stanley
Cups.

And lost tonight's game. At seven minutes, Carleton
slipped a short pass to Pronovost near the Leaf net. The
defenseman tried to bring the play into the corner and safety,
but the puck hopped over his stick, rolling to Red Berenson,
who threw a backhand to the blueline. Wayne Hillman
grabbed the puck, looked up, saw everyone covered, took a
step in, lowered his head and blasted a shot wide of the net,
but not quite clear of the desperate Pronovost. The puck
glanced off Marcel's shin, angling past Bower for the night's
only goal.

When the game ended, Francis made ski tracks across the
ice for Giacomin, throwing himself on the pile of Rangers celebrating the youngster's first shut-out. Afterwards, Giacomin
thanked his coach. "Francis kept me going," he said. "I hear
all those trade rumours about Rangers getting a new goalie,
but Francis kept encouraging me.... I always knew he had
faith in me." Francis in turn praised Giacomin. He was his
man. The Ranger goalie for this season and the next ten
years.

The next day, Francis was on the phone to Imlach. He still
wanted Sawchuk. Punch must've been tempted. The team
was off to a bad start; maybe critics were right, this was a fifth-
place team. Plus, he had Gamble, who'd thrown four shut-
outs in ten NHL starts the previous season, in Rochester to
back up Bower. And Imlach must've remembered how
Sawchuk moped into his office in Peterborough in training
camp and announced his retirement. Terry felt he hadn't
recovered from a summer back operation. Punch talked him
out of it. Still, Sawchuk was thirty-eight and his back could
go at any time. With expansion six months away, the Leafs
would only be able to protect one goalie anyway.

"Yeah, I wanted Sawchuk. And I was willing to offer full
value for him," Francis remembers. "I know how much a great
goalie can lift a team, and Terry was still a great goalie."

Punch never even made Francis an offer. It wasn't his style
to worry about finishing fifth, and rebuilding.

"Punch knew Terry was a great goalie, too, eh?" Francis says. "[Punch] wanted to go all the way and probably figured he needed Sawchuk to get him there."

FIRST PERIOD
No scoring
Penalties—Stanley (high-sticking), Ingarfield (high-sticking), Fleming (elbowing) 4:23; Pappin (slashing) 5:44; Horton (tripping) 17:15; Horton (cross-checking) 19:54

SECOND PERIOD
No scoring
Penalties—Howell (holding) 7:37; Seiling (holding) 16:58

THIRD PERIOD
1. New York, Hillman 2nd (Berenson) 7:14
Penalties: Douglas (high-sticking); Gilbert (high-sticking) 15:01

Shots on goal
Toronto   4   13   7 — 24
New York   4   16   9 — 29

Crowd noise
Evading a Forechecker

"Let's get this straight. Are you telling us that there's nothing that worries you? Nothing that bothers you? How can you write poetry if you're not bothered by anything?"

"Well, I'm bothered when I get up in the morning. My real concern is to discover whether or not I'm in a state of grace. And if I make that investigation and discover that I'm not in a state of grace, I'm better off in bed."

"What do you mean, a state of grace? That's something I've never understood."

"A state of grace is that kind of balance with which you rise to the chaos you find around you. It's not a matter of resolving the chaos, because there is something arrogant and warlike about putting the world in order that kind of…it's like an escaped ski going through the…"

"You've lost me."

—Pierre Berton interviewing Leonard Cohen, from the 1965 NFB film *Ladies and Gentlemen, Leonard Cohen*

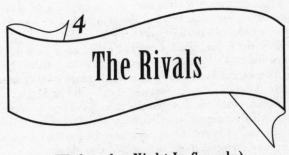

4

The Rivals

(Wednesday Night In Canada)

In grade seven, my science teacher, Mr. Scrim, told us we had molecules swimming on top of our desks. Yeah, doing the backstroke, you can tell by the grain of the wood, I snickered, then got on with business, filling in a sketch of the Big M flipping one past Worsley on the inside of a notebook. Mr. Scrim's story was the last science lesson I even half-listened to; why wonder about electrons when you could dream about hockey or Whit Tucker taking Garney Henley deep?

Dreaming is the natural state of something half-formed, and like every kid I spent my days in moony reverie. Tuesdays and Thursdays were for absent dreaming—studying Canadian Tire catalogues for bike accessories (with an odometer I could compare miles travelled from one year to another!), or conquering squirrels with a Thierry la Fronde slingshot. Wednesdays were reserved for hockey. Habs and Leafs played that night. It took hours of dreaming to get ready.

I'd start after school, sitting on a curb, waiting for the Ottawa *Citizen* to drop off my bundle. Truck appears on an even number, 4:02 say, Leafs'll win, I'd tell myself. Odd number? A tie. To be fair, I'd give Canadiens multiples of five ending on an odd numeral. But if the big white truck did show at 4:15, I'd bail quickly... *Bet's a blubber! Bet's a blubber!*

My work suffered. IGA circulars (roast beef, 49 cents a pound!) that had to be shuffled inside the paper were stuffed in a garbage can. Who had time to properly dispose of the thick baling wire that bundled the original load? I tossed it into the hedge of a nearby Ottawa *Journal* reader.

Why the hurry? Well, I wanted to get my papers done before the civil servants got home. In other cities, fathers had regular jobs, but Hull-Ottawa dads liked to pretend they were in Her Majesty's Secret Service. "I'm a CR3 at D.S.S.," a neighbour would say, then look away to discourage conversation. All that meant was that he was a clerk rated three, Department of Supplies and Services—the guy who emptied the pencil sharpener in the morning. Moony old guys are a bad audience for kids (who can stand to see their younger selves engaged in hopeless longing?), so I'd want to get the crucial part of Wednesday dreaming finished before they got home.

Stopping at a customer's house, I'd grab a paper and run up the laneway. At the edge of the walk, I'd fold the *Citizen* into a tight cylinder, measure the distance to the porch doormat with a swinging arm, close my eyes, then fling the paper in a looping arc. If any part of the paper landed on the mat I considered it a goal in the bank for the Leafs that night. On a good Wednesday, I might score eight goals. Bower could take it from there, I figured.

I wasn't the only one dreaming his heroes to victory on Wednesday night. The weekly battle between Montreal and Toronto was a collision of dreams involving the whole country. In the 60s, Saturday was Hockey Night in Canada. The marquee game was on the tube, inevitably Hull and the Hawks or Howe and the Wings in against the Leafs or Habs. Husbands brought wives to the game. On TV, intermission hosts Ward Cornell and Frank Selke Jr. gussied up in dark evening suits. This was hockey as theatre. By comparison, Wednesday night's contests were clan smokers. In Montreal and Toronto, men went to games with buddies. Across the land, taverns with colour TVs did weekend business. These were the games that excited snowball fights among kids in Fredericton, or heated office debates in Saskatoon.

While Leaf-Canadien games engaged every corner of the Dominion, the epicentre of the rivalry was Upper and Lower Canada. Researching his play, "Les Canadiens," Rick Salutin asked Red Fisher what the Habs meant to Quebec. "If you fight but don't win the real battle against those who are perceived to be the real rulers," Fisher replied, "you try to win elsewhere in a forum in which you're successful. In other words, Les Canadiens." Salutin spent time in bars watching games. "I marvelled at the frenzied involvement of the patrons," he wrote. "I put to my drinking companion this question: 'How come?' She said, 'Canadiens—they're us. Every winter they go...and in the spring they come home conquerors.'"

Toronto was the team and city Montreal most wanted to see conquered.

"During the 60s, Montrealers followed the census nervously," remembers Larry Black, a reporter for *The Independent* of London, who grew up in Montreal. "Every year, Toronto seemed to be gaining on us. There was this sense that an economic shift of power was taking place. Which we thought was totally unfair. We'd been brought up to think Montreal was a vital, cosmopolitan city. And Toronto was this dull, monolithic city where lights went out at ten and you couldn't get a drink Sunday. It seemed inconceivable that we were losing control to this...this less-interesting city."

Leafs personified the city they played in, Hab fans believed.

"Leafs seemed so drab," Black says. "They didn't skate fast or score a lot of goals. They grabbed and held and played defense. Basically, they tried not to lose. To us, that wasn't hockey."

While Montrealers saw Toronto as a city of accountants with pencil shavings coursing their veins, residents of Canada's second city considered Montreal a suburb of Gomorrah. WASP prejudice against the capital of French Canada was evident in much of the journalism of the day, including a 1966 *Weekend Magazine* cover story, "BOOZE,

BROTHELS AND DRUGS," by Clifford W. Harvison, a
retired RCMP officer:

> Montreal was a graft-ridden city. The rot of bribery
> and corruption had spread through all levels of gov-
> ernment. Venality undermined law enforcement and
> tilted, if it did not upset, the scales of justice. Holdups,
> burglaries, assaults—every offense in the calendar of
> crime—occurred with what should have been regard-
> ed as alarming frequency.... Brothels operated openly
> in a red-light district that covered more than a dozen
> blocks...

When the two solitudes collided for the first time this season,
Wednesday November 2, Mahovlich was in Toronto's line-up.
Frank had his $40,000 contract after a two-game hold-out.
Imlach welcomed reporters into his office after the signing to
discuss the deal.

"How much did he get?" someone asked.

"No comment."

"How long is the contract for?"

"No comment."

"Are you satisfied with the compromise you reached?"

"No comment."

Five more questions elicited the same response. Finally,
Punch looked up, smiling. "Anything else you fellows like to
know?"

The conventional wisdom is Imlach rode Mahovlich out of
town. And it's true Punch contributed to the winger's unhappy days in Toronto. He routinely mangled his name ("Ma-hal-
o-vich") and criticised the player after even his finest efforts.
In one playoff game in 1964, Frank scored a pair and assisted
on three more against Montreal. Afterwards, Punch could
only talk about the occasional evenings when the Big M was
the Big Empty.

"Hockey's mostly a Streetcar Named Desire," Imlach said,
"and sometimes Frank misses the train."

"That was Punch," says Milt Dunnell. "He never wanted to
be seen as being wrong. Even when Mahovlich played well,

Punch wanted people to remember he'd been right before in criticising him."

While Imlach tormented Mahovlich, teammates suggest he wasn't the sole cause of the winger's difficulties.

"I thought Frank's biggest problem was that he believed 15,000 people came to the rink 35 times a year to watch him play," says former linemate Billy Harris. "He worried too much and never let anything go. Sports is a tough business. You're not going to always succeed. Everybody has ups and downs. Sometimes, Frank couldn't deal with the downs."

There's a poignant story involving Mahovlich in Harris's memoir, *The Glory Years*. One day, Harris received a call at home. "Billy's not here, take a message?" his mom asked. "Yeah," a small voice said, "tell him the Big M phoned."

Frank was like the lead in one of Scott Young's popular juvenile novels from the period, *A Boy at the Leafs' Camp*—a talented kid blinded by the spotlight of professional sport. But juvenile novels are life-affirming morality plays. The story ends when the kid scores the big goal and the crowd cheers. Twice in his career, in 1964 and 68, Frank scored the big goal, was named one of the three stars, and when he made a post-game twirl around his home rink, the crowd booed. On both occasions, he checked into Toronto General Hospital the next morning, suffering from acute depression.

"The thing about Frank that frustrated people was...well, that he could appear lackadaisical," says Red Kelly. "Frank was a good guy, a nice guy, and oh, he was talented. He had speed and that reach. It was a pleasure to watch him on the ice when he'd take the puck from left to right field in one shift. But sometimes," Kelly sighs, "well, say we were in the other end. Maybe their defenseman had the puck. Frank could be skating beside him, just looking at him. Heck, I'd get so mad I'd yell, 'Get him!' And Frank would get him, finally."

When Kelly is asked why Mahovlich didn't think to check the man himself, he offers a parched laugh. "Geez, I don't know. Nobody knew."

Tonight was one of Mahovlich's good games. Midway through the first, he checked Balon, took two hops to get in gear, then exploded down his wrong wing, shoulders high, legs pumping. At centre, he shifted past Rousseau, jerking the Gardens' crowd to its feet. Defensemen Harris and Tremblay wedged together to bring him down, but Frank burst through them like saloon doors. Now he was in alone on Hodge. The big forward's shot ripped the goalie's glove, dribbling wide. Spreading his legs to fend off Harris's desperate check, Frank reached between his skates to find the rebound and slapped the puck into the empty cage.

The goal put the Leafs up two. Minutes earlier, Brenneman deflected a shot into Hodge's pads. Harris cross-checked him to the ice, but the winger golfed the puck from his knees into the corner of the net.

Although the season was just two weeks old, it was clear something was wrong with Montreal. The Canadiens normally came out like colts escaping a burning stable. But in five games so far, they'd been outshot 53-39 in the opening period. Even in winning (the squeakers over Boston and a 3–0 Worsley shut-out of New York) the Habs looked at sea. In a 5–3 home loss to Chicago, Montreal was "as uncohesive as a symphony orchestra playing a piece by ear," according to Red Fisher. Now here they were down 2–0 to their archest enemies.

"I was afraid this [slump] would happen when I started reading all the reporters giving us first place," a fretful Blake said recently. "Unfortunately we're not playing reporters, we're playing NHL teams…they don't give you anything."

One reason the Habs never suffered prolonged slumps was because they could survive on their power play during the rare stretches the offense faltered.

"We always have a good power play because we take pride in it," J.C. remembers. "We work harder on our power play than any other team, maybe. [Imlach never drilled Leafs on man-advantage situations.] Toe would make us work hard in practice, just working with the puck; passing quickly. Passing is everything on a power play. Once I heard Harvey say, 'No matter how fast you skate, you can pass faster.'"

Before the game, Imlach complimented Armstrong and Conacher on their penalty killing. "No goals in thirteen tries [this season]," Punch chirped. The players were shocked. How could Imlach, a man who never changed fedoras in a winning streak, taunt fate in such a blithe fashion? Punch would ask himself the same question after this game. Early in the second, after Horton was tossed for interference, Rousseau accepted a pass from Béliveau, then dropped back to pass, waiting for a forward to emerge from a tangle in front. When Cournoyer shook free, the puck was on his stick and in the net in an instant.

Led by the swirling attack of the Balon-Richard-Rousseau line and J.C.'s savvy quarterbacking, Montreal began to penetrate Toronto's defense midway in the second period. Balon was sent in alone on successive shifts, but Sawchuk, a master of the geometry of goaltending, offered the shooter impossible angles. Then Henri set up Balon with an empty net. This time the flustered winger tried to shoot before he had the puck (Sawchuk did that to you), firing wide.

Toe was using J.C. more now. Tremblay always played well against Toronto, which was surprising given the Leafs were a physical team, and the knock against Tremblay was he didn't like rough going.

"No, I love playing Toronto," Tremblay says. "They were always big games. Yeah, always Wednesday night, that's right. It was like the play-offs. Blake would be in a bad mood before the game.... You know, you would watch out before we got on an elevator in the hotel. You would look for Toe. If you saw him..."

Harper picks up the story.

"Oh man, if you saw Blake, you'd stop and pretend you had to tie your shoe or something. No one wanted to get onto the elevator with Toe day of a game. He'd be so tense. You'd say hello and he wouldn't say anything. He was thinking about Toronto."

Tremblay laughs. "When Toe takes the elevator, I take the stairs... After being a coach, I understand. A coach, all he can do is worry. A player, he gets to work off the nerves. When I was a player I like being nervous before a big game...[thinking] about what's going to happen. About what? Oh, you would think about what you would do if you got a pass in a situation—a power play, maybe. You could see your-self getting a pass and shooting quick past a goalie… It was all mental preparation."

Inventing dodges to avoid the teacher? Imagining yourself scoring the big goal? Even the Leafs and Canadiens engaged in Wednesday night dreaming.

J.C.'s dreams began coming true midway into this contest. From the second period on, the defenseman was at his master-ful best. Nimble as a cat negotiating a crowded mantlepiece, the slender defender picked his way out of crowds in front of Hodge, then threaded perfect passes to flying wingers. On the power play, Tremblay had Conacher and Armstrong spinning with his Bob Cousy-like, no-look passes. When the Habs were still down 2–1 going into the third, J.C. pulled another crooked arrow out of his crowded quiver of tricks—his patent-ed, change-of-pace flip shot.

"I couldn't shoot like Bobby Hull," he says. "So sometime when we were changing men and I'm up by myself, I just flip the puck over the defense on the net. Maybe I get lucky and it bounce funny past the goalie. You never know." But luck had little to do with J.C.'s trick shot. Other players scored on bouncers, but by accident. "J.C. worked on that shot all the time in practice," Cournoyer recalls. "Sometimes, we laugh at him. But I saw him score with it many time."

J.C. says he scored on maybe twenty-five flip shots in his career. "The trick is you have to get the puck over the defenseman and make sure it bounce in front of the goalie," he explains. "If the puck is flip too high, the goalie can come out and catch it. And it has to be flip, not raised. The puck will come down flat and go right to the goalie if it is raised. A flip though, maybe it hit an edge and bounce a little funny."

In the opening seconds of the third, with Montreal up a man, J.C. surprised a wall of Leaf defenders by lobbing a flip over their heads just as his wingers crossed the blueline. Sawchuk skated from his crease, saw he couldn't catch the dying quail, stopped, fell to one knee, and threw out his glove, like a baseball catcher setting up for a pitch. The puck bounced ten feet in front of him and took a crazy leap over his right shoulder.

Tie game.

A curious move by Imlach almost cost the Leafs even a single point. In the match previous, Shack took a bad penalty late, with the Leafs up 3–2 on Detroit. On the power play, Howe had an open net, but clanked one off the post. A move like Shack's by a Canadien would've resulted in a benching. "Blake had a memory like an elephant," Ferguson says. "One time, Backstrom lost a face-off and it cost us a game, and I don't think Ralphie took another key draw in five years." Punch, however, liked to play wild hunches. With two minutes left, he tapped Shack on the shoulder. Eddie hopped the bench and took a Harpo Marx-like dash at Provost, prompting a two-minute charging call. The Leafs avoided Punch's penalty-killing jinx on this infraction, however, and the eventful, well-played contest ended in a draw.

FIRST PERIOD
1. Toronto, Brenneman 2nd (Pulford, Hillman) 6:45
2. Toronto, Mahovlich 2nd 12:48
Penalties—Shack 0:40; Richard 17:06

SECOND PERIOD
3. Montreal, Cournoyer 2nd (Rousseau, Béliveau) 5:52
Penalties—Horton (interference) 5:26; Harper (roughing) 7:58;
G. Tremblay (roughing), Harper (roughing), Carleton (roughing)
17:08; Pulford (cross-checking) 19:21

THIRD PERIOD
4. Montreal, J.C. Tremblay 1st (Rousseau) 0:33
Penalties—Mahovlich 14:08 (tripping); Shack (charging) 17:59

Shots on goal
Montreal   11   11   12 — 34
Toronto   13   8   9 — 30

Montreal continued its early-season sleepwalk the following weekend against Detroit. At home, the Habs were once again outskated, outshot (12–8), and outscored (1–0) in the first period, but were bailed out in the game's second half by

Rousseau. Number 15 started the team's comeback on Saturday with a poolhall bank shot from behind the net off a Wing defender in the second, then set up Balon and Richard for the go-ahead and insurance goals in the third for a 3–1 win. (In seven games, Rousseau had been involved in two-thirds of Montreal's seventeen goals, with four goals and seven assists.)

On Sunday in Detroit, a thermometer-skinny rookie, Pete Mahovlich, scored his first goal and Howe collected his 626th. Four other Wings also tallied. The Stanley Cup champions played as if the trophy was leashed to their backs. The centres were a step slow. Worsley fanned on a couple of long ones. Laperrière, an on-ice spectator on the three of the first four Detroit goals, watched the last period from the bench. Even Blake seemed to give up without a fight. Normally, after a 6–0 pasting, Toe could be counted on to melt reporters' pens. After this sad effort, however, he sounded resigned to his team's play.

"This had to come," he sighed. "We've been lacking overall effort since the start of the season. Only Rousseau, Richard, and Provost have played at all well. I don't think we ever had as much publicity about being the club to beat— even with those great clubs in the 50s. Maybe it has an effect on the players."

The Leafs, meanwhile, continued behaving like a supermarket cart with a bad wheel that can only travel so far in a straight line before catching an invisible rut and wobbling off track. After finishing with Montreal, the Leafs hopped a train to Detroit for a Thursday game. The team was up 2–1 in the third on goals by Ellis and Shack (both set up nicely by Kelly). Then that wheel started wobbling. With six minutes left, Murray Hall slid a Bruce MacGregor rebound past Gamble. (The pudgie goalie with Elvis sideburns had been summoned when Sawchuk's back stiffened in the warm-up; Bower was out for a month with a bad back.) For the fourth time in six games, Toronto blew a late lead. Once again, the team was lucky to come away with even a tie, as with seconds left, Howe found himself alone with the puck and an empty net.

"How the heck do I explain to Mark [his eleven-year-old

son] how I missed that open net?" Gordie asked afterwards. "I have no excuse. The puck was flat. The goal was empty. I took careful aim and missed by a foot. And that's the second open net I've missed in two games with [the Leafs]."

Through his team's third-period misadventures, Punch remained surprisingly perky. "We're just having bad luck— nothing you can do when you get the bad bounces," he commented after J.C's 100-foot knuckler cost Toronto a win. "We'll start getting some luck soon, wait and see."

Sports figures are often superstitious. With Punch, however, luck was a religion. "He thought two-dollar bills were a bad omen," says Louis Cauz. "If you took out a two-dollar bill in a bar, Punch would go crazy. 'Jesus, what are you trying to do to me?' he'd yell, then grab it and rip it up. And if you ever saw Punch make his way from his office to the bench at the Gardens, you wouldn't know what to think," Cauz continues, laughing. "He'd bang his door in a certain place, leaving, then slap photos on the walls for luck. Then he'd hop along the hallway careful not to step on cracks, whatever. You'd think you were walking behind a lunatic."

The following Saturday and Sunday, Eddie Giacomin made the lunatic look like a prophet, as two bad bounces turned what should've been a one-point home-and-home series into a three-point Leaf weekend.

Saturday, Toronto took a 1–0 lead over the Rangers into the third. When Bob Nevin beat Sawchuk on a penalty shot, the Gardens crowd started chewing their programs—not again! Then with two minutes left, Ellis dumped the puck into the Ranger corner. When the Leaf winger's shot came back at an odd angle thirty feet in front of the net, Giacomin took a few steps out, stopped, reconsidered, then hurried after the puck, arriving at the circle a fraction later than Larry Jeffrey, who slapped the winner into the open net.

The next night, in New York, with Toronto down one and time running out, Horton and Keon tried the same play. This time, Giacomin didn't hesitate, flying out after the corner dump-in. Horton's shot jumped over Eddie's stick and rolled in front of the empty net to a streaking Keon, who calmly tapped in the tying goal.

•••

In a Forum return match with Toronto on Wednesday, November 9, Cournoyer hopped the Montreal bench in the game's second minute, just after the Leafs were nabbed for too many men on the ice. The Habs' power play unit—J.C. and Rousseau back, with Gilles Tremblay, Béliveau, and Cournoyer up front—sent the puck swirling about the periphery of the Leafs' defensive box with quick, short passes. As in last week's game, penalty killers Conacher and Armstrong seemed to be always untangling their feet, forever one pass behind the play.

Seventy-five seconds into the furious merry-go-round, Yvan took a pass from Béliveau to the left of Sawchuk. Because number 12 shot left, he received the puck a split-second faster than most right wingers. With his quick wrists that meant he'd be shooting when other players were teeing up the puck. Just as he had in Toronto on a similar chance, Cournoyer's shot was past Sawchuk before the goalie could turn to face him.

After receiving teammates' hugs, Yvan returned to the end of the Montreal bench, where he remained rooted for the rest of the period.

"When I come up to the Canadiens, there were four right wingers already, all very good players: Rousseau, Provost, Larose, and Roberts," Cournoyer remembers. "Then I come along. We all want to play, but Toe believes in three lines. That's a problem for Jimmy and me. So Toe makes him a penalty killer, and me I play the power play. It work out pretty good. We won the Stanley Cup my first two years in Montreal."

At first, it seemed Montreal would win easily tonight, too. The Balon-Richard-Rousseau line was flying. And Béliveau, who hadn't scored this season, had more bounce in his stride. For the first time in eight games, Montreal outshot a team (13–9) in the opening period. While the Canadiens enjoyed a territorial advantage, the Leafs yielded few clear opportunities. Late in the frame, Armstrong stole a pass in Montreal's zone and slipped the puck in front to Conacher, who beat Hodge low to the stick side. As was often the case in games with Imlach's Leafs, the other team figured it had the contest in hand, only to look up at the end of a period and find the game tied.

The second period was a clone of the first, except the Leafs managed to keep Cournoyer at bay during minors to Baun. At fourteen minutes, Montreal committed another blunder. Conacher, who'd been left unattended in front, banged a corner pass from Stemkowski on net. Hodge got a pad out, but the rebound came to Armstrong—where were Harris and J.C.?—who rapped it in off the far post.

Montreal played its best hockey in the third. After the opening face-off, Henri took a return pass from Rousseau. Crouching low to the ice, he slipped past Horton, cutting in front of Sawchuk. Richard never had an angle to shoot, but his backhand—he always went to the backhand in close—dribbled off Sawchuk's pads free to Balon, who tied the game.

For the next seven minutes, Montreal dominated, and the rink shrank to a sixty-foot patch in front of Sawchuk. With his team sinking into another third period torpor, Punch once again turned Shack free. A big puppy set loose in a wide field, Eddie took off on a rink-long dash and hopped Ferguson, sending him crashing into the boards. Referee John Ashley didn't see the ambush, but hearing the Forum crowd's angry "HEYYY!" turned in time to see the bleeding Ferguson retaliate.

Roberts forechecked the ensuing Leaf power play to a walk. Early in the first period, Jimmy had taken a Zorro-like thrust in the face from Pappin, which left him with a seven-stitch gash in the cheek. This was his first shift back and the little forward hit every Leaf in sight. A minute into the Leaf non-power play, Roberts found himself approaching Pappin and lost his head. Up went his stick. Down went Pappin. Now the Canadiens were two men short.

Mahovlich took an Armstrong pass at the blueline—Toe would scream afterwards he was offside—glided into the Montreal zone, stopped, then dropped the puck to Pappin, who fired a low bullet under Hodge's glove to give the Leafs a 3–2 lead.

In his Toronto *Star* column next day, Red Burnett would compare Sawchuk's performance in the game's final minutes to 1966 Cy Young winner Sandy Koufax closing out a baseball game: once Sawchuk got a late-inning whiff of victory, the game was over. The Habs had one "golden opportunity," as Danny Gallivan would say, to even the score on a power play with seven minutes left. Cournoyer received a pass alone to left of Sawchuk. This time the goalie anticipated the play. When Yvan looked up all he saw was a six-foot goalie advancing upon him. His snap shot kicked off Sawchuk's pad to Richard at the other side of the net. When the speedy pivot wheeled to shoot, Sawchuk had rematerialized and was now hugging the right post.

"What do I do?" a glum Richard reflected after the game. "Do I shoot it hard and try for a deflection? Or do I try and flip it and hope it catches a corner?"

He flipped. Sawchuk caught. And the game was over. The Leafs had beaten the Canadiens on their own ice. "It felt like the end of the world if they came into our rink and beat us," Ferguson says. "I'd be sick until the next game." Throughout Quebec and in Canadien homes across the country, fans went to bed with an ache in their throat. For Leaf rooters, a win in Montreal was a wonderful, unexpected windfall. Like finding a ten-dollar bill in an old coat. They'd go to bed this evening wearing a smile that would last all Thursday.

FIRST PERIOD
1. Montreal, Cournoyer 3rd (Beliveau, G. Tremblay) 3:15
2. Toronto, Conacher 5th (Douglas, Armstrong) 18:42
Penalties—Toronto, too many men on ice (served by Hillman) 1:58; Montreal, too many men on ice (served by Cournoyer) 5:08

SECOND PERIOD
3. Toronto, Armstrong 1st (Conacher, Stemkowski) 14:12
Penalties—Baun (tripping) 8:24; Baun (kneeing) 16:00

THIRD PERIOD
4. Montreal, Balon 2nd (Rousseau, Richard) 0:41
5. Toronto, Pappin 1st (Mahovlich, Armstrong) 9:21
Penalties—Ferguson (cross-checking) 7:57; Roberts (spearing)
9:17; Ellis (interference) 12:30

Shots on goal
Toronto	9	9	7 — 25
Montreal	13	8	13 — 34

NOVEMBER 10 STANDINGS

	P	W	L	T	F	A	Pts
Chicago	7	6	1	0	31	17	12
Toronto	9	3	1	5	23	20	11
Montreal	8	4	3	1	19	20	9
Detroit	9	3	5	1	31	29	7
New York	10	2	5	3	26	31	7
Boston	9	2	5	2	22	35	6

LEAGUE LEADERS

	GP	G	A	Pts	PIM
Ullman, Det.	9	2	12	14	18
Mikita, Chi.	7	5	8	13	2
Rousseau, Mont.	8	4	8	12	4
Goyette, N.Y.	10	0	12	12	2
Henderson, Det.	9	8	3	11	0
Gilbert, N.Y.	10	4	6	10	4
D. Hull, Chi.	7	5	4	9	6
Marshall, N.Y.	10	5	4	9	0
Smith, Det.	9	3	4	7	2
R. Hull, Chi.	7	4	3	7	8

Crowd noise

I portray [Prime Minister Lester Pearson] as a kind of baggy, flappy little mole or tree toad. His voice is a tenor. He doesn't have a real lisp, though it often sounds that way, but he gets his tongue mixed up somehow: it doesn't ride right in the mouth. The "sp" sound in particular bothers him. It's sort of a mushy sound, with a lot of spray and splatter. Of course, I exaggerate his funny little walk: a kind of shuffle, with one leg stiffer than the other. He smites himself on the forehead for emphasis and wipes his hands down his cheeks. But I don't see anything self-important in his posture; there's a chuckly shyness in the midst of it all.

[John Diefenbaker] looks like a big white northern owl, and he has a voice that goes with it: a baritone, stern and rebuking. There's an evangelistic timbre in it, a sort of Bible Belt religiosity—the Old Testament prophet in action. He keeps putting an "aaah" prefix in front of words as if pausing to get the word exactly right. Of course he emphasizes with a lot of head-shakings and jowl-quiverings. He puts his hand on his hips, glaring down and around at the floor as though he's hunting for something and is angry at himself because he can't remember what it is.

—Sunday morning CBC host Rich Little explaining how he "does" his most popular impressions

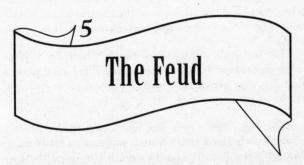

5

The Feud

Three minutes into a November 19 game between Detroit and Chicago, Black Hawk centre Phil Esposito circled the Red Wing net. Looking up, he found Bobby Hull in front, struggling to peel a 160-pound barnacle, Bryan "Bugsy" Watson, off his back. Esposito lobbed the puck into the crease, figuring Bobby might break free. He didn't, but the puck struck a stick and fluttered high, caromming off Hull's knee past goalie Roger Crozier. As Chicago Stadium erupted into a ragged duel of foghorns, Watson chased Hull.

"You gonna take that goal?"

Hull pretended to ignore Watson as the score was announced: "Black Hawk goal, his eighth of the season, scored by number nine…" The message was swallowed by the crowd, but Hull could still hear Watson.

"Don't tell me you think you deserve that goal?"

Hull said nothing, but Watson could tell from the play of his jaw muscles that the Golden Jet was upset. "I kept at him, and he kept getting madder and madder," he said later.

Hull's rage stretched back to the spring play-offs. The then twenty-seven-year-old forward was coming off his best season.

73

With fifty-four goals, Bobby finally broke hockey's four-minute mile, the Rocket's record of fifty goals in a season. Too many of those goals (ten) came against Detroit, figured Watson, the Wings' fractious utility forward.

"Before the playoffs, I went into [coach Sid Abel's] office and volunteered to guard Hull," Watson says. "Paul [Henderson] had been doing it during the season, but he was banged up and anyway I figured we needed him to score, not check."

Hull had dealt with checkers before. The Habs' Provost and a pair of Leaf Ronnies—Stewart and Ellis—all shadowed him. But they played both ways. Watson stuck to Hull like white on rice, remaining close even when Detroit had the puck.

And Bugsy never ever shut up. "Geez, Bobby, haven't scored tonight, have you?" Watson yapped into Hull's ear at face-offs. "Hey Bobby, lookit the score, you're losing," he'd say when the Wings were up. "Christ, I thought you could shoot better'n that," was his happy shout whenever Crozier stopped the Black Hawk star.

Hull only scored twice in the series. "But not when I was guarding him," Watson remembers today, chuckling. The Detroit forward also tallied twice. And the second-place Hawks lost in six to the fourth-place Wings. For Hull it was another distressing end to a glorious season. Bobby was hockey's most compelling performer in the 1960s. Handsome, swift and strong. Chicago's number nine had an almost un-hockey-like glamour about him. Trent Frayne took this snapshot of Bobby at the peak of his fame:

> On TV he was a dimpled pitchman for hair tonic, rubbing his head with Vitalis.... In *Esquire* his muscles bulged from swimsuits and sweaters.... There he was in Hawaii...his tawny pelt glistening, his grin caressing some delicious doll wearing...a Jantzen that just did make the picture. While in work clothes he extolled a Ford tractor.... Back on TV between periods, there he was being interviewed after firing three goals past some hapless goaltender, telling the interviewer

with a...nice warm gratifying touch of humility that it
was fine to score.

Hull's Madison Avenue profile and gaudy scoring records only
made his post-season failures more acute. Sometimes even difficult to watch. Except for the spring of 1961 when Chicago
surprised Montreal and Detroit (and maybe even themselves)
to take the Cup, the abundantly talented Hawks usually made
an early playoff exit. And Hull always seemed to end the season looking like butchered meat.

After finishing a point out of first to Toronto in 1962–63,
the Hawks were sent home by Detroit in the first round. Early
in that series, Hull tried to slip a spinning Bruce MacGregor
and caught a stick on the bridge of the nose.

"People in the stands said it sounded like a rifle shot," Hull
remembered. "It knocked me to my knees, but I was able to
make it to the dressing-room under my own power. When the
doctor finally got there, I was bleeding all over the place.
'Son,' the doctor told me, 'I was on duty for the Graziano-Zale
fights, but I've never seen a nose like that.' He didn't finish
up with me until after midnight."

The next season, Chicago finished a point out of first,
behind Montreal, and were again knocked out by Detroit in
the opening round. The Hawks finally solved the Wings in
the 65 playoffs before losing to the Habs in the finals. In that
Montreal series, Bobby tangled memorably with Ferguson in
game five. Fergy's shoulder caught Bobby in the face, shattering his reconstructed nose. Other players would have stayed
down, but Hull, an immensely strong and courageous man,
sprang to his feet, his face raining blood, and charged his
attacker. Ferguson ducked Hull's blind sallies, then waded in.
After the game, Bobby's face looked like a bag of marbles.

In his book *Thunder and Lightning*, Ferguson offered a sad
coda to the story of his fight with Hull. In the parking lot
after the game, he was approached by a smiling woman. "I
want to thank you," she said without a trace of happiness.
"For what?" Fergy responded. "For teaching my husband a lesson," the woman replied. Ferguson shook his head and walked
away. "Know who that was?" a teammate asked. Ferguson

shrugged. "Joanne Hull. Bobby's wife."

By the fall of 1966, Bobby's blonde hair was thinning and his face marked by more than 200 stitches. He had difficulty breathing out of the ruin that was his nose and bursitis in his right hip made skating a torture. If he was still the best winger in the game, was still the Golden Jet, he no longer played with the joy and abandon of earlier seasons. In training camp he talked of retiring, saying he'd quit just like Sandy Koufax* if he had the money. He was certainly in no mood for Bugsy Watson this November night in Chicago.

After Mikita set up Ken Hodge to make it 2–0 for Chicago, Hull and Watson resumed their feud. It was a typical hockey fight—more taunts than punches were thrown. Watson kept ragging Hull in the penalty box, taking delight when Dean Prentice scored to shave the Chicago lead in half.

In the second period, the two men tangled first shift out when Bobby attempted a pirouette around his check and Watson cross-checked him into the boards. As 20,000 Hawk fans let out an injured roar, Watson himself groaned. "I looked out of the corner of my eye and there was Bobby [on the ice]. I said to myself, 'Here's where I get two minutes.' Then I sneaked a peek at Hull as he was getting up. He swung his stick backwards and something exploded in my head."

Watson lay slumped on the ice for a full five minutes, his head in a spreading halo of blood. He couldn't see out of his right eye and feared the worst. Trainer Lefty Wilson finally told him to relax. The gash was above the eye. Seconds later, a relieved Watson was on his feet, staggering toward the clinic. He didn't even mind the abuse that rained down as he left the ice.

"See, Ted Lindsay once told me that when they boo you on the road to take it as a compliment," he says. "It only means you're doing your job."

Chicago reacted to Watson's blood like feeding sharks. After MacGregor converted a pass from Ted Hampson to tie

---

* After winning his third Cy Young award, Los Angeles Dodgers pitcher Sandy Koufax retired in the fall of 1966. He was just 30 years old and coming off a 27–9 season, but was plagued by an arthritic elbow.

the game early in the third, Chicago went on a ten-minute
scoring frenzy. The free-skating Hull, now double-shifted, was
on the ice for linemate Chico Maki's tip-in from Esposito,
then, minutes later, took a blind pass from the artful Mikita
and wired a wrist shot under the crossbar. Brother Dennis also
scored, golfing a "Louuuuu" Angotti feed past a demoralized
Crozier. Kenny Wharram, on yet another Mikita pass, and
gangly Eric Nesterenko rounded out the Black Hawk scoring.

On nights like this, Chicago seemed to belong in a higher
league. With all their big scorers it was as if the Hawks were
using machine guns; everyone else, single-shot rifles.

"Boy, when they got those big shooters going with those
danged curved sticks and the crowd starting screaming it was
unbelievable," remembers Red Kelly. "You just couldn't stop
them. Other teams would score a couple of goals, then maybe
fall back a little. Not Chicago. Oh, hang, they would roll
right over you. Before you looked around you could be down
three or four goals and the game was over."

It could be argued Detroit's season was over after Chicago's
five-goal outburst, as the Wings would remain curled in a fetal
position for a month. During that time the team would win
one (against Boston) and lose eleven, while being outscored
52–24.

"Yeah [66–67] was a bad year in Detroit," Watson recalls.
"I think we kind of fooled management because of the way we
won those first two games in Montreal and almost stole the
Stanley Cup the previous spring. But remember that season,
we had Doug Barkley and Bill Gadsby, all stars on defense.
And Roger was unbelievable in the nets. Then Doug, who
was one of the five best defensemen in the league when he
lost his eye, and Bill both retired. Roger couldn't handle the
extra work…well, no one could. Management probably
should've retooled the team over the summer, I guess. But,
Christ you gotta remember we'd almost won the Cup."

Teammate Henderson felt the team should've won that
Cup.

"Montreal had a great hockey team, but we lost the series
because we had no discipline," he said in his book *Shooting
For Glory*. "Instead of practicing during the playoffs, we hung

out at the racetrack and the bars. Some of the older guys on the team should have stood up and said, 'Let's start behaving ourselves,' but they didn't. To put it bluntly our coach Sid Abel lost control of the team… Some Red Wings were more familiar with the bars in Detroit than with their homes. Detroit owner Jim Norris had a picture taken of himself and some of the Red Wings smoking cigars after our second win… Montreal coach Toe Blake got his hands on it and put it up in the Canadien dressing-room."

The suggestion that the 60s Wings were chronic under-achievers, a country club more than a hockey team, has been made before. Watson doesn't buy it.

"I'm disappointed in Paul for saying that. Listen, Roger played the best hockey of his life those first two games in Montreal. But the Canadiens were just better than us. Paul knows that. And that stuff about Sid, and the team drinking and all is…well, it's a crock. You think Doug Harvey didn't have a drink or two during all those years Canadiens won the Cup?

"Listen, you want to know why Montreal won, I'll tell you. And this is right from the Canadien players, who told me. After we won those first games, couple of our guys left the Forum smoking cigars. Toe was getting on the Montreal bus, saw us, and flipped.

"'Look, they think they've already won the Cup,' he screams. But it wasn't the screaming that got his guys pumped. On the train to Detroit, Toe goes to Béliveau, [Gilles] Tremblay, and Provost and says, 'I'm going to tell you how we're going to win the Cup, all right?' Course, they're all ears. Then Toe says, 'Jean, I don't care what you do on offense, but if your line can keep the Howe line from scoring I promise you, we win.' And you look it up, neither Gordie or Alex [Delvecchio] or Dean [Prentice] gets a point next four games. And three of those games were in Detroit, where we had last line change."

"I played for Toe [during the 1963–64, 64–65, and 67–68 seasons]. He was the smartest coach I ever had. What he did better than anyone is tell you what you needed to do to win. Nothing else. Winning was all he cared about. But listen, it was more than Toe. There's one simple reason why Montreal won all those Cups, and Detroit, Chicago, New York and Boston didn't win any.

"Because they had to!

"That's right. Look, I started in the Montreal organization when I was fourteen. Scotty Bowman was my coach in Peterborough. You had to win with Scotty. Lose two games in a row, it was a catastrophe.

"Second place was not a consideration. Losing in the finals was not a consideration. You won. Same thing was true through the whole organization. By the time you got to Montreal you thought of yourselves as winners. Champions.

"To play in Montreal was the greatest thrill of my career. Oh, to just ride on the train with that Canadien team—well, it was probably the only time in my life I ever just shut up and listened," laughs Watson, who even today is capable of giving a three-hour interview in forty minutes. "My God, to sit there in a small compartment and listen to Béliveau, Geoffrion, Talbot, and Henri talk hockey. That's all they did, just talk about the great games and players. Always Montreal teams and Canadien players, mind you. Isn't that funny? But that's the way you thought if you were a Canadien—that you were the only team!

"And if you weren't allowed to lose in Peterborough, my God, losing in Montreal was unthinkable. If you did lose, I tell you, you went from the rink home then back to the rink, nowhere else. Why? Because if you walked down any street in Montreal all you saw was disappointed people giving you a look that said, 'How could you?' And, my God, if you lost the Stanley Cup! Well competitors like Henri and Béliveau, they wouldn't show their faces in Montreal over the summer. They just disappeared for four months."

Bugsy's chuckle trails into a sigh.

"What a shock it was to leave the Canadien organization after ten years. Biggest surprise of my pro career was my first training camp in Detroit, listening to Sid talk to the players, first day of camp. He says something like, 'OK boys, let's have a good camp. Remember, we want to get off to a good start so we can make the play-offs, finish high up and take our chances in the playoffs.'

"'Finish high up?' 'Take our chances in the play-offs?' I couldn't believe it! With Montreal, Toe never made any speeches. Didn't have to. Every player knew that the team had to finish first and win the Cup, and that anything short of that was failure. But frankly, Detroit wasn't any different from any other NHL team I played for in my [seventeen-year] career."

The Hull-Watson feud could've ended the day after Hull pitchforked Watson, when Bobby visited the Detroit winger in a Chicago hospital.

"I'm sorry. I intended to hit you, but I didn't mean to hurt you," offered a remorseful Hull.

"Big deal," responded Watson from behind a mummy's head of bandages.

And so the quarrel continued.

In a week, Watson was back in action, sparring with teammates: "Hey Gordie, when you gonna hang 'em up and let some of us young guys play a while?" he kidded Howe upon returning to the Detroit dressing room. Noticing the eighteen-stitch zipper on Watson's nose, Gordie winced, turned to Abel, and remarked, "Sid, when you gonna schedule a few open dates so Bugsy here can rest his face?"

Although Chicago and Detroit wouldn't play again until December, Watson harassed Hull long distance, starting up a collection in his honour in the Detroit Olympia offices: "The Bobby Hull retirement fund," Watson's hand-made box read, "Please donate. Chairman, Bryan Watson. All proceeds to go to Bobby Hull so he can have as much money as Sandy Koufax and retire."

In fact, the feud would continue long after both men left hockey.

"Yeah, over the years I've attended old-timer events with Bobby and a lot of the guys, and he always gives me the cold shoulder," Watson says. "I guess I understand why. We had a weird chemistry. You could say we brought out the worst in each other…. If I had've tried the same thing with Howe, I would've ended up in a hospital, permanently. Another guy like Béliveau, I wouldn't have been able to do it at all…

wouldn't have seemed right. Only way I can explain why I did what I did to Bobby is to say that it worked. Bobby just totally lost his concentration with me. He was more concerned about me than the game."

Watson says he regrets the two never managed to patch things up.

"Listen, Bobby was one of the greatest players of all time and of course I have a lot of respect for him. He has a pretty good sense of humour, too. I remember a couple of years ago I almost cut my arm off in a chainsaw accident. And I heard through the grapevine that one of the guys told Bobby about the accident. He just nodded and said, 'Un-hunh, and how's the chainsaw?'"

DETROIT
Goal—Crozier, Bassen
Defense—Boivin, McCord, Bergman, Marshall
Forwards—Prentice, Delvecchio, Howe, Ullman, Mahovlich, MacGregor, Smith, Watson, Bathgate, Hampson, MacDonald

CHICAGO
Goal—DeJordy, Hall
Defense—Pilote, Jarrett, Van Impe, Ravlich, Stapleton
Forwards—Wharram, Mikita, Hodge, Maki, Esposito, R. Hull, Nesterenko, Angotti, D. Hull, Stanfield, Boyer

FIRST PERIOD
1. Chicago, R. Hull 8th (Esposito, Stapleton) 3:42
2. Chicago, Hodge 3rd (Mikita, Pilote) 8:37
3. Detroit, Prentice 3rd (Boivin, Hampson) 16:50
Penalties—R. Hull and Waton (majors) 13.53

SECOND PERIOD
No scoring
Penalties—None

THIRD PERIOD
4. Detroit, MacGregor 3rd (Hampson) 4:18
5. Chicago, Maki 3rd (Jarrett, Esposito) 8:02
6. Chicago, D. Hull 6th (Angotti, Nesterenko) 9:18
7. Chicago, R. Hull 9th (Mikita, Pilote) 11:14
8. Chicago, Wharram 5th (Mikita, Hodge) 15:16
9. Chicago, Nesterenko 4th (Jarrett, D. Hull) 19:39
Penalties—None

Shots on goal
Detroit   5   12   8 — 25
Chicago   12   13   9 — 34

NOVEMBER 19 STANDINGS

	P	W	L	T	F	A	Pts
Chicago	12	8	2	2	48	27	18
Toronto	14	4	3	7	34	36	15
New York	15	4	6	5	43	43	13
Boston	13	5	5	3	36	41	13
Montreal	12	5	6	1	26	28	11
Detroit	14	4	8	2	43	49	10

LEAGUE LEADERS

	GP	G	A	Pts	PIM
Mikita, Chi.	12	6	15	21	2
Ullman, Det.	14	3	13	16	18
Gilbert, N.Y.	15	8	6	14	4
D. Hull, Chi.	12	6	7	13	6
Rousseau, Mont.	12	4	9	13	16
Goyette, N.Y.	15	0	13	13	2
R. Hull, Chi.	11	9	3	12	15
Henderson, Det.	13	9	3	12	0
Geoffrion, N.Y.	13	3	9	12	6
Marshall, N.Y.	13	6	5	11	2
Howell, N.Y.	15	5	6	11	10

LEAGUE LEADERS (*continued*)

Kelly, Tor.	14	4	7	11	8
Pilote, Chi.	12	2	9	11	14

Crowd noise

November 25 CHUM Hit Parade

1. "Winchester Cathedral," New Vaudeville Band
2. "You Keep Me Hangin' On," The Supremes
3. "Devil With the Blue Dress/Good Golly Miss Molly,"
   Mitch Ryder and the Detroit Wheels
4. "Stop, Stop, Stop," Hollies
5. "Good Vibrations," Beach Boys
6. "Born Free," Roger Williams
7. "Look Through Any Window," Mamas and Papas
8. "Walk Away Renee," Left Banke
9. "Mellow Yellow," Donovan
10. "Lady Godiva," Peter and Gordon
11. "Last Train to Clarksville," Monkees
12. "I'm Your Puppet," James and Bobby Purify
13. "Coming on Strong," Brenda Lee
14. "That's Life," Frank Sinatra
15. "Holy Cow," Lee Dorsey
16. "Poor Side of Town," Johnny Rivers
17. "Psychotic Reaction," Count Five
18. "Rain on the Roof," Lovin' Spoonful
19. "96 Tears," ? & the Mysterians
20. "On This Side of Goodbye," The Righteous Brothers

Local bands playing Montreal high school dances

Bartholomew Plus Three; The Beau Gests; The Bohemians;
The Dirty Shames; Family Dog; Fyve; The Haunted;
The Hidden; The Inn Crowd; Jamie and the Jesters;
The Jaybees; Junior Hamilton and the Senators; The Kreatures;
The Luvs; MG and the Escorts; The Munks; Our Generation;
The Rabble; The Raving Mad; Rembrandt; Simple Simon and
the Piemen; The Stix and Stones; Les Sultanes;
MikeThornhill and the Exciters; TR '5's;
Trixie and the Inmates; Trybe; and the Underdogs.

6
Clashing Cultures

Nineteen-year-old art school dropout Joan Anderson arrived in Toronto in 1963. She got a job at Simpson's, and paddled with her guitar up Yonge Street to Yorkville every night after work. Soon she was getting $10 gigs at coffee houses like the Penny Farthing. Anderson married, separated, moved to Greenwich Village, found a manager, and was discovered, all inside 24 months. Judy Collins would record three of her songs on her next album, including "Both Sides Now," the number she closed with during her week-long, November stay at Yorkville's premiere folk club, The Riverboat.

Joni Mitchell was one of a score of artists working Toronto's flourishing folk scene this month. Neil Young left Yorkville (and a job as a stock boy at Coles on Yonge Street) for California in March, but Gordon Lightfoot, Ian and Sylvia, Phil Ochs, John Lee Hooker, and Arlo Guthrie (with a single-song set, "Alice's Restaurant") all played here in November.

The jazz scene was just as fertile. The fabulous Thelonious Monk splonked away a week at the Colonial Tavern recently. While Art Blakey, with Jazz Messengers Chuck Mangione and

Chick Corea, played the refurbished Towne. Stanley Turrentine and June Christy had stays in the swank Plaza Room. And Willie the Lion Smith roared through a string of dates at The Golden Nugget. The Leafs hung out at another downtown jazz club, George's Spaghetti House, where trumpeter Maynard Ferguson regularly threatened glassware with his upper register blowing.

Maybe the hottest music in town could be found at the scruffy Le Coq D'Or—Ronnie Hawkins' rompin' ground. His old band was now backing Dylan, but Ronnie still did his funky camel walk three sets a night in Toronto's most infamous Yonge Street bar. According to participants, after-hours parties were the stuff of Nero. "Let's not call them orgies," Hawkins said, "let's just say it's seven or eight people in love."

Hawkins' old drummer, Levon Helm, maintains "Toronto was swinging at least a year before…London." Helm was raised in Turkey Scratch, Arkansas, and never made it to England, but his claim has some substance. Go Go Givens was about to get the heave. And yes, the city continued to exhibit flashes of old-maid decorousness—in Montreal, strip joints letterboxed dancers' breasts in marquee posters; here, the Victory Burlesk on Spadina felt compelled to block out faces, as well—still, Toronto was undergoing something of a renaissance.

Right now, filmmaker Michael Snow was editing the underground film classic, *Wavelength*. Painters Jack Chambers and Harold Town were in their primes. Northrop Frye and Marshall McLuhan lectured at U of T. And the self-proclaimed "Canadian Publisher," Jack McClelland, had recently convinced a twenty-seven-year-old poet, Margaret Atwood, to try her hand at novels.

This was also the golden age of TV in Canada. "Wojeck," the story of a coroner who gave a damn, had just completed a successful run. Now viewers were raving about a TV politician who gave a damn: "Quentin Durgens, M.P." "This Hour Has Seven Days" had been yanked by the CBC in the spring, but this remained an era of nervy public affairs programming. A recent episode of "Nightspot" opened with a skit of a hooker being interviewed on inflation. "Well," she said, slumped against a lamp-post, "it's definitely getting harder to make ends meet."

A November episode of another Toronto-based program, "Umbrella!" had Canadians rubbing their eyes. A Margaret Laurence interview was followed by "Eddie Shack's Nightmare." CBC called the film "a surrealistic fantasy." Eddie, dressed in Leaf blue, lay trapped on a brass bed, while about him swirled a jazz band, modern dancers armed with custard pies, and a gingham-bikinied temptress (CBC staffer Barbara Amiel taking her baby steps as a Canadian media personality). "They called me a while ago," Eddie told reporters, rolling his eyes—the class tough forced to perform in the school play. "I wasn't interested. But I said if the Gardens would OK it, I'd do the show. I guess they did."

If Toronto wasn't quite the hick town Montrealers imagined, neither was Canada's largest city the criminal jungle of Clifford W. Harvison's fervid imagination. Studying 1967 crime statistics, it's a toss up which city is most (or least) virtuous. Assaults are the same. We find twice as many prostitution busts in Toronto (712 to 340). Montreal has more murders (36 to 22). One stat, however, catches the eye with the impact of a Baun elbow: There are twice as many robberies in Montreal (20,609 to 10,391).

In the 60s, Montrealers enjoyed robberies the same way that Londoners, in Orwell's time, appreciated a good murder. Spectacular bank heists were routine front-page news. In early November, after a thrilling six-month chase punctuated by gunfights, kidnappings, and a giddy spree of robberies, Quebec's Clyde Barrow, André Daoust, was cornered in a Montreal motel.

"I want to speak to a reporter," the twenty-four-year-old media-savvy folk hero demanded from his tear-gassed room. "Nothing doing, throw out that gun," police shouted. André swallowed a handful of bennies, threw away his 357 magnum pistol and stumbled outside. When police cuffed him, he snarled, "Keep your dirty hands off me" Jimmy Cagney style, then collapsed into a thirty-six-hour stupor.

Weeks later, shotgun-wielding bandits made headlines—"Holdup Goes Haywire"—at the Versailles Shopping Centre.

After looting the Bank of Commerce of $12,000, Richard Lortie and Yvon Dubrueil smashed their way out a bank window. While escaping, Lortie took a shard of glass in the leg. Outside, Dubrueil gunned the getaway car before his limping partner made it inside. Lortie, still clutching a shotgun, fell under the car and was dragged thirty feet. When Dubrueil braked to check his partner, Lortie blew a fist-size hole in his chest. Both men were dead before police arrived.

But the story doesn't end there. Two relatives of one bandit then fell into an argument with police. When a scuffle broke out, a brother officer drew his gun and raced to the scene, slipped on a scalp of ice and shot himself in the leg.

Still, the best Montreal crime story of 1966 didn't involve guns or bank robbers. The Montreal *Star*'s Bruce Taylor wrote in a recent column: "We've heard of some unusual thefts in our years in this dodge, but this one has to be the weirdest. A man living in St. Hillaire had his lake stolen. A small lake on high ground stocked with trout. Someone dug a sluice and drained it off to lower ground, stealing the trout."

One Montrealer unlikely to steal from either a commercial or river bank was Jean Béliveau. Opening game of the season, Béliveau even returned a goal that didn't belong to him. Incredibly, Big Jean still hadn't registered a goal in fifteen contests. Teammates weren't scoring either. Going into their November 30 game against Toronto, the Habs hadn't scored more than three goals in a game this season.

After the team's 3–2 loss to Toronto three weeks earlier, Montreal dropped a weekend pair to New York and Boston. At home against the Rangers, Boom Boom beat Gump on a breakaway ("I put a deke on him, hoo boy, he was out for coffee with cream and sugar"), and Gilbert added two more in an easy 6–3 New York win. The next night in Boston, Gerry Cheevers held the Canadiens to a goal in a 2–1 victory. Six days later, Toronto humiliated the Habs 5–1. Montreal finally ended a two-week slide the next night, edging the Rangers 2–1 in a game Hodge and the Canadiens were outshot 44–21.

The following week, Montreal failed to impress while taking two from the free-falling Wings. "I shouldn't say this," a

depressed Sid Abel observed after Gump shut out his club
3–0, "but I don't think I've ever seen Montreal play a worse
game." Any suggestion the tiny winning streak meant the
Habs had turned a corner was dispelled by a mid-week contest
in Chicago that saw Montreal outshot 12–4 and outscored
4–0 in the first period on the way to a 5–0 drubbing.

The low point in the Canadiens' miserable November,
however, remained the Toronto loss. Blake was mute afterwards. "Toronto won 5–1. Béliveau played three shifts. I have
nothing else to say," he told reporters, then quit the Gardens
for the team bus, where he waited for his last-place club to
shower and change.

That Toe should mention the slumping Béliveau's participation in the Canadiens' humiliating loss was an indication of
his frustration. "Béliveau was a special member of the
Canadiens," Red Fisher recalls. "Over the years, Toe inevitably
crossed swords with most players. Even a fierce competitor and
consummate team man like Henri had his rounds with Toe.
Having said that, I can't recall even hearing of Toe getting
into a disagreement with Jean. There was a feeling, I think,
that because he always gave an honest effort, and carried himself with such distinction, that he was above reproach.

"Also, you have to remember that Toe was above all else
an astute coach," Fisher continues, "and as a purely practical
matter, it wouldn't have been useful to discredit Jean because
the whole team—all of hockey, really—looked up to him.
Jean symbolized the best traditions of the Canadiens."

Blake knew the Captain could untangle the little personality kinks that beset a team; difficulties that otherwise
would've been his to solve. One problem was Blake himself.
The coach was often remote. A player sometimes passed
Blake and offered a cheery hello, only to have Toe stare
through him as if he were a smudged window. "Tell me, am I
headed for Quebec City?" the troubled player would ask
Béliveau. Jean would sit his teammate down and tell him a
story:

"One summer, this is in the late 50s when we are
Cup champion every year, I am out playing golf here

in Montreal. I look up and see Toe walking ahead.
Well, I had been with the Canadiens a while, I was
feeling good. So I walk up and say, "Hello Coach." He
walks past like he doesn't know me. At first I was
upset, but look, ten year later, I'm still here."

Although he wasn't a dressing-room Patton, like Ted Lindsay,
the Captain could control his team with the smallest of ges-
tures. After one game, a rookie peeled off his Canadiens
sweater, flinging it away. Rising to his full height, Béliveau
marched over and lifted the discarded jersey. A hush fell on
the dressing room as he turned to confront the young player.
"This sweater," Béliveau said gravely, "never lands on the
floor again."

"Jean Béliveau was the Montreal Canadiens," Ferguson
says. "The way he carried himself, with such dignity, that's the
way we tried to behave in public. Every time he walked into
the room or stepped onto the ice you realized, hey, I'm with
the Canadiens, that's special."

The Leafs had a captain, too. George Armstrong. The
Chief had none of Béliveau's solemn nobility. "On the first
day of camp in Peterborough, George would get pissed and go
into his drunken-Indian act [Armstrong was part Ojibway],"
recalls Louis Cauz. "He'd take out his teeth and slump on a
bar stool and start moaning, 'Ugh, white man's fire water ruin
Indian.' Stuff like that."

"Early on, George was a bad drinker," says Billy Harris. "At
one point he had three car accidents in four summers back
home up north. But when he made captain in 1958, he
changed. It was a responsibility that he took seriously and
made him a better man. For one thing, he stopped the heavy
boozing."

"After that first night of clowning," Cauz says, "George
would lay off the sauce and concentrate on work. He seemed
to set the tone in practices during training camp."

"He never had the natural ability of a lot of players,"
Harris says. "He wasn't a terrific skater. It was all sweat and
hard work with George. I remember those morning practices
when I didn't feel like working, I'd look over and see George

pumping and groaning as he skated past, and I'd think, geez, better get back to work. A lot of the so-called Imlach work ethic was Armstrong."

"Armstrong didn't stand up in the middle of the room and make speeches," says George Gross. "But he was a terrific leader. Many times I'd come into the dressing room and see him talking quietly to Mahovlich in the corner, and Frank nodding."

Sometimes it seemed Béliveau descended from a cloud to play the game. "He was like a priest, maybe," J.C. says. "You might be doing something, then when Béliveau comes you stop…you know it's not right." The Chief, however, was decidedly of this earth. One night, he was at a show with Harris, a frequent guest in Punch's doghouse. They were in a line-up, Harris in back of Army, when the Chief decided to lighten Harris's spirits with horseplay. Reaching back, George grabbed his teammate's crotch and sang, "Check your bags, Mr. Harris?" No response. So Army gave it another honk, then turned to find a nervous stranger in a fedora. Harris, seated twenty yards away, was watching all this, killing himself laughing.

Armstrong was peerless defensively and a clutch scorer (in the Leafs' Cup-winning springs he counted twenty goals and assists in forty-five games), but his greatest contribution came off ice, keeping peace between his mulish teammates and hard-headed coach. "George was the only player who had influence on Imlach," Gross suggests. Brian Conacher adds, "He was the ham in the sandwich between Imlach and players. That fall in training camp, George came up to me one day after a work-out. Maybe he figured I was skeptical about some of the things that were going on. Anyway, he says, 'You may wonder why we're doing this. No one works as hard as we do. No one is in as good shape as we are. If it comes to the sixth or seventh game in the play-offs, I guarantee you we'll end up on top.'"

The Chief did Imlach's bidding for a decade without becoming a management stooge. How? Well, maybe the answer to that puzzle comes with the resolution of another Leaf mystery: Who swiped Punch's Florsheims back in 1963?

"Sounds like Armstrong," Allan Stanley says today, laughing.

No one noticed, but helmets came to the NHL on this, the fourth meeting of the season between Montreal and Toronto. Oh, players had worn them before. Howe, Mikita and Kelly donned head gear after injuries. But on this the last day of November, 1966, two Canadiens stepped onto Gardens ice wearing permanent head gear.

"I got knocked out when my head hit the ice after Reggie Fleming hit me [in Montreal's 6–3 loss to the Rangers]," J.C. remembers. "I told Toe I want to wear a helmet. He said, 'OK, you're hurt, if you want to wear a helmet for a while, OK, but I think you could be hurting yourself if you wear the helmet always. You will become a target. People will think you're afraid.'

"Even though I told Toe I'd think about it, in my mind I decided to wear a helmet after that injury…. Players say all kind of thing about helmets," J.C says. "'It slip over your face so you can't see.' 'You get too hot and the sweat fall in your eyes.' But it was no problem except nobody else was wearing it, so they didn't want me to."

Alas, J.C.'s first game in a helmet did little to change Blake's prejudice against head gear. On Tremblay's first shift, Horton intercepted a pass, flew down the boards, dodged Laperrière, then, seeing Gump had the angle covered, lobbed one at the net. The puck hit J.C., who had a hold of but no control over the hard-charging Pappin, and skipped into the empty cage.

On his next shift, J.C. retreated behind the net then appeared to become unstuck in time. While Tremblay gazed into the future, the brutal present arrived in the form of Shack, who left the ice to pancake number three into the boards. With J.C. falling, Eddie sent a quick pass out front to Brenneman and it was two-zip, Leafs. Toe had some words for the clock after pulling J.C. Except for a few spins on the power play, Tremblay would spend the night on his backside, polishing the bench.

On his previous visit to the Gardens, John Ferguson drifted

into position for a face-off, only to have Kent Douglas greet him with a smirk. "Got you handcuffed, huh?" the defenseman remarked. Six weeks into the season, word was out that Blake told Ferguson to cut down on the rough stuff. "We want you to hit people, just try not to get as many stupid penalties," Toe said. Blake's order turned Fergy into a scarecrow. He wasn't getting penalties, but neither was he hitting, skating, or shooting; like Béliveau, Fergy was scoreless so far.

Tonight, Fergy couldn't take it any more. "My blood always got boiling when we played Toronto," he says. "Especially if we were losing." After Brenneman's goal, number 22 hopped the boards and charged the Leaf end, elbows and shoulders twitching. After walloping Conacher, he wheeled in search of Shack. Sure enough, Fast Eddie was Geronimoing his way. Ferguson buzzed Shack's flat-top—wwwhooshh!—with the shaft of his stick, then wrestled his decade-long sparring partner to the ice.

"Shack was the most aggressive guy on the Leafs, although he didn't necessarily try to take on the biggest guys on other teams," Ferguson says. "It was my job to look after him. I didn't have anything against him, though."

An incident this season, however, suggests Fergy had a special mad-on for Leafs' number 23. Before a game, Ferguson dined out at George's Spaghetti House, the jazz club on Sherbourne and Dundas, with teammate Duff. After the players' meals arrived, a murmur rippled the room and Duff's face brightened. "Hiya Shackie, how are you?" he shouted. Seeing Eddie bound toward the table, Ferguson felt a cold fury descend upon him.

"I put down my knife and fork, threw my money on the table and left," he says. "I couldn't sit at the same table with Shack. He was a Maple Leaf. He was the enemy. People ask me about Shack and those games. Yeah, we went at it a lot, I guess, and we used to play each other every week back then. But seriously, I didn't have anything against him. He was a Leaf. I hated them all."

To prove his loathing for Toronto was entirely democratic, Ferguson took on three more Leafs at the end of the first period. With time running out, he put a Killer Kowalski sleeper hold on Kelly, then tried to make a shish kebab out of Jeffrey. After the prelims, he waded through linesmen to tangle with Baun.

"On every successful team you have a role player who gets the team going," Béliveau says. "Fergy was important to us, not only because he was the policeman who let us play Canadien hockey, but because when we were in a slump, he would get us going with his ah,"—Jean searches for the right word—"excitement."

The Habs got some excitement going midway in the second with good work from Béliveau's line. Jean threw a smart pass between Pronovost's legs onto the stick of a cutting Provost. Claude's tap shot from a sharp angle slid past Sawchuk, off the far post, yo-yoing back along the goal line. The twisting goalie threw his blocker on the puck just as it appeared to wobble over the line.

Goal judge Eddie Mepham's right hand jerked instinctively to the brown-switched metal box in front of him. Although the red light flashed, referee Art Skov waved the play off, then huddled with fellow officials. A few minutes later, he pointed to centre ice. The goal stood.

Leafs mounted a protest. Punch stood on the bench, hands on his hips, fedora back, screaming. Sawchuk skated to centre, gesturing with his stick. "I was hopping," Terry said afterwards, "but [Skov] told me it'd cost me a misconduct and I can't afford $50. But that puck still hasn't crossed the line!"

Skov took a few minutes of grief, then blew his whistle to resume play. A few shifts later, Ferguson found Henri at centre. The Toronto Star's Red Burnett described what happened next: "Leafs were still visibly upset and shaky defensively when Richard tied it up at the 12:33 mark…and there was no doubt about that score. He took a pass from Ferguson, left Horton as if he were fast-frozen, walked in and deked Sawchuk out of his suit before slipping the puck into the net."

The rest of the period was frantic back-and-forth action. Keon was flying. Richard, too. And the Béliveau-Gilles Tremblay combination showed some of the old magic when Jean sailed over the Leaf line, split Stanley and Hillman, then threw a blind backhand to his wing that Gilles Tremblay collected and fired in one motion, forcing Sawchuk into an acrobatic glove save.

Then, inexplicably, for the second game in a row against Toronto, the Habs faltered in the final period. Stanley and Horton (Foster Hewitt's first star tonight), along with Pronovost and Baun kept Montreal circling and spinning in their own zone. The Canadiens' defense played well, too, especially Harper and Harris. A tie seemed inevitable. Then Léon Rochefort committed a cardinal sin. The defensive specialist was in for Rousseau (Montreal's other helmeted player had been in Toe's bad books since leaving a game in Detroit with a nosebleed). Léon had played well this evening, but with ten minutes left he threw a cross-ice pass in his own end. Stanley, who'd been laying back like an old bass in the weeds, grabbed the puck and fed Stemkowski, who quickly relayed to Conacher high in the slot.

"Shoot, shoot," Stemkowski yelled. Conacher fired a low shot at Worsley's stick side. "It wasn't a real hard shot, but it caught Worsley by surprise. He was back in his net," Lionel Conacher's grandson said. "It was a nice feeling when that red light glowed."

The goal gave the Leafs a 3–2 win and a tie for second place with the surprising Rangers (both teams were four back of Chicago). The Habs fell to fifth. What was wrong with the Canadiens? Everybody wanted to know.

"That's easy, their main problem is that the schedule has forced them to play the Toronto Maple Leafs four times," Imlach crowed. "We beat 'em three and the other game was a tie."

Then Punch proceeded to squeeze seven first-person references into a one-paragraph explanation of his team's recent success: "Things have been working out surprisingly well. I've been playing four forward lines, mixing the rookies with some of the old guys. I have Brenneman playing with Pulford and Shack. I have Pappin playing with Keon and Mahovlich. I have Ellis and Jeffrey playing with Kelly. I have Conacher and Stemkowski playing with Armstrong…. I'm exactly where I want to be right now."

The Habs weren't. "Canadiens are in a crisis…the worst

since the early 40s," Jacques Beauchamp reported in Montréal *Matin*. Canadiens had spent much of November in last place. They'd be there still if not for the miserable play of Detroit. "Let's face it, this is getting embarrassing," Toe said upon arriving back in Montreal. "Here it is December and we're in fifth place." He shook his head. "Fifth place!"

FIRST PERIOD
1. Toronto, Horton 2nd 1:38
2. Toronto, Brenneman 4th (Shack) 4:01
Penalties—Ferguson (high-sticking) 5:52; Armstrong (hooking) 8:37; Armstrong (interference) 14:32; Ferguson (high-sticking), Jeffrey (high-sticking) 19:47

SECOND PERIOD
3. Montreal, Provost 3rd (Béliveau, Talbot) 10:50
4. Montreal, Richard 6th (Ferguson, Laperrière) 12:33
Penalties—Conacher (charging) 7:06

THIRD PERIOD
5. Toronto, Conacher 6th (Stanley, Stemkowski) 11:00
Penalties—Backstrom (holding) 11:39; Provost (hooking) 15:30

Shots on goal
Montreal   14   17   5 — 36
Toronto   14   12   12 — 38

For much of the fall, Lili St. Cyr was in at Champs Show Bar on Crescent Street, performing her Dance of the Seven Veils, the same act that turned men into boiling tea kettles at the Gayety in the 40s. Actually, Lili didn't get into town much these days. Nudie shows were dying in Montreal. The movies had killed them. Right now, *Mondo Nudo* ("You'll stare in amazement") was playing at the Strand. Stella Stevens, fresh from a bubble bath and wearing only a few islands of suds, could be seen wrestling Dino in *The Silencers* at Loew's. The city's hottest night club was more like another recent movie—*Fantastic Voyage*, which played for months at the Capitol.

"Total environment—that's what I aim at. Total experi-

ence," Jean Paul Mousseau informed a recent visitor to Le
Mousse Spacethèque disco at Crescent and Burnside. "Here
all the senses are at play."

Especially vision. Four pivoting slide projectors sprayed zoo
animals and bikinied girls across the jackets and dresses of
frugging patrons. The blinking, swirling images and psychedelic music, from The Beatles' "Revolver" to Jefferson
Airplane's "Surrealistic Pillow," left even wallflowers standing
in corners feeling as if they were riding the aisleway of a moving bus. For at Le Mousse Spacethèque even the air was
turned on (Mousseau spiked the air-conditioning with lavender). Dawdling next to the club's leopard-skin bar, Mousseau
explained his nightclub's philosophy:

"Stimulation. People need it. So many people are content
just to be spectators. Life is participation…. Remember the
old dances: You had to learn steps. You had to do everything
the right way." He watched Mousse Spacethèquers sway like
trees in a windstorm on the dance floor. "Look at these people. They're daring, the way they feel the music… They are
part of their environment."

Yvan Cournoyer was a regular part of Le Spacethèque's environment. "Deadeye Dude of Crescent Street," *Sports Illustrated*
called him. "He speaks of the cavelike La Licorne and the
space-age Mousse Spacethèque with relish and admits that
dancing is another favourite pastime," the magazine reported.
Sports Illustrated's photographer caught the cherubic winger at
his parents' home in Lachine, sorting through clothes that
spilled from his closet onto a long metal rack. Like many
affluent Montrealers of his generation, the twenty-two-year-
old was something of a clothes pony, with hundreds of mod
outfits: double-breasted Edwardian blazers; epauletted pea
jackets; polka dot and striped shirts; and a rainbow variety of
hip-hugging slacks. Then there was his car, a $7,100 Corvette
Stingray (with automatic windows!).

"Yvan was a swinger, oh sure," J.C. laughs. "The rest of us
were too old to swing, even then."

"Never heard of Le Mousse Spacethèque," Yvan says quickly today.

Space-age disco on Crescent and Burnside, he's reminded. Wild light shows. Lavender in the air-conditioning.

"Oh no. We work pretty hard back then. Practice all the time, then the games. During the playoff we're away in the Laurentians. No time for that kind of thing."

In the summer then, relaxing.

"What is it? Le Mousse Spacethèque? No way."

Thirty years later, Yvan still acts like the Habs are mired in their December, 1966, slump and he's afraid Toe might read something that will embarrass the team. "When you play on the Canadiens you have responsibilities," he says. "To the team. To the city. All the fans. Management expects you to behave a certain way. There was a different atmosphere maybe than other teams."

Certainly a different atmosphere than existed on the Leafs. The rivalry between Montreal and Toronto played out at many levels. Most were obvious to fans. The clubs had different styles of play. Canadiens flew, Leafs marched; every match was a race between the tortoise and the hare. Then there was a clash of cultures: Canadiens represented Lower Canada (twelve players came from Quebec). Leafs flew the Upper Canadian flag (thirteen skaters came from Ontario). But there was another cultural difference that was lost on fans following the teams on TV.

"I was just a young guy when I got a job working in publicity for the Rangers," remembers John Halligan. "And what an eye-opener it was to see how the Leafs did business with Harold Ballard and Stafford Smythe running things. The carrying on. Boy, sometimes on the road you'd look into the wrong room and, oh my God, there were orgies going on! It was unbelievable. This is the Toronto Maple Leafs?" I asked myself. Imlach loathed Smythe and had nothing to do with Harold and Stafford's toga parties, but he also played hard on the road. "Punch liked the ladies," Louis Cauz says. "He used to invite me to go with him when he went out on the town. I was young, single. Anyone saw us with a girl, they'd figure she was with me."

The Canadiens were different, Halligan says.

"No comparison between the two teams. Management and

players, [the Canadiens] were consummate professionals. The whole organization had such class. And you know guys like Blake or Béliveau would never sit still for any of Smythe and Ballard's nonsense."

"The one thing that Toe would not let you do is embarrass him or the team," Cournoyer recalls. "That was because of his pride, eh? He was very proud. He would become upset if you make the team look like a joke. Very, very upset."

Right now, Blake was upset with his team's record. He'd shouted himself hoarse, scheduled extra practices, given days off...nothing worked. What could he do to lift players out of their torpor? Three days after the team's 3–2, November 30 loss to the Leafs, a brooding Blake entered the Forum dressing room. In a few hours, Habs would take the ice for a game with the first-place Black Hawks. He silently paced the floor until he was sure he had everyone's attention.

"Ralph," he finally called out to number six, Ralph Backstrom, "I've got something to say to you."

Players braced themselves. Ralph was in a slump, with only one goal and three assists in seventeen games.

"You know, about a month ago, we decided to have our door painted at home, so the painter carefully removed the 'two' and the 'zero' and the 'six' from the front door. He did a pretty good job. Everything looked nice, except for one thing: The painter forgot to put back our address.

"You know, weeks went by," Toe continued, pacing, "and the mailman was going past our door and nobody could blame him because how was he supposed to know that our number was 206 if the numbers weren't there? The delivery men would come up our street but they couldn't deliver the parcels and our groceries because the numbers weren't there. So for weeks we were missing mail and deliveries and hell, how long was this going to go on? Finally, I got hold of the painter and I said to him, 'Listen, Dugal, how long is this going to go on? When am I going to get back the numbers'?

"'Well, I tell you,'" he said, 'I've got the 'two' and I've got the 'oh,' but I can't find the 'six.' No, sir, I can't find it.'

"'It's funny you mention that, Dugal,' I told him, 'because we've got a 'six' on our club and I haven't been able to find him for the last two months either.'"

Blake's team exploded with laughter. Charlie Hodge got a particular kick out of the story.

"What are you laughing at, Charlie?" Toe snapped. "I could say the same thing about all the numbers between one and thirty."

Blake ended his talk by saying, "Whatever happens tonight, give the fans a show. Give them some entertainment. It's the least they deserve."

And so the players went out and gave Forum fans, including Prime Minister Pearson, an outstanding display of two-way hockey. The newly minted Larose-Backstrom-Ferguson line out-muscled and out-skated Mikita's unit. Balon-Richard-Provost never let Esposito or Hull see the puck. And both Duff and Béliveau, on beautiful set-ups from the helmeted Rousseau, scored their first goals of the season. Béliveau had an open side on his goal, but slapped the puck into Denis DeJordy's pads; after collecting the rebound, he lobbed a second shot into the goalie's chest protector before finally poking the puck home. "If I didn't score on the third shot I would've retired," he joked after the Canadien's 3–1 win.

The next night, in New York, Habs outshot the Rangers every period (and 43–25 overall). Backstrom's line looked after the scoring, with Larose counting two and Ferguson getting his first marker of the year in a 3–1 win. Only fabulous netminding by Giacomin kept it close. "That, gentlemen, was a perfect game," Emile Francis observed when it was all over.

Punch Imlach was as high as old cheese coming into the Forum, Wednesday, December 7. His Leafs had scored thirteen goals in weekend games, knocking off Detroit at home, 5–2, and drubbing the Bruins 8–3, Sunday night in Boston. Now they were in first place. First place! All Punch had hoped for was to stay in contention the first twenty games of the schedule.

"I'm gonna play four lines," he'd announced as the team entered a sixteen-games-in-thirty-three-days stretch in November. "We should be in good shape if we play 500 hockey. Oh, we could win more if I went with three, but it could cost us at the end of the season."

During that period the team was 9–3–4. Sawchuk, Stanley, Kelly, Ellis, and the surprising Conacher were the most dependable performers early on. But in the last two weeks, Horton had rounded into form, and the Mahovlich-Keon-Pappin line was functioning at peak efficiency. Frank led scorers during the streak with eight goals. Most were highlight reel material.

With his team down one late in Detroit, Frank grabbed the puck in his end, dashed the length of the ice, and rocketed one over Crozier's shoulder. "I didn't see the puck until I turned around," the goalie said. The night after the team's 5–1 November massacre of the Habs, Frank whipped a third-period blast past Glenn Hall to give his club a 2–2 tie. Three days later, the Hawks were in Toronto, up 2–0 in the second, when Mahovlich received a penalty shot. Reay replaced DeJordy with Hall, then argued with referee Bill Friday when Hall wasn't allowed a warm-up. Five agonizing minutes later, Friday moved to centre and pointed to Mahovlich. The crowd, which was already standing, climbed to its toes and leaned forward.

The Big M scooped the puck at centre and was at the Hawk blueline in three strides, then killed the engines and coasted, head up, the rest of the way in. Hall moved out, stopped, started backpedaling. When the goalie changed gears, Mahovlich leaned into a wrist shot that was past Hall's glove before he moved. In the third period, Frank scored again to salt away a 6–3 Leaf win.

"Mahovlich has the hardest shot in the league," Toronto goal judge Eddie Mepham used to say. "I've seen them all, ya know. Frank's shot is the hardest. Even harder than Hull's. Some of Frank's shots I don't see until the net bulges."

But Punch wasn't crowing about Mahovlich's shot when the team arrived in Montreal. "Our goaltending is the reason we're in first place," he said. "Sawchuk has been fantastic. I think he's playing the best hockey in his career right now. Even better than he was playing with Detroit in the 50s."

Sawchuk agreed. "You know my back was so bad [before a lower back operation] I'd been walking hunched over for

years," he said. "When I arrived in camp everyone looked at
me and said, 'Terry have you grown or something?' Truth was
I was just standing up, so I suddenly looked two inches
taller.... I feel great now, and I think I'm playing my best
hockey in ten years."

The Leafs started quickly this contest. One minute in,
Ferguson scratched an itchy elbow on Baun's noggin and was
gone for two. On the power play, Kelly dropped a soft pass to
Pappin, who golfed a low drive past Worsley. The Leafs carried the play for the next five minutes, twice burying Gump
under multibody pile-ups. The Habs didn't get a chance until
midway through the period, when the team finally managed a
flurry of weak shots on Sawchuk.

Unfortunately for Toronto, most of these efforts resulted in
goals. Richard tipped a Provost shot past the flopping
Sawchuk to tie the game. Two minutes later, Ferguson flattened Baun behind the Leaf net, then shovelled a pass out to
Larose, who swatted another one beyond the falling Leaf netminder. Baun charged Fergy after the goal, yanking his feet
out. During the Habs' power play, Conacher and Armstrong
kept Montreal outside the blueline. The way Sawchuk was
playing, however, even that wasn't enough. Cournoyer, out
for his second skate of the game, looked up at centre ice, saw
linemates heading off, then threw all of his 170 pounds into a
slapshot. One hundred and twenty feet later, Sawchuk waved
at Montreal's third goal.

After the game, Yvan was offended by suggestions that his
two-line blast was a cheapie. "I got all of it. And it was right
off the post. It was my best shot," he protested. Today,
Cournoyer still feels no one appreciated how hard he worked
to perfect his shooting.

"I could skate, sure. But a lot of hockey players can skate
fast. My Dad told me when I was young, 'Yvan, you are too
small [5'7"] for the NHL. You need something else.' So I
worked on my shot. My Dad worked in a machine shop. He
made me ten steel pucks, one-two pounds each. I shoot in the
basement every day until Dad told me to stop. I had demol-
ished everything.

"Finally, I got a few bales of hay and brought them downstairs, and I would shoot at the hay. Wrist shot—first ten right, then ten left, then ten backhand. I would do this every day for hours, from when I was fourteen to sixteen. Later I didn't do it so much because I felt I had the shot. But even when I was with the Canadiens, I can still remember working out in the summer in the basement, practicing my shot."

Teammates teased Yvan about his extra shooting. Especially when the left-handed shooter worked on his right-handed shot. "I remember one game, everybody was laughing at me in practice because I was working on my right shot. 'What are you shooting from the right, you never score that way,' they said. Later in the game I was skating down my wing, on the backhand. At the last second, I thought, I'll show them, so I switch [to my forehand] and put it high in the top corner. Then I came back to the bench, boy, was I laughing. 'Is that such a funny joke, now?' I screamed. 'Is it still funny, all my practicing?'"

Horton, the best Leaf on the ice tonight, beat Worsley on a blueline drive late in the first to keep it close, but early in the second, Larose scored on a thirty-foot slapper Sawchuk might've pocketed on a better night.

Again, Leafs fought back on the power play. Armstrong took a Mahovlich pass behind the Montreal cage, cut around Laperrière, then outwaited a falling Hodge before lifting a back hand into the top corner. (Worsley had injured a knee in a first-period pile-up.) For seven minutes, the 4–3 game was a fast-rocking teeter-totter. Hodge made a nice toe save on Ellis. Then Backstrom's line pounced, with Ferguson just missing, banging one off the boards. Finally the teeter-totter broke. Rousseau flew down the boards, found himself alone, saw Baun churning his way, then flicked a desperation shot from the far boards and leapt out of the way. Sawchuk, moving as if under water, fell to trap the puck, only to have it trickle through his pads for the fifth Montreal goal.

Bower mopped up in the third, surrendering a goal on a dandy thirty-foot Béliveau wrist shot. Although the outcome was decided, the rivals still had scores to settle: Hillman ran Ferguson. Roberts tried to collect Pappin's scalp. Harris looked after unfinished business with Shack. (Canadiens remembered how Eddie had split Henri's skull with a coco butt in last spring's semis.) Midway through the period, Harris caught Shack from behind, driving an elbow into his neck. Shack hit the ice with enough force to open a two-and-a-half-inch gash in his forehead. By the time Leaf trainer Bobby Haggert got to him, the ice surrounding the fallen winger looked like the late stages of a Newfoundland seal harvest.

Imlach didn't complain about Shack's injury after Montreal's 6–3 win. And he brushed off Sawchuk's shaky performance, saying, "the way he's played, he's entitled to an off night." In truth, Punch was concerned about his goalie. Minutes earlier, Sawchuk stepped into the shower and felt a stab of pain in his back. Horton caught him as he collapsed, then carried his moaning teammate back to the dressing-room.

The next morning, Sawchuk was walking like Groucho Marx again. He phoned his wife in Detroit. "She cried when I told her about my back. Things always happen when they are going well for me," he told teammates. By Friday, the goalie was in the Toronto General, undergoing tests. When he returned to the Gardens, a morose Sawchuk told Imlach he wanted to quit. Punch nodded, said he understood, and when his unhappy goalie fell silent, hockey's biggest advocate of The Power of Positive Thinking began his sales job:

"Listen, Terry, you've worked too hard to get where you are now," Imlach said. "Before this injury you were feeling the best you have in years. Playing the best, too. I've never seen you play better. You owe it to yourself, and you owe it to your family, to give it another shot."

Of course, Punch had an ulterior reason for saying all this. If Sawchuk was indeed the reason the club was in first place, where would they be without him? Well, Leafs would find out soon enough. Sawchuk was gone for at least two months, maybe longer.

FIRST PERIOD
1. Toronto, Pappin 5th (Kelly, Jeffrey) 1:54
2. Montreal, Richard 7th (Provost, Laperrière) 8:41
3. Montreal, Larose 5th (Ferguson, Harris) 11:27
4. Montreal, Cournoyer 7th 12:06
5. Toronto, Horton 3rd (Jeffrey, Ellis) 18:56
Penalties—Ferguson (elbowing) 1:12;
Pappin (cross-checking) 3:56; Baun (tripping) 11:27;
Richard (tripping) 12:33; Larose (elbowing) 17:12;
Conacher (interference) 20:00

SECOND PERIOD
6. Montreal, Larose 6th (J.C. Tremblay, Ferguson) 4:51
7. Toronto, Armstrong 3rd (Mahovlich, Keon) 7:53
8. Montreal, Rousseau 6th (Béliveau, Laperrière) 14:54
Penalties—Backstrom (cross-checking) 5:59;
Harper (holding) 19:04

THIRD PERIOD
9. Montreal, Béliveau 2nd (Duff, J.C. Tremblay) 15:32
Penalties—Hillman (boarding) 1:42; Duff (tripping) 4:03;
Roberts (boarding) 4:55; Harris (major, elbowing) 8:01;
Mahovlich (hooking) 8:15; Stemkowski (tripping) 14:27

Shots on goal
Toronto   10   8   8 — 26
Montreal   9   8   8 — 25

DECEMBER 8 STANDINGS

	P	W	L	T	F	A	Pts
Toronto	21	9	7	7	63	59	25
Chicago	19	11	6	2	67	50	24
New York	22	9	7	6	69	55	24
Montreal	19	10	8	1	46	48	21
Boston	21	6	11	4	62	72	16
Detroit	20	5	13	2	54	73	12

MONTREAL/TORONTO SCORING

	GP	G	A	Pts	PIM
Rousseau, Montreal	19	6	14	20	16
Keon, Toronto	21	6	13	19	0
Kelly, Toronto	21	6	9	15	0
Mahovlich, Toronto	19	8	6	14	21
Jeffrey, Toronto	21	3	10	13	10
Richard, Montreal	19	7	5	12	8
Ellis, Toronto	21	6	6	12	2
Conacher, Toronto	21	7	3	10	13
Shack, Toronto	21	4	6	10	16
Cournoyer, Montreal	19	7	2	9	4
Pulford, Toronto	18	3	6	9	8
Brenneman, Toronto	20	5	3	8	2
Armstrong, Toronto	21	3	5	8	12
J.C. Tremblay, Montreal	13	1	7	8	0
Béliveau, Montreal	15	2	6	7	2
Larose, Montreal	18	6	1	7	14
Balon, Montreal	19	4	3	7	2
Provost, Montreal	19	4	3	7	10
Douglas, Toronto	17	1	6	7	13
Ferguson, Montreal	19	1	6	7	34
Laperrière, Montreal	19	0	7	7	8
Pappin, Toronto	20	4	2	6	18
Horton, Toronto	21	3	3	6	12
Backstrom, Montreal	18	1	5	6	6
Stemkowski, Toronto	20	1	5	6	10
Stanley, Toronto	20	0	5	5	8
Rochefort, Montreal	16	2	1	3	4
G. Tremblay, Montreal	13	1	2	3	6
Talbot, Montreal	19	2	1	3	10
Duff, Montreal	11	1	2	3	9
Harris, Montreal	19	1	2	3	23
L. Hillman, Toronto	18	0	3	3	12
Harper, Montreal	19	0	2	2	44
Baun, Toronto	14	0	2	2	14
Carleton, Toronto	5	1	0	1	14
Price, Montreal	6	0	1	1	4
Roberts, Montreal	19	0	0	0	6

Crowd noise
Strikes

This was the most tumultuous year in Canadian labour history. Over 4,000,000 man-days were lost to strikes. Railway workers struck. Air Canada mechanics walked out. Toronto housewives picketed a grocery store. University students in Montreal staged a downtown sit-in to fight rising transportation costs. ("Bus drivers are fat enough already," read one protestor's sign.) In November, 3,000 Toronto city workers stayed home. Garbage piled high. Sewage backed up. Some residents went without water. In Montreal, not a day passed without labour difficulty. At one point, the city's Catholic teachers, police brotherhood, white collar employees, and hospital workers were all on strike. Labour troubles literally followed some Montrealers to the grave, when, in late November, members of the city's Building Services Union picketed Mount Royal Cemetery.

7

Three Little Indians

After Clancy signed Mahovlich, all but one NHLer was in the fold. Glenn Hall remained a hold-out into the season's second week. Glenn had "retired" to work on his farm outside Edmonton. He was painting the barn whenever Black Hawk GM Tommy Ivan called. Coach Reay figured otherwise. "Glenn must have the biggest barn in Canada because he started painting it a year ago," Reay observed. The coach predicted the building's second coat would dry in a jiffy if the goalie received the right salary offer. Sure enough, in early November, Hall signed a one-year, $40,000 deal.

The Mahovlich and Hall hold-outs were the most publicized pre-season hockey labour disputes, but not, as it turned out, the most consequential. In early October, three members of the minor league Springfield Indians, Bill White, Dale Rolfe, and Dave Amadio, marched...well, crept doe-like was probably more like it, into club owner Eddie Shore's office.

"Eddie, we...that is the boys and I figure we deserve a raise," White said, hoping to sound firm.

"Oh, you do, do you?"

Springfield's best defenders told Shore they wanted $500

more, each, or they wouldn't play.

"Eddie gave it to them, no problem," remembers team captain Brian Kilrea, "which should've been our first clue something was up."

Shore was hockey's Ty Cobb, a brilliant but sour defenseman with Boston in the 30s. The Hall-of-Famer went mad with power when he bought the AHL Indians in 1939. (The league was hockey's top minor league circuit; most teams had affiliations with NHL clubs.) With age, Shore's wondrous physical constitution began to buckle and cleave (by 1966, he'd suffered four heart attacks) and his madness ripened. Eddie was now an impossible tightwad. He even kept tabs on broken sticks.

"That's the twenty-second stick you've broken this year, Mister," a red-faced Shore would scream. "I told you beginning of the season that was all you'd get. From now on every stick you break will be taken out of your salary!"

The Indians wore ratty, pre-war equipment. Some were forced to work rink clean-up crews, sweeping, painting seats, and blowing up balloons. And there was no medical coverage. Players were yanked from hospitals when the meter ran too high.

"Many's the time one of our guys was in the hospital," Kilrea recalls. "Shore would come in and say, 'Let's go.' 'But, Eddie, the doc says I can't leave for two weeks!' player'd say. Eddie, he'd grab the guy by the arm, 'I say you're fine, come on! let's go!'"

Shore sometimes bypassed the medical profession entirely. Winger John Bobenic once approached Shore complaining of a knee injury. "Maybe I better see a doctor," he suggested. "Nonsense. Get up on the table and let's have a look," Shore shouted. "Now pull up your pant leg." Bobenic about fainted when Shore pulled a penknife from his jacket and started probing his injured knee. "Was that ever painful. The knife wasn't even sharp," he recalled.

Any Shore story, no matter how gruesome or seemingly far-fetched, can be topped. During Indian alumni get-togethers, Kilrea likes to tell the one about Shore giving goalie Jacques Caron a back rub.

"The team was gathered in the dressing room, minutes before the game," Kilrea begins. "We were cramped together, twenty-some guys in this room as wide as a bus, with a training table in the middle and three light bulbs hangin' from the ceiling. Now, Jack [Caron], he bein' the goalie, he's just to the left of the door, first guy you'd see when you walk in. So when Eddie opens the door—what's this?—he sees Jack cricking his neck, trying to get loose for the game.

"'Something wrong, Mr. Caron?' Eddie asks.

"'No, no, no,' Jack says, real nervous. See, Eddie liked to think he was a chiropractor. He wasn't, a course. And man, those back rubs, they were torture.

"'On the table, Mr. Caron,' Eddie shouts.

"'No, no, I'm fine.'

"'You've got a crick in your neck. I'm going to relieve the pain. Now get on the goddamn table.'"

To say players did whatever Shore asked because he was boss doesn't quite get at the truth. "Oh, he was a fierce-lookin' guy—he'd scare you to death to look at him when he was mad," Kilrea explains. "And he was still a strong man." Even at sixty-five, with all his heart trouble, the trim, kneecap-bald Shore could crack walnuts with his handshake. Finally, there were his black, unblinking eyes. "It was like you were looking at a shark," former Indian goalie Bruce Gamble used to say, shuddering.

"Jack, you could see he was scared a the back rub," Kilrea continues, laughing, "but he was more scared a Shore, so he jumped on that table. Now Eddie, he gets those big hands a his around Jack's neck and he tells him 'R-e-l-a-x, r-e-l-a-x.' Which is impossible under the circumstances, right? Anyway, Eddie keeps yanking and pulling on Jack's neck, and Jack, he's so stiff, his arse hops off the table every time Eddie yanks.

"'Keep your arse down and relax. R-E-L-A-X!' Eddie yells.

"Now, Jack starts screaming he's so upset and worried. Eddie, he's yelling back. And the rest a us guys, well, the room's so small we're only a couple of feet away, right? We're all trying not to laugh cause this strikes us as funny. Finally, when Shore starts to get really mad and is yanking at Jack's neck like he's strangling him, Dennis Olson, our best forward, he pipes up, 'Hey Eddie, one a those necks ever come off in your hand?'

"The rest of us, we just explode laughin'. Couldn't help it. But when Shore turns around, things got quiet real quick. Suddenly, we were all trying to hide behind our sticks.

"'Did you say something, Mr. Olson?'

"Course when the game starts, Dennis takes one shift, then Shore sends word down and [Olson] is stuck the end of the bench the rest a the night. And after the game, coach tells him he has to show up at eight the next morning for practice. Shore's orders. Dennis tells me this later in the dressing room, I give him a look, you know, tough luck there, pal. But me, I was feeling pretty cocky. See, we won 4–1 and I was on for all the goals, their one and all a ours. I think I got a goal and three assists. Anyway, after I shower, the coach comes up to me and says, 'Brian, report for practice, eight o'clock sharp tomorrow morning.'

"'What?' I says, 'How come? I got a goal and three assists.'"

"Mr. Shore says to tell you, 'There are two ends to a rink.'"

"Well," Kilrea laughs, "that was Eddie, he got you one way or another, but he always got you."

Shore got White, Rolfe and Amadio just before Christmas. After a Saturday, December 17 game, the players received letters announcing they'd been suspended a week, without pay, for "indifferent play." As it happened, the Indians were off a week, so Shore didn't have to find and pay three new players. The fines amounted to $1,500, the same $500 each of the men had bargained for months earlier.

"It was a horseshit fine," Kilrea says. "Everybody knew it. Shore. Us. The league. Oh yeah, the league knew. But back then, Shore was the league. [The AHL President, Jack Butterfield was not only Shore's nephew, but also the Indians' GM.] Shore did what he wanted, how he wanted. Nobody ever challenged him."

Until now.

The Indians had a booster club gathering the night after the suspensions. During the party, White, Rolfe and Amadio asked captain Kilrea to intervene on their behalf.

"I said, 'Fine, but you know all that's gonna happen is I'll probably get myself suspended, too. That's fine,' I says, 'but if I do this I want everybody behind me, OK?' So I went to every player in that room and asked if they'd support me if I talked to Eddie. 'Sure, Killer,' everyone said, to a man."

The evening was a social occasion. Players had a few beers. No one defined what "support" Kilrea could expect. That became evident next day at practice, when Kilrea confronted Shore.

"Eddie, I represent the three suspended guys."

"You represent fuck-all," was Shore's lightning reply.

A light-headed Kilrea returned to the dressing room and explained to his teammates what happened. "We were all there, even White, Rolfe, and Amadio, 'cause Eddie made them practice even though they were suspended. We decided not to go out on the rink to practice as a way of protesting the suspensions. It was pretty tense in that dressing room while we waited for Shore to find out, I tell you. Don't forget, a lot a guys had kids and it was around Christmas. There were bills coming up. Some of the young guys were scared, I could tell. Hell, we were all scared. Finally, Shore walks in.

"'So it's all of youse, is it?' he says, and oh, he was mad. 'Well, stick around, I got letters for everybody.'

"After that, I told the guys, 'Fellas, go home, this looks like it could get ugly. I'll be in touch.'"

As predicted, Shore suspended Kilrea for "indifferent play." What happened next, however, was something players never anticipated.

"Next day, oh geez, the press starts phoning from all over North America," Kilrea says. "'What about the strike?' 'What about the walkout?' they want to know. Christ, now we were really scared. See, we figured we could maybe get Eddie to back down quietly. We never in a million years figured this was going to blow up into a big story. See, in Springfield, playing for Eddie, you figured you'd dropped off the side of the earth. Nobody seemed to care about what Shore did. All the crazy stuff that was going on."

Only AHL players knew about the crazy stuff: During practice, Shore sometimes placed awkward skaters in harnesses strung to clotheslines in the rafters. Whenever the player's form offended the owner, Shore pulled a cord and the player was borne aloft, like Peter Pan. Goalies were forced to work out with nooses, hung from crossbars, strung around their necks (this to encourage the Bill Durnan stand-up goalie technique). On an off day, Bobenic once bought a fishing rod and thought he'd try a few casts in the abandoned arena. Third or fourth cast, he got his plug tangled in the rafters. After a few fruitless pulls, he decided to snap the line. Then Shore walked in.

"What do you think you're doing, Mr. Bobenic?"

"Ah, trying out my new fishing rod, Eddie. Got the plug caught up there, see. Just gonna give it a yank and break it."

"You will do nothing of the sort."

Minutes later, Bobenic found himself on a tottering extension ladder, forty feet in the air, trying to keep his hands from shaking long enough to unsnarl a tangled lure.

"You ask us why we took it?" Kilrea says. "Because we had no choice. Shore owned us. There wasn't anything we could do about it. That's the way hockey was those days. AHL, NHL, all hockey. Anyway, I went to this friend a mine, a lawyer who'd done some work for me before, and I showed him my contract, and asked if Shore could get away with the suspensions. He looked at the contract, read it twice, then shook his head. 'Killer,' he says, 'if Shore ordered you to play in just a bowtie and shorts, I'm afraid that's what you'd have to do.'"

The only way out for Shore's players was to pray for a trade. Bruce Gamble sat out a year to force Shore to swap him. Bobenic got off easier. "Mr. Bobenic, you have been traded to Ottawa," Shore announced one day. "I didn't give him time to change his mind," Bobenic said. "I threw my clothes into my car and drove five miles out of Springfield before I stopped to pack my bags."

For Kilrea and teammates, there was little hope of Shore swinging a fifty-player deal. They were stuck in Springfield. Maybe even out of work.

"I'm at home that night after dealing with the press all day," Kilrea recalls. "Phone rings. My wife answers. She says, 'Un-hunh, just a minute, he's right here.' I'm thinking, oh boy, another bloody reporter. She walks in and says, 'Brian, it's a Clarence Campbell.' Doesn't even know who he is, right? I grab the phone.

"'Brian Kilrea?'

"'Yes.'

"'This is Clarence Campbell, President of the National Hockey League. Mr. Kilrea, I must say I'm very, very disappointed with what's going on there in Springfield.' Later, he says, 'Mr. Kilrea, if you and your players do not report back to work tomorrow morning, you will never work in hockey again. Not as a player. A coach. Even a referee. Is that clear?'"

Next day when the Indians met at a motel outside Springfield, all that was clear to Kilrea was that he and his teammates needed help, fast.

"Some the young guys had got phone calls from Shore's doctor, night before, telling them they better get back or else they'd be out of hockey, forever. Some of the guys were really panicking. There was no doubt in my mind that we were about to give in. No doubt about it."

Another time, that might've been the end of it. In 1957, Ted Lindsay, Doug Harvey, Fern Flaman, Gus Mortson, Jim Thomson, and Bill Gadsby tried to establish a players' association, but were drowned like kittens by Campbell and the owners. (Within four years all had been traded or were out of hockey.) In the press, the players sank without a ripple. By the mid-60s, however, labour unrest was commonplace. Authority figures were routinely under attack.

"Shore, perhaps the finest defenceman of all time, has been linked with every tight-fisted story imaginable, and most of them are true," Red Fisher wrote in a Montreal *Star* column. "He has been criticized, demeaned and lashed in the public prints since his Springfield players walked out earlier this week… The league directorate…has a responsibility to investigate the situation fully."

Kilrea says players didn't realize how charged the situation was. "We weren't lawyers. What'd we know? Alls we wanted was to play hockey. We didn't think our guys getting suspended was fair, so we tried to do something about it. We never dreamed about starting a players' union, nothing like that.

We were just sitting around in a motel room, sweating, trying to do something to save our careers. Then, I'll always remember this, Bill White says, 'Hey, how about we get in touch with Eagleson? You know, the guy looked after Bobby Orr's contract.' We looked at each other. What did we have to lose?"

In 1966, Alan Eagleson was a thirty-three-year-old lawyer trying to get his foot in the castle door. Any castle would do. He did legal work for a few Leafs, and represented Carl Brewer in the player's 1964 contract talks with Imlach.* He was also Orr's agent. But hockey couldn't even be considered his top sporting interest. The Eagle was president of the Toronto Rifles Continental football team. In fact, he'd spent most of the fall working on a new North American TV deal for the league. "The Continental League will be bigger than the CFL in five years," he predicted. Eagleson also dabbled in politics, running for the Tories against Liberal Red Kelly in the 1965 federal election. ("What was Eagleson like to run against?" Kelly says. "Oh, I'd have to say 'Great.' Beat him a lot easier than the fella before him.")

Although busy, Eagleson dropped everything when Kilrea called.

"Got right through, didn't have to wait on line, or anything," Kilrea remembers. "'Killer, sounds like you've got problems there,' Eagleson says. 'That's right,' I says. 'We never figured it'd get out of hand like this big, we got all these papers phoning us. Clarence Campbell says we'll never play again. We could really use some help. We're wondering...'

"'I can get on a plane and be there tonight,' he says."

Eagleson's appearance was no less dramatic than the last-reel cavalry charge in a western movie, Kilrea believes. "Sure

---

* From Net Worth, by David Cruise and Alison Griffiths, here's Brewer's account of Punch's response to the news Eagleson would be acting as his agent: "'Can he fucking play hockey?' Imlach demanded. 'He's a lawyer not a hockey player,' Brewer said, sagging. 'If he can goddamn well play hockey, I might talk to him. But I'm not going to waste my time on some son of a bitch who can't play hockey.' 'But Punch, he's my lawyer. Don't you understand? He's not another hockey player. He's my lawyer.' 'That doesn't matter shit to me! I'm not gonna talk with the son of a bitch if he can't play hockey! And that's that!'"

it was a rescue. Cause we were about to give in. If Eagleson didn't show up and go to bat for us, there is absolutely no doubt in my mind that we would've caved in. And Shore would've been worse, a bigger cheapskate than ever. But Al convinced us that we could win."

Eagleson told the players their fight wasn't hopeless. Shore's was. It wasn't simply them against Shore and all of hockey. No, it was the whole world against Shore.

"What Eagleson told us was that Shore would have to go to court against all of us, and that we'd beat him," Kilrea says. "Cause we'd get all these affidavits from players saying some of the illegal medical stuff he'd been doing. And all the monkeying around he did with players' contracts—the phony fines and whatnot. Basically, Eagleson said he'd expose Eddie to the world."

Before Eagleson met with Shore, however, players wanted to give it one more shot. "To try to sort it out in the family," Kilrea says. Next night, Kilrea and teammate Gerry Foley drove to the rink with a short list of player demands.

"We found Eddie in his office," Kilrea remembers. "'So what is it that you want?' he snarls.

"'Mr. Shore, we want proper medical, some new equipment, and no more fines,' we said.

"'Not one fucking iota,' Eddie says, and he was trembling he was so mad. I started to say something, then all of a sudden he give me an awful, awful look. 'Mr. Kilrea,' he says, 'I'm giving you sixty seconds to get off my grounds!' Didn't take me that long, I tell you. I was out the door in three seconds.

"Honest to God I was afraid for my life," Kilrea says. "See, I knew that Eddie kept guns around the rink. For security reasons, like bringing cash home after the game, stuff like that. And I was afraid that the old bugger might cook up some excuse, that I was a burglar maybe, and shoot me." He chuckles. "You couldn't a put it past him."

Recent stories suggest Eagleson never confronted Shore and that the strike was defused by Shore's nephew, Jack Butterfield. Kilrea disagrees. "That's crazy. No, Eagleson met with Shore," he says. A meeting between the two men took place at the Springfield arena, Thursday, December 22, a

Canadian Press story confirms. During a stiff, half-hour rink-side chat, neither Shore nor Eagleson backed down. Afterwards, The Eagle flew back to Toronto for Christmas. And the players waited to see what Shore would do.

"We were supposed to play Sunday night, and there was a deadline, three o'clock Saturday," Kilrea recalls. "By that time, Shore knew he had to lift the suspensions or all hell was going to break loose. We wouldn't play. The game would have to be cancelled. God knows what woulda happened then.

"I remember I was listening to the radio at my home that Saturday afternoon. Two o'clock news comes on, guy on the radio says Eddie is stepping down for health reasons and goin' to Florida. Oh, what a relief that was. We'd won! But I tell ya, I wasn't happy because we'd beaten Shore, I was happy because we were going to play hockey again. None of us really wanted to strike. I remember Eagleson telling us before he left, 'You guys want to go home, I'll guarantee you'll be free agents next year.' Which would've been expansion year in the NHL. 'No way,' we said. 'We're hockey players. Alls we want to do is play hockey.'"

Kilrea says that the Sunday night game the Indians played against Don Cherry's Rochester Americans remains one of his sweetest hockey memories: "They were the best team in the AHL that year. But that night we were just fantastic. Like we were horses just let out of the corral, you know. We just skated, skated, skated all night. I think we beat them 10–2. That night, as far as I was concerned, was the only good part of the whole damned week."

Two weeks after his success in Springfield, Eagleson began selling NHL players on the advantages of a union. A few months later, the NHL Players Association was born. "Yeah, no doubt about it, The Eagle made his reputation with hockey players that winter in Springfield," Kilrea says. In 1994, the NHL Players Association that emerged from the Shore-Eagleson conflict was locked out by management for refusing to accept a salary cap. Kilrea says he sided with owners on that labour dispute.

"No, I don't see any irony there," he says. "Maybe we did

start the NHL Players Association with what we did back in Springfield. It was time for an association back then. Owners could get away with murder. Not just in the AHL, but the NHL, too. Way I look at it, what we did is cut the pendulum loose, and maybe it's gone too far in the other direction now. Man, when I think of what the players have today—the money, the benefits, how they can look after their family with a few good years. And then I look back at what we had. God Amighty! I mean we didn't even have good medical, or proper equipment. Well, I don't know how else to put it—I think they're so fortunate. Just so fortunate."

That Kilrea now sides with an old enemy isn't surprising. He's management himself these days—GM of the Junior OHA Ottawa 67s. In fact, virtually all participants of the Springfield players strike have changed jerseys. Eagleson, a worker hero in 1966, and the founding president of the NHL Players Association, would ultimately be accused of misappropriation of membership funds. Now The Eagle is sweating out an extradition proceeding to determine whether he must travel to the United States to stand trial for racketeering.

Such King-of-the-Castle climbs and tumbles are the way of the world—a game that young and old men have played forever. Indeed, 1966 was not the first professional hockey strike. In 1934, Boston GM Art Ross tried to trim the last-place Bruins' payroll. Several players received substantial pay cuts. One Bruin refused to accept Ross's decree. It wasn't fair, he said, then packed his bags and returned home to his Alberta farm. A horrified NHL President Frank Calder suspended the player "indefinitely." Ross maintained the Bruins would get along without their defector, no problems. After a sorry exhibition season and a 6–1 opening game drubbing by the Leafs, he changed his mind. And so Eddie Shore was welcomed back to Boston, at full salary, after a one-game strike.

Crowd noise

Christmas presents

Man From U.N.C.L.E. six-piece "Napoleon Solo" Gun!
A cap firing automatic (caps not included) with clip-loading
magazine—converts into rifle with stock silencer, telescopic sight,
U.N.C.L.E. badge and "membership" card. $4.44

Hands-Down Game—Pick a card, match a pair—and Hands
Down! Action a mile-a-minute! Cards for four players,
colour-keyed, all-plastic, unbreakable Slam-o-matic unit. $4.97

Trik-Trak Set—9 unique cars! Vary the layouts as you wish.
The battery-operated racing cars will follow the course you set.
Scenic backgrounds. (Batteries not included.) $6.99

Easy-Bake Oven. Perfect for the "little mother." Three baking
pans slide through enclosed oven and cooling chamber on grooved
rolls. Heavy plastic exterior, vented top uses two 100-watt bulbs
(not included), kitchen utensils, and mixes. $14.77

Sno-Cone Machine—Who wants a kiddy-cone?
Sturdy all-plastic dessert-maker comes with ice-crusher,
re-usable cones, and assorted mmm-mnn good flavours. $6.99

—Ad copy taken from Christmas flyers, 1966

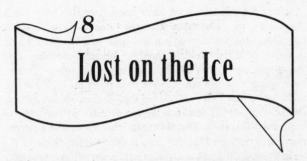

8
Lost on the Ice

Stepping from his car in the church parking lot on Christmas Eve, minutes before midnight mass, a Montrealer might've looked up at the clear, ocean-deep sky and muttered, "Guess the weatherman was wrong, doesn't look like snow." The city was supposed to get four or five inches. No matter, it'd be a white Christmas. Sidewalks downtown were rimmed with hard, calf-high banks of boot-chiselled ice. Suburban lawns lay snug under a pearly fleece.

The first dancing flakes appeared as mass started. In five minutes, the snow was coming down fast, sideways, a sure sign of a blizzard. By the time church doors re-opened, shortly after midnight, everything was a fresh, gleaming white. Returning to the parking lot, parishioners were giddy with confusion: cars had been reduced to identical frosted snowscapes. High spirits gave way to frustration, however, when Dad nosed the Impala into traffic. What was normally a ten or fifteen minute drive home now took an hour. Turns were an adventure in geometry. Hills were worse than impossible. The number 64 (Windsor) and 125 (Victoria) had to abandon their routes because groaning buses couldn't negotiate steep climbs.

By two o'clock, families were finally home, around the tree, cups of Ovaltine warm in hand, following the storm's progress through the theatre screen of the living-room picture window. Hard to believe, but it was coming down harder. Winds of up to fifty-five miles an hour whipped swirling ghosts up and down the street.

It was still coming down eight hours later. Ten inches fell overnight, plus the wind brought unused snow in from Labrador. Families, decked out in bright new ski-jackets and mukluks, attacked the driveway on Christmas morning. But shovelling was futile, like raking leaves in a forest. By the time you got to the street, snow had piled up back on the walk. Just when Dad pronounced the job done, hours later, a city plow grumbled past, leaving a waist-high pyramid at the foot of the driveway. This was hard, chunky snow—a potential heart attack for Dad. Another hour of work for kids.

It snowed off and on all day. After every flurry, sons and daughters were turned out of the house for another round of shovelling. Not that anyone was about to take the car out. Parents stayed home, basting the turkey, with an ear tuned to the radio for the latest storm news. Thirteen inches had fallen by dinner. Quebec police reported thousands of traffic accidents, including twenty-eight fatalities. Tens of thousands of Quebec travellers were stranded in motels and inns, their cars lost in the ice. More than a thousand poor souls were trapped at Dorval Airport.

By midweek, Montreal was almost back to normal. City plows reclaimed the suburbs. You could leave for work and arrive home same day. Then late Thursday morning, incredibly, unbelievably, another blizzard hit. Businesses closed at noon, but few downtown workers beat the storm home. This snow was wet. Roads and highways turned to ice under the polish of spinning tires. Even buses with chained tires pirouetted around corners. Police estimated another thousand traffic accidents.

It was still snowing on Friday. A foot of snow fell in less than twenty-four hours. This time the city stayed on the canvas. Businesses remained closed. Cars hid in the garage. The only sound on most streets was the scratch of shovels. By evening, snowbanks were parallel with the roof. But it wasn't until the next day, a bright, still Saturday morning, that you appreciated how much snow had fallen.

"I remember when the street was finally clear, Dad coming inside the house to ask me to help him get the car out the driveway," remembers a forty-three-year-old Montrealer. I didn't understand. I didn't drive; why'd he need me? Dad laughed and said, 'C'mon, you'll see.' When we got outside, the snowbanks were more than twice, three times as high I was—twenty feet in places. Dad pointed to the end of the driveway, which was a tunnel almost. 'Go stand at the end and tell me when I can pull out onto the road. The banks are so high, I can't see if a truck is coming.'"

A Montrealer in her early forties recalls, "That morning I let our dog out the side door, because the snow had drifted right to the top of the back door—you couldn't get it open. A little while later I called her, and she wouldn't come. Where could she be? The yard was fenced in. I got dressed and went out to look, and oh, my God, I realized the snow was so high there weren't any hedges or fences anymore! All the backyards had come together into one big field. Our dog had walked right over a ten-foot hedge and disappeared onto some other street."

The Canadiens skidded into a ditch even before holiday storms hit. Going into their December 21 game against Toronto, the Habs were spinning their wheels in fourth, eight points back of Chicago and New York, five behind Toronto. After downing Toronto 6–3 three weeks earlier, the team had its way with the lowly Wings, winning 5–1 behind a Larose hat trick. (Claude had scored seven goals in three games since Blake threatened demotion.) The team appeared to be on its way, having won four straight by a score of 17–5. "The mystery isn't why we're playing well now," Toe said after the Detroit win, "it's why we were playing so badly before."

Then the Canadiens dropped two road games, losing 4–2 to New York and 2–1 to Chicago. The only good sign in the losses was Béliveau's aggressive play. The Captain had a goal and assist against Giacomin, and bulled past three Hawks to set up Rousseau in Chicago. Late that game he even got into a scrap, clipping Mikita for four stitches. The incident didn't end there, of course, as the six-team league was governed by Old Testament law. Three nights later, Chicago was in Montreal. In the first period, Béliveau and Mikita skated away from play in Chicago's end. Seconds later, big Jean was sliding across the ice, his face twisted in pain.

"When that hooked stick of Mikita hit me above the eye I was afraid," he remembers. "I was sure it was my career, because when he hit me, my eye felt like an explosion. That was a very difficult night in the hospital."

The Habs tied that game on a late goal by Duff, but the point was costly. Béliveau was out indefinitely. The following morning, doctors repaired cartilage in Worsley's right knee. Gump would be gone three to six weeks.

The rest of the Canadiens trained on down to Boston where the mystery that was their season deepened. The Bruins were ripe for picking. The team had managed a point in six games, and had scored a single goal in the last seven periods.

"By Christmas I realized we had a pretty bad team," recalls Harry Sinden. "Our forwards were puny and most of them just weren't much good, other than Bucyk and Westfall. And I know everyone was in love with Marotte, but I didn't think much of him. Other than Orr, our defense wasn't much good at all. We lost because other teams were better. If we won a game that year it was because Orr won it for us or the other team didn't come to play."

That night, without Orr, who was out with a knee injury, Boston trimmed Montreal 3–1. For the second time this season, Toe skipped the post-game press conference, storming out before his players finished dressing.

After Toronto's early December loss to Montreal, the Leafs rebounded at home against Chicago, winning 5–3. "The Quiet Line"—Jeffrey-Kelly-Ellis—counted four goals, including Ellis's first NHL hat trick. But it was the thirty-nine-year-old Kelly who drew post-game raves. "I get the chance, I'll draft him," Red Sullivan, GM of the expansion Pittsburgh

Penguins promised. "He can play five years at centre, five more at defense, then another five as goalie, by then he'd be about Bower's age, I guess."

Bower was in nets next night in Detroit. Well, for fifty-seven minutes anyway. The goalie wasn't removed because of bad play. With the team down 3–1, and three minutes to go, Punch just decided to pull Johnny and go with six attackers. It was an unorthodox move that was typical of Imlach.

"Sometimes we thought Punch just did things to attract attention, to remind everybody that he was coach," says Billy Harris. "There was no tactical reason for some of his [on-ice] moves. And I can't remember many of them working."

This one didn't either, as Leafs dropped into a shell to protect their empty net. Then again, maybe it did. The restless Imlach perked up the last 180 seconds of a dull contest. Perhaps that was all he wanted. Suddenly there was a game again. For 162 seconds, the crowd was on its feet, shrieking "shoooot" whenever a Red Wing touched the puck. With twenty seconds left, Norm Ullman and Howe broke behind the Leaf defense. Ullman passed up an easy goal, slipping the puck to number nine, who, on his third chance at an empty Toronto net this season, finally scored.

The Leafs weren't much better at home the following Wednesday against Boston. One-all, late in the game, the crowd was grumpy and Imlach "sizzled like an overcooked veal cutlet," according to Dick Beddoes. "End of the game I'm going to make you stay here and watch this fucking thing all over again on tape, just so you can see what fans have to put up with," Punch promised players in the second intermission. But with five minutes left, Mahovlich popped a short Keon pass past Cheevers. After the win, Leafs skedaddled out the dressing-room before Imlach had a chance to get the projector out. "That's the fastest they've moved all day," Punch groused as the last player whistled past, his hair still wet from the shower.

Unfortunately, that kind of effort wasn't good enough the following weekend against New York and Chicago. Leafs were beaten 3–1 both nights. Bower injured his shoulder in Detroit, so Gary "Suitcase" Smith was brought up from

Rochester to play in Chicago. Everyone thought the orange-haired netminder earned his nickname because of his penchant for on-ice travel. If Jacques Plante was an adventurer who tested Blake's patience by journeying to the circle to poke away loose pucks, Smith was hockey's Columbus, an explorer who antagonized the coaching fraternity's flat-earth society by occasionally sailing past the blueline, stickhandling to centre before dumping the puck.

"Got that move from watching Cesare Maniago play for the Hull-Ottawa Canadiens," the Ottawa-born goalie says. "Maniago used to skate way out. I remember one time, on a delayed penalty, Maniago skated to the other net lookin' for a pass to score. I thought that was fantastic. My dream was to score a goal."

The nickname "Suitcase" actually came from the travel Smith did as a rookie in 1964–65. He started the season in Rochester, then was sent to Victoria, Tulsa, then back to Rochester, and on to Toronto. In the spring, Imlach lent him to Boston before the goalie returned finally to Rochester. "Leafs had three good goalies in the minors," Smith explains. "Doug Simmons in Tulsa, Cheevers in Rochester, and Al Smith in Victoria. So I didn't really have a team. Instead I got sent from one team to the other if someone got hurt. Then Eddie Johnston broke his arm and Jack Norris was the only goalie Boston had in its system, so Toronto loaned me there for a buck. Yeah, a dollar…sort of makes you stop and think, doesn't it?

"That was a bit of a shock, playing for another organization. See when I was a junior goalie in Toronto, I used to spend a lot of time at the Gardens as Leaf practice goalie. Also, I got ten bucks a night to sit up in the press box in case a goalie got hurt. I got to know everybody. I have to say Imlach scared me. I was young, I didn't know what to think of the guy. I'd be hanging around the dressing room during intermission, and see him go in and yell at the players, really ream them. Then he'd come into his office, laughing away. 'Boy, I really gave it to them,' he'd tell his assistant [John Anderson]. Then he'd flip on the TV and watch "Hockey Night in Canada."

"Players were great. I was a kid, but they went out of their way to make me feel comfortable. Another thing that struck me about Leaf players was their professionalism. Class, you might say. They wore a shirt and tie to the rink. And there were practices every day, even travel days. In Boston, players dressed how they wanted, and it didn't seem there was ever any ice to practice on. You know I was with the team twenty days and I think there was only one practice, at Harvard University."

Smith was delighted to be journeying with Toronto to Montreal this holiday season. "Boy, was I ever. Know why? I got my parents a TV for Christmas—a big colour job," he says. "I thought hey, wouldn't it be great if the first time they got to see me on TV it would be against Montreal, in colour."

And what a game Mr. and Mrs. Smith saw on their new fiddle-free Philco. The first period of the December 21 contest took nearly an hour, and included three goals, five fights, and one incident that left even Danny Gallivan stumped for an appropriate adjective.

Twenty seconds in, Kelly hit Hodge in the face with a shot. Little Charlie did a backwards somersault and landed, as sportswriters used to say, in Queersville. After a lot of rubbing and blinking, Hodge pronounced himself OK. The crowd gave him a nice hand. Seconds later, he was slow on an Ellis rebound and Jeffrey scored. The Forum crowd turned quickly: "Toe, the man can't see! Get him off the ice!"

Before Kelly's line departed, Jeffrey was tossed for hooking. A minute later, Henri fired a shot off Gamble's glove. The puck trickled to an opening that was quickly filled by Cournoyer. One-all. Minutes later, Ferguson and Shack collided. After catching a spear in the thorax, Ferguson whacked his nemesis on the shoulders with his stick. Shack went down as if he'd been knighted by a guillotine. Fergy grabbed the puck and raced to the Leaf net. At the circle he flipped to Backstrom, who fired a low shot wide of Gamble's left pad to make it 2–1. With that, number 22 doubled back to Shack, dropped his gloves and pummelled the still-dazed Leaf. When Kent Douglas came to help his fallen mate, Fergy was still in a murderous trance. After a half-minute of sweater-tugging, Montreal's policeman got his arm loose and connected with four chopping rights, driving Douglas to his knees.

In the undercard, Larose and Baun, and Backstrom and the suddenly revived Shack clashed. Montreal and Toronto papers had Shack outpointing Backstrom, while Larose was the consensus winner in the other battle, delivering the fight's only knock-down. (Baun later claimed he'd been suckered. Could be. Larose had a reputation for getting his best lick in before a fight actually started.)

One Leaf who wasn't about to take Ferguson's bullying sitting down was "Suitcase" Smith. "I wanted to show everybody I was a team guy, eh?" he says, "so I stood up at the bench, yelling my head off, 'Hey Ferguson, you're an asshole, y'hear me—a big, dumb asshole! Yeah, come on over here, ya jerk ya!' I was really giving it to him, swearing away. Suddenly, I feel Punch behind me. All of a sudden he's lifting the towel off my shoulders.

"'Go get 'em, kid,' he says.

"'Who?' I says, my face going all red.

"'Ferguson. You want him. Go get him.'

"'But, Punch, he's in the penalty box.'

"'Oh, they'll let him out eventually, don't worry about that. C'mon get out there. I'm putting you in the nets.'

The big (6'4" 230 lbs) goalie made some fine stops early, including a gliding kick save on Duff. "I was pumped," Smith remembers, "there I was, a twenty-one-year-old kid playing in the Forum for the Leafs, all of Canada watching, a dream come true, eh? And my parents were watching back home on colour TV. I figured this might be the only time they ever see me play in the NHL. I wanted to do something spectacular!"

At the game's thirteen-minute mark the goalie snared an easy shot from the far boards. "I looked up and saw clear ice. And something in my head said, 'Go for it!' I skated about ten yards with the puck in my glove, then dropped it and kept going. You know I remember it now as if it was a dream, like I only remember funny details. I remember the crowd noise, this loud buzz. Then as I got past the blueline I remember waiting for J.C. Tremblay to come check me. See, times I

skated out before, the defenseman always came for me. But
J.C. kept skating backwards, giving me more room. If he
comes to check me, I pass off to a forward, right. But he kept
going back, and I kept skating. Now I'm past centre and the
crowd's screaming, and I thought, fuck it! I'm gonna go for a
goal. So I look down to make sure I still have the puck, and
that's when J.C. hit me. Jesus, he probably didn't hit three
guys his whole career, but he hit me that night.

"All of a sudden I didn't have the puck anymore and I'm
way, way the hell out of the net. I'm lost, spinning around.
First time I spin around I can see Punch on the bench, pulling
his hat over his head. Second time I spin around I see the
puck in our end and Marcel Pronovost making a diving save. I
tried to get back in the nets but for some reason I couldn't
seem to skate. I think I fell a couple of more times on the way
back to the net."

The Leafs' lost Suitcase caused a commotion right through
to the first intermission. Jacques Plante was rushed into the
French TV studio and asked to comment. "C'est fantastique,"
he said. English TV analyst Dick Irvin later told Smith that
the goalie's dash left Danny Gallivan speechless for the first
time in his career.

"But none the Leafs said anything to me, not on the ice, or
after the period was over," he recalls. "Probably because they
were pros, eh? Once the play was over, it was over. They still
had a game to win."

A Toronto win looked unlikely midway through the second period. With Horton off, Cournoyer pounced on a Duff
rebound to make it 3–1. While Montreal celebrated, Ferguson
hopped off the bench and kabonged Conacher.

"The man is a maniac," the Leaf winger said later.

"I thought he was going to attack Henri," Fergy explained
with a shrug. When it was suggested he'd initiated the Shack
fight with a high stick, the forward smiled. "I guess maybe I
did, but the referee didn't call it. All I know is this night really brightened up my Christmas. Now I feel nothing but good-
will toward those poor little Leafs. I don't know what it is, but
they rile me something awful."

Another Leaf penalty led to Montreal's third man advantage. J.C., Rousseau, Béliveau, and Duff kept the puck spinning in faster circles. Finally, Cournoyer tipped in a Duff pass to make it 4–1.

"Cournoyer," Smith groans. "I remember when Yvan went into the Hall of Fame, on TV they put together a clip of him scoring ten goals; I think all of them were against me. But you had to look close because I was wearing a different uniform every time—Toronto, Oakland, Chicago, Vancouver. Fact is, I always had trouble with him. Even in junior and oldtimer games. He was so damned fast, skating and shooting."

The Leafs got back into the game when Mahovlich slipped a Kelly pass back to Douglas, who loaded and fired a pea past Hodge. Early in the third, the Big M had a chance to pull the game tighter when he broke in on Hodge. The little goalie was deked, but stretched to make a toe save. After that, the Leafs sagged, managing one shot on Hodge the rest of the way. With the game decided, the Forum crowd organized a petition to give Cournoyer a regular shift.

"Y-van! Y-van! Y-van!" they chanted. The little winger had three goals in as many shifts. What would he do if Toe left him on the ice for a whole period? But Blake thought nothing of individual records. In February, 1964, he benched Rousseau late in a game with Detroit after the winger scored five goals. The team was ahead, Toe figured, time to play my defensive specialists.

"People would ask if I was mad only playing the power play, but they don't understand what it was like before expansion," Cournoyer says. "Back then, one or two rookies made it to the NHL in a year. My first year, everybody was saying it was a really great rookie year because Ellis, Crozier, Bergman, Hodge and me all made it. Yes, I remember that night, scoring three goals on the power play and the crowd calling for me. But I wasn't mad, no way. I was happy because I knew I had done my job."

So it was defensive specialist Roberts, not Cournoyer, who received extra playing time in the third. Yvan's impatient fans had to accept that Blake knew what he was doing when Roberts got his first goal of the year, a long shot from the boards that fooled Smith. Two minutes later, Backstrom completed the scoring, threading his way through the Leafs as if he were negotiating a pylon drill in practice.

"Geez, six goals? How many bad ones did I let in?" Smith asks. One, maybe two tops, he's told. He doesn't believe it. "If another team, even the Canadiens, scored six goals against that team, the goaltending couldn't have been much," he says. "Games I played for Toronto I can't remember the other team getting that many good chances, let alone goals."

Smith, who would later play on a series of expansion teams, says he's always treasured the games he played as a Leaf.

"It was wonderful because you got to see how a great hockey team performs," he says, sighing. "I remember my first game against New York, I think they won 2–1 and one of their goals was kicked in. Anyway, they only had maybe three decent chances all night. Oh, and to see how Horton and Stanley worked together. Never a mistake. Never a man left open. They were fantastic. And all the forwards backchecked. I remember thinking at the end of the game, 'Geez, this isn't too hard at all.' Later, when I played on some expansion teams," he laughs, "then I learned how hard goaltending could be!"

Smith is asked what his parents thought of their Christmas gift after watching their son's part in Montreal's Canadiens 6–2 shellacking of Toronto.

"They loved it! Except maybe the reception was bad, eh? Especially that time the goalie skated way the hell out and got knocked on his butt."

What did Punch think of the goalie's mid-ice adventure?

"Don't know, he never told me," Suitcase laughs. "Morning after the Montreal game I was sent back to Victoria."

FIRST PERIOD
1. Toronto, Jeffrey 6th (Ellis, Pronovost) 0:39
2. Montreal, Cournoyer 8th (Richard, Rousseau) 1:57
3. Montreal, Backstrom 2nd (Ferguson, Larose) 5:23

Penalties—Jeffrey (hooking) 0:57; Shack (roughing),
Baun (major, fighting), Douglas (major, fighting),
Backstrom (roughing), Larose (major, fighting),
Ferguson (roughing, major, fighting) 5:23;
Horton (holding) 13:26; Armstrong (interference) 16:14

SECOND PERIOD
4. Montreal, Cournoyer 9th (Richard, Duff) 6:13
5. Montreal, Cournoyer 10th (Duff, Rousseau) 15:24
6. Toronto, Douglas 2nd (Mahovlich, Kelly) 16:43
Penalties—Harper (major, fighting),
Stemkowski (major, fighting) 4:18; Horton (holding) 5:21;
Ferguson (high-sticking) 6:13;
Montreal (too many men on the ice, served by Cournoyer) 12:37;
Pulford (holding), Pappin (misconduct) 14:36; Backstrom (interference)
16:17

THIRD PERIOD
7. Montreal, Roberts 1st (Rousseau, J.C. Tremblay) 17:19
8. Montreal, Backstrom 3rd (Larose, Harper) 19:42
Penalties—None

Shots on goal
Toronto   9   9   5 — 23
Montreal   14   9   8 — 31

DECEMBER 22 STANDINGS

	P	W	L	T	F	A	Pts
Chicago	26	15	7	4	97	69	34
New York	28	14	8	6	89	65	34
Toronto	27	11	9	7	75	79	29
Montreal	25	12	11	2	65	64	26
Boston	27	7	15	5	71	100	19
Detroit	27	8	17	2	75	93	18

LEAGUE LEADERS

	GP	G	A	Pts	PIM
Mikita, Chi.	26	14	29	43	2
Wharram, Chi.	26	16	13	29	13
Rousseau, Mont.	25	8	19	27	20
Gilbert, N.Y.	28	16	10	26	4
Goyette, N.Y.	28	3	23	26	4
Ullman, Det.	27	8	17	25	20
Howe, Det.	27	7	17	24	8
Marshall, N.Y.	28	14	9	23	2
D. Hull, Chi.	26	12	11	23	8
Geoffrion, N.Y.	25	7	15	22	8
Pilote, Chi.	26	4	18	22	24

Crowd noise

Montreal English-language top ten TV programs, January 1967

1. Dean Martin (Thursday, 10:00 p.m.)
2. Jackie Gleason (Saturday, 7:00 p.m.)
3. Batman (Tuesday, 8:30 p.m.) *
4. Saturday Night Hockey
5. Wednesday Night Hockey
6. Bonanza (Sunday, 9:00 p.m.)
7. Get Smart (Friday, 8:00 p.m.)
8. Tommy Hunter Show (Friday, 8:30 p.m.)
9. The Man From U.N.C.L.E. (Thursday, 8:00 p.m.)
10. Walt Disney (Sunday, 6:00 p.m.)

* Batman cartoon balloon expressions for a sock to the jaw:
"BIFF! BAP! WHAP! ZWAPP! SW-A-A-P! POW!
K-POW! KER-POW! KLONK! ZOKK! URKK!
THHWACK! BOI-OI-ING! and EEE-YOW!

9

Here's Boom Boom

The Rangers were in first place in January. The Rangers! It hardly seemed possible. But Giacomin was the NHL's best netminder in the first half of the season. And with his perfectly timed one-leg curtsies, defenseman Harry Howell might've been the league's second-best puck blocker. ("Howell stopped more shots than Giacomin," Dennis Hull moaned after Chicago dropped a 1–0 Christmas decision to New York.) In addition to having hockey's best nicknames, Hot Rod Gilbert and Boom Boom Geoffrion were top ten scorers. So were Marshall and Goyette. Gunboats Fleming, Kurtenbach, Neilson, and Hadfield patrolled the corners with murderous aplomb. And so the Rangers were in first, somebodys at last. Even American network TV took notice. Early in the new year, Giacomin and Boomer appeared on Johnny Carson's "Tonight Show," which was then shot in New York.

Televisions only went up to channel 13 in 1967, but Montrealers and Torontonians with rabbit ears on their sets, and cable subscribers across the country* had no problem

*In 1963, cable companies began using microwave in Canada, extending service to isolated and remote areas. According to CRTC statistics, one in ten Canadians were using cable by 1968.

dropping in on Johnny and his hockey guests in early January.

"I was really surprised by what doing that show meant," recalls Giacomin. "Geez, it seems everybody back home [Sudbury] saw it. But the thing that really got me was next year, in expansion. I'd be in Los Angeles or St. Louis, and a person would come up to me on the street, recognizing me. Only they wouldn't say, 'Hey, aren't you the goalie for the Rangers?' they'd say, 'Hey, aren't you the guy who was on Johnny Carson?' And that was a year later."

The night they appeared, Giacomin and Boomer were surprised backstage by Tiny Tim. While Johnny traded quips with chortling sidekick Ed McMahon, Tiny orbited the Ranger stars in a manic flutter. "Tiny Tim was a guest that night, and he was a big hockey fan," explains former Ranger head of promotions John Halligan. "He charged up to the guys with that high voice of his and said, 'Oh, Mr. Geoffrion, Mr. Giacomin, such a pleasure to meet you! You're both so wonderful.' Didn't faze the guys a bit. Especially Bernie. He was a natural when it came to these sorts of things."

After prying themselves loose from the ukeleled crooner, the players joined Johnny on stage. Following a brief chat, hockey clips were shown. While the crowd applauded the crunching hits and spectacular toe saves, it was Geoffrion's commentary that drew the biggest response. Carson and the audience lapped up Boomer's gruff baritone and fractured beerhall English. What they couldn't understand was that Geoffrion spoke French in the same corkscrew fashion. A week earlier, Boomer slayed teammates by limping into the dressing-room after a game. "Oh-oh," he shuddered, clutching the inside of his thigh, "Boys, I'm afraid it's the lions." A pretty good Boomerism. But French Quebecers could top that any day. Everyone in Montreal remembered how when he was a Canadien, Geoffrion startled a TV reporter by saying, "Oi-yoy, j'ai une blessure à la laine," meaning, "Boy, do I have a wool injury." (What Boomer meant to say was "j'ai une blessure à l'aine," or "I have a groin injury.")

When the interview ended, Johnny cut to a commercial, and his crew hauled a hockey net on stage. Giacomin donned goalie pads, grabbed his blocker, glove, and stick, and assumed his position in net. Boomer, who was wearing his Ranger jersey over suit pants, lined up five pucks a foot apart about twenty-five feet from the net. When the show came back from break, the players executed a smart shooting drill.

"It was something we did every day at practice," Giacomin says, "Bernie was supposed to shoot one low on the left side that I get with a pad, another up high I take with my blocker, one between the legs, then two more low and high on the right side."

Boomer snapped off five quick screamers. Giacomin expertly turned the shots aside. The audience applauded wildly, as if it had witnessed a vaudeville knife-thrower trace the silhouette of his beautiful assistant with daggers. Carson turned on his toe and mouthed "wow" to the camera.

After another commercial, the program returned to find Carson in the nets, fully upholstered in a goalie outfit, mask included. In a soft voice, Giacomin explained to Carson the classic, getting-ready-for-a-face-off goalie stance.

"Hey, how come I have to wear a mask, if [Giacomin] didn't?" Carson asked Geoffrion.

"Because he's tough," Boom Boom barked.

The crowd exploded with laughter. Johnny milked the gag by turning to the camera and doing a Jack Benny slow burn. Then Geoffrion assumed his shooting position. Carson squared himself. The "Tonight Show" drummer did a firing squad drum roll. Finally, Boomer rifled a shot three feet over Johnny's head right through a stage wall and out of the studio. Just as Geoffrion leaned into his second shot, Carson rearranged himself, bringing his catching glove down to cover his groin. More laughter. A smiling Giacomin tried to point out that Johnny was out of position.

"Oh shut up," Carson yelled in mock hysterics, "you do it your way, and I'll do it mine."

The segment, which lasted twenty minutes, ended when Boomer fired a shot into Carson's open glove hand, exciting a delighted squeal from the crowd. As soon as the floor director cut to the commercial, Giacomin was rushed out of 30 Rockefeller Plaza.

"What nobody knew was that for the last fifteen minutes

or so, I felt like I was dying," Eddie says. "What happened was that Bernie's second shot caught me right in the friggin' adam's apple. Boy, did it hurt. Bernie had that heavy shot, eh. Other guys when you catch their shot in the hand, you seem to snare the puck. Same shot from Bernie went right through your hand. Man, after that shot in the throat, I couldn't swallow. I could barely talk the rest of the way, which is why it sounded like I was whispering."

So why didn't he even flinch when he was hit?

"Well, national TV, everybody watching, as a goalie you never want to let the shooter know he got you. But boy, did it hurt. I didn't play all week. It was my only injury all year."

The Saturday before the All Star break, New York visited Chicago for a showdown with the second-place Hawks. The season series was tied at three wins each, with a seventh game tied. Chicago had blown Giacomin out 6–3 in New York's home opener. Two weeks later, the Hawks clipped Maniago and the Rangers 3–1. Later in November, when Chicago visited New York again, Giacomin was back in nets.

"But really we had a new goalie," says Emile Francis. "Giacomin changed...after a certain incident. What happened is I sent him down [to Baltimore] for a week just after the season started. He wasn't doing too good. Oh, he'd be great for a game or two, then he'd have a bad period and the crowd'd get on him, throwing the garbage. You could see he was depressed, so I sent him down to get his confidence.

"He's back up, first game, we're playing Boston, at home, up a couple, when Maniago catches one in the mouth. I put Eddie in and the crowd give it to him good. I can see he's fightin' the puck so second intermission I go to Maniago. 'You're back in,' I say. 'No,' he says, 'the mouth is too bad.' I just looked at him. Next period, they get a bad goal on Eddie and the crowd starts. Then, wouldn't you know, late in the game, Eddie goes out to get a puck, darn it if a bad hop doesn't bounce over his stick. Bingo, it's tied. Now the garbage starts coming down. Game's over, I was so disgusted with the way we played I call a meetin' for next morning to show the guys the game film.

"We're sitting down that morning, geez the projector explodes in flames. Fire all over the place. Now I'm gettin' frustrated, eh? I look at Eddie in front of everyone and say, 'From now on you're my goalie, anyone throws garbage at you, pick it up and throw it back. They throw two pieces, I'll be there behind you to throw the other one back.' Son-of-a-gun, a week later he's the best goalie in hockey. Mentally tough, focussed. That's when we took off."

The new, improved Giacomin beat the Black Hawks 4–1 at home and 5–0 in Chicago. Then came the Christmas whitewashing, again in Chicago. Eddie had yielded one goal to the powerful Hawks in nine periods. The clubs met again December 27, in New York. Giacomin played another strong game and Rangers were up 2-1 in the third on goals by Gilbert and Geoffrion. Then Mikita banged one in off the post. The Rangers carried play rest of the way, but with time running out, Esposito won a face-off to Hull and the puck was in the net, giving Chicago a 3–2 win.

"It was a rough game, but we went down with a fight," Francis said afterwards. "See Fleming out there handling Hodge at the buzzer. And Hadfield sticking it to Pilote. That told me our guys hated losing. That's what you want to see."

"We had some rough games against Chicago my first couple of years," recalls Giacomin. "They were a good offensive team and you had to play them tough. I had a hard time against them. I'll tell you this straight out: those Hull boys tried to injure you to intimidate you. At first, they got to me, especially Bobby. What he tried to do was drill me between the eyes first shift. Wasting one. Then when he had me standing, backing away from the high one, next shot would be low off the post. That kind of stuff rattles a rookie. But with experience, you use it to your advantage. After a while, first time Bobby came down, I'd think, here it comes, then duck. Sure enough it'd be over my head. Next time, I'd think, low, glove side, and there it'd be."

Not many goalies were guessing right on Bobby these days. Number nine was skating easily, his hip free of pain. And he was in one of those grooves where every shot glanced off a post or zipped under a crossbar. He'd scored eight goals in five games, including one on a lightning tear through the entire Red Wing club a few nights earlier.

"Bobby you had to treat different from other players. Especially when he was going good," Giacomin remembers. "He had the best shot in the league. And he was so quick. Whenever he got the puck, even if it was at his blueline, you had to be ready. He was on you so fast. I bet if you look back he scored the first goal of a lot of games because if you hadn't played Chicago in a while you forgot how quick he was and how hard he could shoot."

It was a Hull, but not Bobby, who opened scoring when the clubs met on Saturday, January 12 in Chicago. Six minutes into an energetic first period, Dennis gathered a pass at centre, lumbered to the Ranger blueline, then threw himself into a slapshot that appeared to be on a flight path over the net until it refracted through some invisible medium in front of Giacomin, dipping off the goalie's shoulder into the net.

"Those friggin' curved sticks," Giacomin sighs. "Today you can only get away with a half-inch curve. But they were an inch-and-a-half back then, like bananas. And what the blade did was it cupped the puck so shots would take off high, like a wedge shot in golf. Then what'd happen is, and I still can't explain this, at fifty feet or so the puck would dip. You'd reach to catch something that wasn't there. Or you'd think it was over the net and the puck might drop under the crossbar. It was awful. You had to relearn how to play goal. It wasn't good enough to throw a glove or blocker out. When the Hawks started shooting, and most of them had the curved stick, you had to throw your body in front of every shot.

"Worst thing about curved sticks," he continues, "is they played with your head. I always say as a goalie you don't want to think, you want to concentrate. Don't think about fans or how much you want to win, just get purely into the game and react using your God-given talents. But then when a knuckle-ball got by you your concentration was shot. You started thinking, 'geez, that shouldn't have gone in, what am I gonna do here?' All of a sudden you start hearing the fans and you're off your game."

Tonight, Giacomin fought back, stopping Esposito and

Wharram close-in, then, cool as a Calypso dancer, snapping up a Mikita blast behind his ear. As the period ended, he went on the offensive, skating to the circle to lecture Nesterenko on his lawless ways in front of the net. Ranger teammates were also frisky. Hadfield got his stick up with Hull, and Kurtenbach and Fleming wrestled Mikita and Wharram.

"You wanted to hit that Chicago team," Francis says. "[Bobby] Hull of course. But the guy who worried me was Mikita. Oh, he was a dandy. Thing was, Hull was great, but if you tied him up, you shut his line down. Now Mikita, he was one those guys who made four other guys better. Like Gretzky. You could tie him up and he'd make one of those sneaky passes to Wharram or Mohns. You wanted to hit him so he was lookin' for you, not teammates."

Rangers came out hitting in the second, with Neilson flattening Mohns. But Giacomin lost another puck to physics when Maki's blueline slapshot bent under his blocker. In all the subsequent confetti and crowd whoops (every home goal in Chicago Stadium was New Year's Eve), Eddie lost focus. Now he was thinking, not concentrating. Hawks pounced, throwing three by him in ten minutes. Mohns broke up a power play, then lobbed the puck over Neilson's head, scooting around the defensemen and collecting his own pass before pretzelling Giacomin and ramming the puck home. Mikita scored on a shot from the circle. Then number nine beat Giacomin with a turn-around slapshot from fifty feet. Eddie had the blast measured, but the puck was a wet bar of soap in his hand and jumped free to the back of the net.

"Ever see a catcher call for a fastball and the pitcher throw him a curve?" Giacomin asks. "Ball skips by. Well, that's what trying to catch one of those pucks from a curved stick was like. It was unfair. Dangerous, too, when you consider most goalies weren't wearing masks. I remember complaining to Glenn Hall. 'Geez, you're lucky,' I said, 'you don't have to put up with those friggin' slapshots from the Hulls.' He rolled his eyes. 'You kidding,' he said, 'I have to put up with them every day at practice!' Except I know he didn't. Whenever Bobby or Dennis wound up, Glenn would skate out of the net and cuss them out. 'Wanna shoot like that? Go fire at DeJordy,' he'd say. No goalie liked facing a shot from curved sticks. Like I said, they were unfair. That's why they banned them. But it sure was murder when they were around."

Rangers had a murderer in their line-up, too. Gilbert had been using a Northland with a wow in the blade for two seasons. He'd tried introducing it to Geoffrion, but Boom Boom waved him away. "Never mind," he said, "Danny, my eleven-year-old son uses one. He's trying to teach me." Geoffrion didn't play this game. His "lions" were roaring again. Rod, however, did collect two second-period goals. On the second score, Hall failed to corral a tricky Gilbert long shot, and the winger tapped home his own rebound.

The duel of the banana blades ended in the third when the Black Hawks fell into a Leaf-like defensive shell (Van Impe and Pat Stapleton were even called for holding). Chicago frequently relieved pressure by icing the puck, an old Leaf tactic. The Rangers continued scrapping, carrying the play the final twenty minutes, and Kurtenbach managed a goal on a goalmouth scramble, but a Chicago victory was never in doubt.

"That was the year Chicago had everything," Francis remembers. "They had the two goalies, so you knew Hall was gonna be fresh for the playoffs. Pilote was a beauty back there on the blueline. He reminded me of Harvey on a power play: He saw the whole ice and could make the perfect pass. Stapleton was a good rushing defenseman. Who else'd they have back there? Van Impe and Jarrett, that's your muscle right there. Offense was just great. The Mikita line and the Hull line. Then they had Red Hay's checkin'. And a good bench. Well, they seemed to have the best of everything the second half, didn't they—goaltending, defense, goal scorers, checkers. Oh, they were a great team, no doubt about it."

FIRST PERIOD
1. Chicago, D. Hull 14th (Hay, Jarrett) 6:42
Penalties—Stapleton 6:42; Brown 14:32; MacNeil 16:23

SECOND PERIOD
2. Chicago, Maki 5th (Esposito, Stapleton) 3:00
3. Chicago, Mohns 10th 5:29
4. Chicago, Mikita 18th (Jarrett, Pilote) 11:37
5. New York, Gilbert 21st (Hadfield) 13:52
6. Chicago, R. Hull 24th (Esposito, Jarrett) 15:42
7. New York, Gilbert 22nd (Hicke) 17:41
Penalties—Van Impe 3:46

THIRD PERIOD
8. New York, Kurtenbach 7th (Hadfield, Hicke) 3:25
Penalties—Van Impe 2:49; Hay 4:40; Stapleton 14:54

Shots on goal

New York	8	10	8 —	26
Chicago	15	12	7 —	35

FIRST HALF STANDINGS

	P	W	L	T	F	A	Pts
Chicago	37	21	11	5	131	94	47
New York	39	20	12	7	112	87	47
Toronto	37	17	12	8	99	100	42
Montreal	36	16	16	4	92	88	36
Detroit	39	13	23	3	107	130	29
Boston	38	8	22	7	92	134	25

FIRST HALF SCORING

	GP	G	A	Pts	PIM
Mikita, Chi.	37	19	36	55	4
Wharram, Chi.	37	19	19	38	17
R. Hull, Chi.	36	26	11	37	23
Ullman, Det.	39	14	21	35	22
Rousseau, Mont.	36	9	26	35	4
Goyette, N.Y.	39	4	31	35	4

FIRST HALF SCORING (*continued*)

Howe, Det.	39	13	21	34	18
Gilbert, N.Y.	39	22	11	33	6
Keon, Tor.	34	9	19	28	0
Ellis, Tor.	37	14	13	27	6
Geoffrion, N.Y.	33	11	16	27	10
Martin, Bos.	38	11	16	27	29
Delvecchio, Det.	39	8	19	27	4
Pilote, Chi.	37	4	23	27	46
Marshall, N.Y.	39	15	11	26	4
D. Hull, Chi.	37	14	12	26	10
Esposito, Chi.	36	8	17	25	22
Kelly, Tor.	32	8	16	24	2
Mohns, Chi.	29	10	14	24	25
Nevin, N.Y.	36	11	13	24	6
Hadfield, N.Y.	39	7	17	24	29
F. Mahovlich, Tor.	35	12	11	23	27
Howell, N.Y.	39	8	15	23	28
Richard, Mont.	36	8	15	23	16
Hampson, Det.	34	8	15	23	2
Kurtenbach, N.Y.	29	7	16	23	17

GOALKEEPERS' RECORDS

	GP	GA	SO	AVG.
New York				
Giacomin	38	79	6	2.13
Maniago	3	8	0	4.14
(New York totals)	39	87	6	2.23
Montreal				
Hodge	24	53	3	2.27
Bauman	1	1	0	1.00
Worsley	13	34	1	2.91
(Montreal totals)	36	88	4	2.44
Chicago				
Hall	21	43	1	2.38
DeJordy	19	51	1	2.69
(Chicago totals)	39	94	2	2.54

GOALKEEPERS' RECORDS (*continued*)

Toronto				
Sawchuk	14	29	0	2.38
Bower	11	26	1	2.64
Gamble	14	33	0	2.73
G. Smith	2	7	0	3.63
A. Smith	1	5	0	5.00
(Toronto totals)	37	100	1	2.70
Detroit				
Crozier	33	105	4	3.32
Gardner	2	6	0	3.00
Bassen	7	19	0	3.52
(Detroit totals)	39	130	4	3.33
Boston				
Cheevers	22	72	1	3.33
Johnston	16	50	0	3.68
Parent	3	12	0	4.34
(Boston totals)	38	154	1	3.53

Crowd noise
Ca-na-da: A Centennial Song

"Ca-na-daa,
(One little, two little, three Canadians ...)
we love thee.
(... four little, five little, six provinces)
Ca-na-daa,
proud and free.
North! South! East! West!
there'll be happy times;
church bells will ring, ring, ring.
It's the hundredth anniversary of
Con-fed-er-a-tion,
everybody sing together!"

(Repeat until 1968)

—Words and music by Bobby Gimby

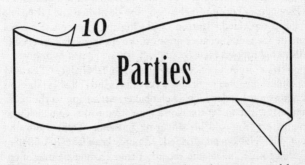

10

Parties

The last night of 1966 was plug-the-car-in cold in Canada's capital. Nevertheless, more than 2,000 Ottawans, all of them wearing long johns, dickies, scarves, toques, and something more serious than church gloves, left home after supper for the big outdoor Centennial party on Parliament Hill. Hurrying down Wellington Street you could even *hear* how cold it was: Galoshes squeaked treading hard-packed snow. Chunks of ice tinkled when booted up against snowbanks. As soon as kids complained about the lung-searing cold, Dad reassured them, "Steady troops, we'll be warming up by that brand new Centennial flame before you know it."

Before anything happens in Ottawa there are at least two speeches: the first in English, the second in mangled French (or vice versa). Tonight, Prime Minister Lester Pearson and the Queen, in a taped message broadcast on a monitor the size of a drive-in screen, made Centennial addresses. After speeches the flame was to be lit. Then fireworks. The Queen spoke first. Sitting at home in Halifax or Medicine Hat, watching the festivities on the tube, you could hear her fine.

On the Hill, however, CBC forgot to pipe the TV broadcast through the public address system. For quivering spectators it was a little like listening to a goldfish for a half hour.

"Typical CBC," someone shouted, "don't adjust your set." The crowd, already miffed because the Corporation had neglected to provide public seating, joined in a mock cheer. (Raspberries continued through next day when the *Globe and Mail* complained, "Instead of placing the Centennial symbol or the Canadian coat of arms on the speaker's dais, the CBC displayed its own crest.")

After the Queen's message, Prime Minister Pearson stepped between State Secretary Judy LaMarsh and Opposition Leader John Diefenbaker, advancing to the podium. "Tonight we let the world know that this is Canada's year in history," he told his shivering audience. Then the sound cut out. The crowd groaned. Minutes later, the P.A. system jolted to life, "...let the record of that chapter be one of co-operation and not conflict, of dedication and not division, of service, not self..." then crashed for the night.

The party took off soon as the Prime Minister finished his speech (you could tell because his lips stopped moving). A choir burst into "O Canada." Everyone joined in. Well, almost everyone. Diefenbaker, a staunch opponent of Canada's new patriotic jingle (he was a "God Save the Queen" man), studied the sky, his mouth a straight line, waiting for the display of unblushing republicanism to pass. The crowd ended the song with a loud cheer. Our smiling Prime Minister descended the stage, accepted a torch and proceeded to the Centennial flame.

"Dad, I can't see what's happening!" kids complained as Pearson dipped from view. Because the monument was ground level and hidden behind cameras at the back of a huge CBC tent, only a handful got to see the big "whoosh." Little matter, soon as the flame caught life an explosion of fireworks stained the sky high over the Peace Tower. Some disintegrating rockets stretched so high that kids, craning their necks, just about tumbled backwards. The crowd broke formation as the singing and rocketry continued. Hundreds chased Pearson and Diefenbaker, who strolled together back to the Centre

Block. Many party-goers were bold enough to venture forth and shake the leaders' hands.

"Happy New Year, Mr. Prime Minister," "Happy New Year, Sir," they shouted. "And a Happy Centennial to you, too," Pearson responded, smiling.

By then most dads had jogged back to the Ford to warm up the car. But teenage revellers hung around to usher in the arrival of 1967. By midnight everyone present had a turn in the CBC tent. What a way to usher in Canada's second century: crowded into a big glorified hockey change shack, warming your stinging hands and toes up against the world's biggest pot bellied stove, a bathtub-sized Centennial flame.

Although the NHL was fifty years old in 1966–67, there were no fireworks at the January All Star game in Montreal. No speeches, esteemed guests, or elaborate pre-game ceremonies. Just lots of bellyaching. For the first time the league scheduled the contest mid-season. Previously the game had been held at the end of the exhibition schedule. Players arrived in the Cup-winning city a few days early, had a scrimmage or two, donned their white jerseys (with numbers front and back and two gold stars near the armpits), then hit the ice. If the All Stars weren't at mid-season form, well, neither were the champs.

This season there was a scant two-day break between Sunday's games and Wednesday's All Star affair. Some players arrived in Montreal the morning of the match.

"This isn't fair," charged All Star coach Sid Abel. "Our guys don't even get to shake hands [before going on the ice], and the Canadiens have been playing together for four months."

Boston's Ted Green didn't show at all. "I don't deserve to be in the game," he said. "I'm not having much of a year. Why don't they take Orr?" Why indeed? Orr was the third leading point-getter among defensemen in recent voting. Oh, he was an All Star all right, but on the 1966–67 first-half All Star team, and though we were now three weeks into 1967, the NHL was just getting around to playing the 1965–66 game.

"This is stupid," complained All Star goalie Glenn Hall. "First-half All Stars should be playing the Canadiens, not last year's All Stars. Some of those guys don't even want to play." Joked Bobby Hull: "They're not going to let us use the kid [Orr], and we're not going to have a practice. Are the Canadiens going to let us use skates and sticks out there tonight?"

Yes, but as it turned out, without much effectiveness. Coach Abel started the game with Hull, Mikita, and Howe up front. Blake matched the Dream Line with Larose, Backstrom, and Ferguson. The Canadien trio, Montreal's best line of late, won every shift from the Hall-of-Famers, digging in corners, hustling at mid-ice, and hitting the blueline in precise formation. (Without the benefit of practice, the Stars negotiated the blueline like Laurel and Hardy entering a doorway, unsure who should go first.)

Hall, crouched in his familiar cobra weave, kept the All Stars in the game early, making a dashing pad save on Rousseau and flicking a Provost try over the net with an elbow. The All Stars played a conservative first period, icing the puck and settling for shots outside the circle. But with five minutes left, the All Stars lost even their defensive composure when Ranger defensemen Howell and Neilson chased the puck in the corner. Quiet as a burglar, Henri slipped into the slot and redirected a smart Rousseau pass beyond Hall.

On the next shift Ferguson and Larose were on the prowl, thumping in the corner. After uncovering a loose puck, Claude wheeled into the circle and fired a shot in the direction of the net. The puck zigged off Ferguson's hip then zagged off Pilote's leg, eluding Hall.

The second period dragged as the Canadiens, playing with a comfortable 2–0 lead, concentrated on checking, careful not to press too deep and let the All Stars back in the game with a three-on-two break. None was forthcoming, although Hull did make a nifty rush, forcing Hodge into a good save on an early power play. Then came the play of the game. Midway through the period, Ferguson bumped Ullman behind the Montreal net, then, seconds later, collided with him again in front of Hodge. Innocent stuff as far as hockey fights go, but unusual for an All Star game, which was held to be an exhibition as much as a contest. What happened next was a real breach of etiquette. Just as the altercation had simmered to the jawing stage, Ferguson, visited by an unexplained fury, launched an overhand right that caught Ullman on the button. The Detroit centre was asleep before he hit the ice.

As Ferguson explained after the game, the fight was all Ullman's fault. The Red Wing had done everything short of pull a gun on him. "He slashed me behind the net and broke my stick," Fergy argued. "Then I hit him with a good shoulder check and he cross-checked me under the chin. So I just zinged him one right on the nose."

Allan Stanley, Green's replacement this night, laughs hearing Ferguson's account of his fight with Ullman. "Yeah, can't you just see Normie attacking Ferguson in an All Star game? That was Fergy, though. He was a real Westerner—a real cowboy. He shot first and asked questions later. You never saw a guy get in a fight any quicker than him. That's why he won so many of them, I guess. He could get mad faster than the other fella."

After the game, Ferguson bristled at a suggestion that punching out another player violated the spirit of All Star competition. "Whenever I put on the Montreal Canadien uniform I want to win," he said. "Doesn't matter who we're playing, the Toronto Maple Leafs or the All Stars, they're the enemy, and I want to beat them."

The All Stars, proud, talented men all, wanted to win the game as well, but when it became apparent that wasn't likely, they pursued what is always a secondary objective in games of this kind. "You want to do two things in an All Star game," Mikita explained. "You'd like to win, of course, because you're a professional, but you don't want to get hurt for exactly the same reason. You're a professional and you still have a half season of hockey to play."

So the All Stars played the third period in the manner of a driver whose insurance has lapsed. Although they recorded fifteen shots on rookie call-up, Gary Bauman, most were from well out. Canadiens weren't exactly putting on a show either. Toe gave André Boudrias and Noel Price lots of ice time, resting regulars. Fewer than half the crowd were still around when Ferguson shovelled a Richard pass through Giacomin's pads with eight seconds left. A reporter in the press box shook his head after the game and commented, "Boy, that third period was rougher than the third day of a Polish wedding."

ALL STARS
Goal—Hall (Chicago), Giacomin (New York)
Defense—Stanley (Toronto), Howell (New York), Neilson (New York), Pilote (Chicago), Stapleton (Chicago)
Forwards—Mikita (Chicago), Howe (Detroit), Hull (Chicago), Keon (Toronto), Gilbert (New York), Mahovlich (Toronto), Ullman (Detroit), Delvecchio (Detroit), Nevin (New York), Oliver (Boston)

MONTREAL
Goal—Hodge, Bauman
Defense—Laperrière, J.C. Tremblay, Harris, Harper, Talbot, Price
Forwards—Backstrom, Ferguson, Larose, Richard, Rousseau, Duff, Cournoyer, Provost, Balon, G. Tremblay, Boudrias

FIRST PERIOD
1. Montreal, Richard (Rousseau, Harper) 14:03
2. Montreal, Ferguson (Larose) 15:59
Penalties—None

SECOND PERIOD
No scoring:
Penalties—Howell (kneeing) 6:58; Richard (tripping) 7:19; Ferguson (roughing) 10:00

THIRD PERIOD
3. Montreal, Ferguson (Richard, Rousseau) 19:52
Penalties—None

Shots on goal
Montreal   14   7   9 — 30
All Stars   10   10   15 — 35

Crowd noise
Canadian humour, circa 1967

"Say, what do you think of that Red China?"
"Well, I've always felt it goes best with white linen."

—Wayne and Shuster routine

"The trouble with taking out a librarian is that
you have to return them in fourteen days."

"One has this awful choice in husbands:
too true to be good and too good to be true."

"A Canadian is a man who puts his empties
in someone else's garbage can."

—Richard Needham's lecture circuit patter

"If Judy LaMarsh married Howdy Doody
she'd be Judy Doody."

—coffee break joke

11
A Month in a Sand Trap

Imlach and Clancy were in vintage form after the Leafs trimmed the Bruins 3–0 on Christmas Eve at the Gardens. First star Johnny Bower had collapsed at his locker and was installing his teeth when King arrived in the dressing-room, loaded with gifts. Kent Douglas was first to open his Christmas present. What a surprise! A blue tie dotted with silver maple leaves, same as last year.

"Say what you like about these Leaf ties, but they're so wide you can use 'em for a scarf," Douglas observed. "In a pinch they're wide enough to make a swell vest."

While Clancy duelled with the players ("What ya get me, ya miserable bum?"), Scrooge arrived. "Good news, there's a big blizzard in Boston, so we can't fly," Imlach said, offering the thinnest of smiles. "We bus into Buffalo and take a train from there. Bus leaves in an hour, so you got time to get a sandwich." Horton pealed off a soggy blue legging and threw it on the floor. "Happy Hanukkah," he groaned.

The team had to take the milk run from Buffalo to Boston. Fifteen hours on buses and trains. Players were understand-ably grumpy. Punch, however, was perversely cheerful. "I'm not always a mean old shit," he cackled. "Those kids in Boston have to have snow for Christmas and that's just what I'm giving them."

Instead of complaining, the Leafs should've been grateful. Punch booked a sleeper on the Boston train. The last sleeper, Boston GM Milt Schmidt soon discovered. "Flip a coin to see which team gets the sleeper," he suggested. "Geez, Milt, it's better to give than receive," Punch replied, pretending astonishment, "and we thought you'd like to do the giving."

The Boston players passed the night rolling on tables in the dining car, lurching awake whenever the train stopped. Later that evening, the Bruins looked like they were still searching for sleep as Leafs pushed them aside 4–2.

Despite the weekend sweep, Imlach was in a foul mood. The schedule-maker had given Toronto a week off, but Punch kept up a daily practice grind. During workouts, he was particularly hard on Mahovlich. The Big M was in a slump, with two goals in fifteen games. Nobody knew why. He certainly hadn't lost his shot, as Bower discovered Monday. Johnny got a mitt on a Mahovlich blast, then sprang from the net, cursing. He couldn't make a fist. His hand was broken, he discovered later. He'd be out a month.

The next morning, Imlach lit into the Big M at the end of a ninety-minute skate. "In case you're interested, Ma-hal-o-vich, you're back at two o'clock," he hollered. Frank was spared the indignity of practicing alone by the appearance of a few volunteers, spares like goalie Al Smith, who wanted to work on their game. Smith regretted showing up as soon as Mahovlich started working on his shot. After snaring a bullet, he left the net, shaking his hand. Imlach hollered for him to get back. "Catch the damn puck right, hand doesn't hurt," he said.

After practice, Punch astonished Louis Cauz with the suggestion he might send Pulford down. Pully hadn't rounded into form after a training-camp knee injury. Normally a dependable twenty-goal-a-year man, he had four goals at Christmas.

"Do teams send players of Pulford's magnitude to the minors?" the reporter asked. "Detroit sent Bathgate to Pittsburgh," Punch replied. "And he won the Hart Trophy.

No player on this team has ever won the Hart, the most important trophy in hockey. It's only common sense. If you or I weren't doing the job, what'd happen?"

Punch suggested Pulford and linemates Shack and Brenneman were letting the team down. "Two goals a game [they allow]," he said, "which means we've got to score three goals and the other guys play perfect. No way."

On New Year's Eve, the Hawks were in town. The game wasn't much of a party for Leaf fans. The Hull and Mikita lines smoked four by Al Smith before the game was half over. Fans booed whenever Mahovlich appeared. By the third period, they were cheering Chicago goals. Foster Hewitt named The Scooter Line all three stars in a 5–1 Hawk win. Imlach was in a vile mood afterwards. "Sixteen, seventeen, eighteen," he hissed as the last Leafs straggled into the dressing room. "Hmmn, everybody here. Not one of you was named a star."

Next day the Leafs regrouped, defeating the Rangers 2–1 in New York. It was a classic Toronto road win. The Rangers were hot, having taken nine of twelve. Gamble was terrific, however, and the team parlayed a few counterattacks into goals by Conacher and Keon, then went into a variation on basketball's four-corner stall for a period and a half, frustrating even New York reporters.

"Rarely has a team been so outplayed and yet managed to stay on top," New York *Times*' Gerald Eskenazi wrote. "The Blues took twenty-one shots on Gamble in the first period, nine in the second, and closed with thirteen in the final period. While they were taking their forty-three shots, Leafs clutched and grabbed, bouncing with the Rangers' momentum… Of sixty-seven face-offs…forty were held in Toronto's end. Which meant, of course, Leafs were icing the puck, or holding it against the boards, or unable to stop the Ranger attack, except at crucial moments."

Despite the win, Punch remained in a funk. When New York visited Toronto the following Wednesday, Imlach's pep talk was, "Fuck up another one here and it'll cost you five dollars each, price of a blue seat."

Gamble and Giacomin were outstanding that night, and the game ended 1–1. Ellis scored the Leaf goal, but lost his centre, Kelly, the team's best forward so far this season. The redhead tried to slip between Nevin and Howell and wrecked his knee on a turnstile of Ranger hips. Three to five weeks, doctors figured.

The next weekend, Mahovlich and Pulford ended scoring droughts, leading the team to a 5–2 win over Boston. On Sunday, Detroit handled Toronto 3–1. Players arrived back in Toronto in the early morning utterly dispirited. After two games and twelve hours of travel in forty-eight hours, they had to face a nine a.m. skating marathon.

"I believe that no one ever died from hard work," Conacher says. "Practices are important. But what Punch held wasn't practice, it was punishment, plain and simple. We didn't work on our power play or some facet of the game we were having problems with. [Punch] skated us until we dropped. Hour after hour, you just skated and skated. Now me, I was young, didn't smoke or drink, but some guys looked awful afterwards."

Imlach deked into his favourite Montreal men's shop, Tony the Tailor, before Wednesday's game, picking out an eye-popping white fur fedora. The last time in at the Forum, he had worn a grey felt top and the team had been bombed, 6–2. Clearly a change in tactics was in order.

The Canadiens started fast this night. Cournoyer collected a power play goal on the team's second shot. The Leafs then fell into their Alamo defense for the duration. With the score 1–1 late, Toronto began to tire. The Habs crowded Gamble. Rousseau, J.C., and Fergy had chances. Then Pulford took a tripping penalty. Béliveau and Rousseau were in close. Somehow the Leafs hung on. With time running out, Montreal launched a furious final assault, but no red shirt could break free of the mucilaginous Leaf checking. Pulford finally cleared to centre. Ellis gathered the puck and tried to swing around Laperrière, but was steered into the boards. In desperation, the winger slapped at the puck.

After the game, a long-faced Charlie Hodge explained what happened next: "It hit my pad and went straight up in the air," the goalie said. "I reached for it and lost it and then [Jeffrey] bumped me and I pulled it into the net with me."

In the Leaf dressing-room, Punch jigged around newsmen. "A lucky break, that's what it was," he sang. "I love coming into this town and getting a little break like that. That puts me six points ahead of them and that ain't bad." The exhausted Leafs must've loved that. They kill themselves three hours to stretch "his" lead.

On Saturday, Toronto roughed up Detroit 5–2. Gamble was marvellous, and what was now the team's big line—Mahovlich, Keon, and Ellis—each contributed a goal. Prior to Sunday's game with the Black Hawks, a Chicago reporter asked Imlach about Mikita's chances of winning the Lady Byng trophy, handed out to the league's most gentlemanly player.

"Shouldn't even be a vote," Punch cracked, "just give it to my team." This wasn't a compliment. Lady Byng was a pejorative in Imlach's book. "Some of my guys are playing like Little Lord Fauntleroy," he said. Why Punch was being so churlish is hard to figure. Bower, Sawchuk, and Kelly were out. Baun had missed most of the season. Stanley was playing with a cracked rib. Still, his team had won six, lost two, and tied one in the last three weeks. Leafs must've wondered what Punch would do if they ever fell into a slump.

If so, they didn't have to wait long to find out. Chicago shut Toronto down 4–0 that night, then Detroit thumped them 6–2. The next Saturday, the Red Wings were in town. Abel's team hadn't won on the road yet (kids in Windsor now called them the Detroit Dead Things). Punch started Horton on right wing that night. When number seven scored, Imlach glowed right through his Swiss yodeller's cap. Conacher and Pronovost added first period markers to give Toronto a 3–0 bulge. Then Leafs just rolled over and died. Led by the HUM line (Henderson, Ullman, and MacGregor), Detroit scored five unanswered goals on the way to a 5–4 win. Next night in Boston, Punch switched back to his grey fedora, but his team was outshot 42–18, and beaten 3–1.

"Least Gamble played well," a reporter said to Imlach.

"He's paid to block shots," Punch growled.

The next week, Punch whipped players on ice and in the papers. "The guys we're paying big money aren't performing,"

Punch told newsmen. "Look what Mikita and Hull are doing. Then look at Mah-ol-ovich and Pulford and the rest of our guys. End of story." Punch chewed Pappin's backside one work-out. "Punch yelled at Jim in practice, listen you blan-kety-blank," Conacher remembers, "you better do something out there soon, cause I got five guys down in Rochester dyin' for your job." Days later, Pappin was gone.

Wednesday, January 25, the Canadiens were in town, searching for their first win in Toronto this season. They found it, too, sailing to an easy 3–1 victory. Cournoyer notched another power play goal. Gilles Tremblay also scored during a man advantage. Larose finished Toronto off in the third, slapping a Backstrom draw over Gamble's shoulder. Fans were so upset some even booed Shack when Punch let him out of the doghouse for his nightly walk.

Toronto closed out January with a weekend series against Chicago. Neither game was close. Saturday, the Hawks bombed Leafs 5–2. In Chicago, it was 5–1. The Scooter Line notched seven goals. Hull's line grabbed two more. Bobby also knocked Baun out of Saturday's match when he blasted a slapshot off the defenseman's toe. So far this season, Hull had thirty goals and three broken toes (he'd also splintered Ed Westfall and Oliver's feet).

The losing streak stood at seven. There was no joy in Leafdom. This fan went into a wretched, month-long sulk. Radio stations were telling Leaf jokes, calling the team the Maple Loafs and Maple Laffs.

"I can't think of a worse place to play hockey when you're losing," Ellis says. "Boston or Chicago you could probably get away from your job. No one would recognize you on the street. In Toronto, everywhere we'd go people would ask, 'Hey, what's wrong with the team?' It got so you'd leave the house go to the rink to practice, then come home. You would-n't want to go out. And you'd hear the stuff on the radio and TV, read it in the paper. I didn't have kids at the time, but I remember some guys telling me that their kids were getting picked on at school. Can you imagine that? Like I said, Toronto is a miserable place to lose."

The club did get some encouragement. One prominent fan

sent a telegram. "You're a good hockey team," the message read, "as good as you were when you won three straight Stanley Cups, so shake it off." The communique remained pinned to the team bulletin board until Imlach discovered it came from Alan Eagleson. "I don't know who pinned that fucking nonsense up," he screamed, "but I'll fire anyone who lets that bastard in here again." (When The Eagle visited the Gardens in January to drum up support for a players' union, Imlach threw him off the premises.)

Punch was impossible these days—Captain Bligh with a toothache. After the Sunday loss in Chicago, he put the team through four practices in a thirty-hour stretch before the Leafs flew to Montreal for a Wednesday game.

Leafs started well that night, with Baun banking one off a Hab defenseman for a goal. Then Cournoyer retaliated with a pair of power play markers (he had ten goals against Leafs this season, all with a man advantage). After that, Bower, in his second game back, settled into form and the game fell into a classic see-saw Montreal-Toronto battle. The turning point came early in the second period: Ellis and the just-activated Kelly poured over the Montreal blueline, with only Harper back. Kelly faked then lateralled to Ellis, who fired it past Hodge, clank! off the goalpost. Harper cleared to Gilles Tremblay, who raced down wing and ripped a high shot that Bower got an arm on, reached for—but not as fast as Richard, who bunted a short rebound into the top corner.

Then Montreal took over.

"They were the most emotional team, and the best team we ever played," remembers Stanley. "Sometimes all they had to do was score a nice goal and they caught fire. After that they came at you in waves. Ten minutes later, you'd look up at the clock and geez, they'd scored three more." When Leafs next looked up this night it was 7–1 Montreal, and the crazy trumpeter who entertained at Canadien home games was playing a medley of Herb Alpert songs.

"I'm going to make [Leafs] walk back to Toronto," Imlach said after the game. He might've, too, but then they would've missed his nine o'clock morning practice.

The following Sunday, the Leafs dropped another road

game to the Rangers, 4–1. "If you saw them during that slump you wouldn't have given them a snowball's chance you-know-where in the playoffs," says Emile Francis. "No spirit, eh? They were just waiting to get beat." The losing streak now stood at nine. The team had been outscored 21–5 in its last four games. "You hear those numbers and shake your head," Francis says. "That team was too good defensively to be playing like that. There was something wrong there, no doubt about it."

"What happened was the young guys quit on Punch," Kelly says. Since Kelly was forty at the time, "young guys" could mean anyone other than Bower. He refuses to name names, however, saying only, "We got into a slump. Punch got mad at the guys. And I guess the young guys got mad back.

"Oh, I know a lot of players disagreed with the way Punch did things," Kelly continues. "I didn't agree with everything myself. Point is as a coach you're never going to be able to please everybody. Way I looked at it, and I think a few veterans felt the same, was this: When you get into a car to go somewhere there might be a hundred different roads you can take to get there. In the end, you judge the driver not on how he got there, but if he got there. Punch, he might've taken some funny roads, but he ended up the right place at the end of the day. And that's the only way you can judge a coach. Was Punch successful? Yes. Well, that meant you paid attention to what he said.

"But the young guys got mad, like I say. That's natural enough. But some of them, I think, they may have let their anger get in the way of their play. They probably didn't think they were, and I know they didn't want to, but they did."

The young guys agree, but plead extenuating circumstances.

"I think what happened was that Punch got so down on the team, made life so oppressive, that we lost our focus," remembers Conacher. "From my perspective, it wasn't so much that the young guys disliked Imlach. Many did, that's true, but I don't know that that's the point. I was just a role player on that team, not one of the big stars, certainly. As a rookie in those days, you just sat there and did what you were asked. But I could see what was going on. And I think what happened was that by [Punch] working us so hard and yelling and screaming all the time, after a while it felt like everything we did we did because Punch was forcing us to do it. Maybe some veterans could take that constant aggravation, they'd learned to live with Punch. But most of the players became lethargic. The constant negativity just got to us to the point that we hated to go to the rink in the morning. Ultimately, I think the individual player has to have the desire to play well and win. A coach can't force that on him."

Stanley chuckles remembering the long-ago family squabble.

"Listen, players getting mad at Punch was nothing new," he says. "The team had rough patches with Punch over the years. This was one of them. As a veteran maybe you had a tendency to let stuff wash over you. Coaches getting mad when we lost was something I'd got used to. Yeah, Punch worked us hard. Real hard when we lost. You see, he believed to play the game right you had to work hard and working hard isn't something you can turn off and on like a tap. It's something you work at and work at until you don't think about it anymore. You just play hard without thinking.

"Did Punch get out of hand now and then? Oh, I don't know. Let me tell you a story about Punch and his practices. [In the spring of 1964] we had a tough play-off series with Montreal. Beat them in seven games. Then we played Detroit in the finals and it was another tough battle. Went seven games and there were some overtimes. I know we won the sixth game in overtime in Detroit. Anyway, after that game the boys were exhausted. Seventh game was back in Toronto two days later. Now the Wings, Sid Abel, he told his players to go to the track on the off day. Relax, forget about hockey for a while, and come back refreshed in Toronto. Us? Well, Punch worked us hard the next day. So what happens seventh game? We handle them, I think the score was 4–0. The only easy game we had in the whole play-offs. Now, tell me if the way Punch worked us was wrong?"

Imlach called the team's next match the most important game of the season. Red Wings, winners of six straight, were in. If Detroit won, Leafs dropped to fifth.

"It's D-Day. It's not a skirmish, it's a battle," Punch told the troops after a vigorous ninety-minute skate. "As Churchill said, 'I expect every man to do his duty.'" Imlach paused. "It was Churchill who said that, wasn't it…or was it Lord Nelson at Trafalgar?" Just then, Pulford emerged from the shower, towel draped over his shoulder. "Nelson," the McMaster grad said, then walked away.

Punch wasn't winning anything these days.

Lord Nelson went down this night 5–2. The game was over in the second period when Ullman netted three in two shifts. Toronto had lost ten in a row. "Any of you guys want to rene-gotiate contracts for next year, my office is open," Punch offered after the game. When the players left, he turned morose. "Worst run I've ever had in hockey," Punch told reporters. "Never lost this many straight in even cribbage or gin rummy."

"[The slump] ate him up," says George Gross. "Punch loved putting on a show in Toronto. And when the team went on a losing streak, he took it harder than anyone, believe me. For Leafs to lose ten in a row, well, it made him sick. I would bet he had many sleepless nights, worrying, fig-uring out what needed to be done to turn the season around. Punch prided himself on being a hockey man who could look at a team, see what's wrong, and fix it."

During a month-long losing streak that saw his team outscored 47–15, Imlach tried everything: Shuffling lines. Moving defensemen to forward. Benching forwards. Demoting Pappin for two weeks. Sending Douglas down for good. Bringing up Hillman, Walton, Dick Gamble, and junior star Gary Unger. Going with four lines. Three lines. Four goalies. Nothing worked.

Then there were the moves not made. Suddenly, everyone wanted to trade. Boston offered Oliver and Green for Pulford and Douglas. Detroit proposed a Floyd Smith-Pappin swap. But Smith was a right winger, and with Mahovlich and Jeffrey slumping, Leafs needed help on the left side. Imlach liked Oliver, but he already had too many centres, with Keon in place, Walton aboard, Kelly back, and Stemkowski playing better. Imlach loved Green, and his defense was battered. But Green was hurt, too, out for the year. He'd help next season, but Punch wanted to win now. Next year he'd figure something else.

So he stood pat. Well, almost. Somewhere in the grey hours between Wednesday's game and Thursday's practice, Punch stitched together a new line. Centre Pulford was shifted to left wing, alongside Stemkowski. Pappin moved in on the right side. If it worked, Punch had found room for his extra centre and a good two-way left winger. (With two playmakers feeding him, maybe Pappin would finally start hitting the net.) Imlach made one other decision that night. Stanley, Baun, and Pronovost had suffered injury-plagued seasons. Hillman was healthy, skating and hitting hard. From now on, he'd get more ice time.

When the fifth-place Leafs took the ice on Saturday, February 11 to face the league-leading Black Hawks, the starting defense was Horton and Hillman. Stemkowski's unit was out second and played so well it was soon double-shifted. Toronto scored early, with Keon chipping a Conacher pass over DeJordy's shoulder. Minutes later, the Scooter Line made like the Harlem Globetrotters, throwing together a series of no-look passes that culminated in Mikita sliding the puck into an empty net. Then Hull announced his presence with a blue-line slapshot that put a full sail in the net back of Gamble.

Tonight, however, the Leafs refused to roll over. Seconds before the period ended, Hillman collected an Armstrong pass and flipped a shot between DeJordy's legs. In the middle frame, Baun, Hillman, and Pulford started thumping. Stemkowski was bowling over everyone in sight.

"I'll get you," snarled Pilote, picking himself up after a Stemkowski knock. On the next shift out, the big centreman crashed Pierre into the boards again. "Want me, here I am," he roared.

Soon the Hawks had difficulty moving the puck. The Leafs capitalized late in the period when Stemkowski converted a Chicago turnover into the go-ahead goal. Toronto carried the play for the rest of the game, skating and banging hard. In search of the tying goal, Hawks cheated, double shifting Hull

on the Mikita line. Late in the second, Bobby caught Gamble
with a close-in slapper that spun the goalie around. The crowd
let out a startled gasp, as if it'd witnessed a car crash. On the
first shift of the third period, Bobby took a Mikita pass at full
speed, dipped past his check, and ripped a slapshot into the
roof of the net. The Hawks were still celebrating when
Hillman broke up a play at the enemy blueline, throwing a low
shot at the Chicago net. DeJordy got a pad out, but Kelly
knocked home the rebound just before Doug Jarrett flattened
him.

The teams traded chances for the next ten minutes.
Mahovlich almost netted the clincher, but banged a Kelly
pass loudly off the boards. Armstrong forced DeJordy into a
big save. Gamble foiled Wharram in close. Then the Golden
Jet got another chance with eight minutes left. He was idling
in front of the net when Hay, digging in the corner, tossed a
pass into the slot. The puck was off Bobby's stick and in the
net before Gamble turned around.

As the deliciously tense game entered its final minutes a
strangely familiar sound washed over the Toronto arena. At
first it was just teenagers up in the greys.

"Go Leafs Go, Go Leafs Go."

Soon even Bay Streeters enjoying company freebies in the
blues had picked up the chant.

"Go Leafs Go, Go Leafs Go."

The team pressed, but couldn't get the winning goal. Then
again, neither did the Hawks. The game ended in a 4–4 tie.
The losing streak was finally over.

The next night, in Boston, Bower held his team in the first
period, turning aside eighteen shots. Kelly and Bucyk traded
goals in the second. Then early in the third, Stemkowski
tipped a Pappin blast past Johnston to give Toronto its first
win in twenty-nine days.

The following Wednesday, the Rangers visited Toronto.
Mahovlich beat Giacomin on a fifty-foot slapshot to open the
game. On the next shift, Frank set up the rampaging Hillman.
Soon Leaf goals were coming from everywhere. Armstrong,
with his first in a month, Stanley, Conacher and Pappin all
tallied in the second period as the Leafs rolled to a 6–0 win.

After spending a month in a sand trap, Leafs were now treading on plush, rolling green. On the morning of the next game, a Saturday encounter with Boston, Imlach and Clancy were in the Leaf dressing-room, passing a few aimless hours. King went on about how good things were all of a sudden: Pulford, Stemkowski, and Pappin were playing fine as silk— and how about that Hillman? Old Punch had figured his way out of another mess, that's for sure. The mastermind looked gloomy, however. Which wasn't unusual. Imlach's life was full of valleys. Today he felt particularly bad. His face was the colour of porridge.

"Christ, I feel lousy," Imlach said. He touched the left side of his chest. "Got a congested feeling right here." Then grabbed his left arm. "And a lot of pain here."

"Better see a doctor," Clancy said.

"Fuck it—I got a hockey game tonight."

As players strolled in, Imlach and Clancy wandered to the Gardens commissary for tea. Punch was a big tea drinker, often going through two pots the day of a game. Somewhere around his third or fourth cup, Dr. Tate McPhedran, a Leaf club doctor, dropped by. Imlach mentioned how he was feeling. McPhedran examined him right away. "I think you better be admitted to a hospital," he said.

"Damn it, doc, you know I got a hockey game tonight."

"This afternoon."

At two-thirty, Clancy dropped Imlach off at the hospital. Three hours later, King received a call at the rink. "They got me locked up," Punch said. "Will you run the club tonight?"

Leafs won that game 5–3, coming back from 2–0, and 3–2 deficits. Orr and Walton, with a goal and assist each, dazzled. Horton was superb, controlling play in the Leaf end and scoring the clincher late in the third. But all eyes were on Clancy at the Leaf bench. Where was Punch? Rumours swept the city: "He entered the hospital Friday," one radio station announced. "Imlach's at home with the flu," it was reported on the late night TV news.

The Leaf medical staff, doctors McPhedran and Hugh Smythe, were vague. "He's exhausted and in for tests," Smythe said. He wouldn't divulge the name of the hospital.

"We hear he had pain on his left side and arm," a reporter said. "Does that mean heart trouble?"

"Pain in the arms, yes," Smythe confirmed. "Chest, some. But don't run around making this sound serious. Punch is mainly exhausted."

"So how long has he been exhausted?"

"Since last August," Smythe said, smiling.

As hard as he drove his Maple Leafs, Imlach was tougher on himself. If the team wasn't winning, it wasn't unusual for him to skip a night's sleep to talk and drink over problems (because of a bad stomach, he'd be knocking back scotch and milks during these marathon sessions). Next day, he'd be back in the saddle, tilting at windmills. During the slump, Imlach became so obsessed with the team's troubles that he admitted to Clancy one day, "Christ, you know it's getting so bad I forgot to eat all yesterday."

Imlach had run his team into the ground. But the Leafs were a tough, flinty bunch. After all, Punch had forged the team in his own image. The players bounced back. In fact, thanks to some adroit manoeuvres by their coach, the club looked better than ever. But the eternally restless Imlach lacked his team's physical constitution. "Even though he swaggered around, Punch was never really a healthy guy," Louis Cauz says. "He had stomach problems, heart problems, a hernia, gallstones. Hell, maybe that's why he swaggered, to fool everybody."

"I was completely exhausted," Imlach would tell Scott Young. "I think maybe if I'd let it go on further, I would have been really sick."

Leafs had survived without key players all season. Now they'd be without their coach for at least two weeks. Just when they'd started to turn things around. Who knew how it would affect them? A bigger question right now was where was Imlach? Nobody even knew which hospital he was staying at, let alone how seriously he was ailing, or what he had to say for himself. Nature abhors a vacuum, and the Toronto hockey media had just lost the source, if not the focus, of all their stories. The race was on to find Imlach.

"Yeah, it was a big mystery," the *Globe*'s Cauz remembers. "I thought to myself, 'wouldn't it be something if I could find Punch and talk to him? Wouldn't that be a scoop?' So I went down to the Gardens [Monday morning], started nosing around. Nobody says anything, of course. But I hang around. Then I see King on the phone and I just walk past him with my ear out, you know. 'Yeah, Toronto General,' I hear him say. So I circle around, pretend to tie my shoe or something, then I hear King go, 'Yeah, room 352,' or whatever the hell it was.

"Now I'm excited." He waves his hand grandly, imagining headlines. "'PUNCH FOUND!'…or maybe, 'MR. IMLACH, I PRESUME!' You know, something dramatic. I walk into the Toronto General in a trench coat with a clipboard under my arm, like I'm a doctor. Up I go to room whatever, then I just stroll in, like I work there. And there's Punch in bed."

The two men's first exchange hardly brings back memory of reporter Stanley's climactic meeting with the lost missionary, Dr. Livingstone:

"Hey there, Punch," Cauz offered pleasantly.

"Cauz, you son-of-a-bitch, what the hell you doing here?" Imlach shouted.

"He gave me shit for a few minutes, but I could tell he was glad to see me. He was probably lonely in there by himself," Cauz recalls. Predictably, Imlach downplayed his physical problems. "Ah, I'm going to be OK soon as I get away from these fucking doctors," the reporter remembers Imlach saying. Then Punch asked his guest about the team and the last few games. (Doctors hadn't allowed him a TV, or even a radio, in his room.) Twenty minutes later, Punch told Cauz, "Listen, you better get out now before my wife shows up. Christ, if Dodo catches you here, she'll kill both of us."

"Overall, he looked to be in not too bad shape," Cauz remembers. "Christ, I'd seen him look worse after the Leafs lost some hockey games."

FEBRUARY 20 STANDINGS

	G	W	L	T	F	A	Pts
Chicago	52	31	13	8	196	124	70
New York	52	25	19	8	145	133	58
Montreal	51	22	22	7	130	136	51
Toronto	50	20	21	9	131	151	49
Detroit	53	22	28	3	164	171	47
Boston	54	15	32	7	137	182	37

SCORING LEADERS

	GP	G	A	Pts
Mikita, Chi.	52	28	48	76	12
B. Hull, Chi.	51	38	18	56	27
Ullman, Det.	54	22	33	55	26
Wharram, Chi.	52	26	28	54	17
Goyette, N.Y.	52	10	38	48	4
Howe, Det.	53	18	29	47	31
Rousseau, Mont.	51	12	34	46	38
Mohns, Chi.	46	19	24	43	52
Esposito, Chi.	52	14	26	40	26
Delvecchio, Det.	53	13	26	39	6

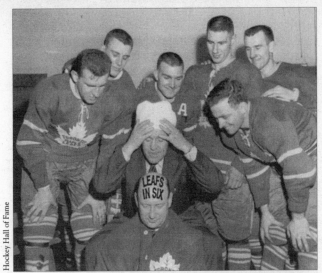

Punch in 1959, back when everybody loved him.

Toe Blake, the heart and soul of the Canadiens.

King Clancy (left) and Red Kelly (right) at Leaf camp, 1966.

The Globe and Mail

Opposite page, top: A very young Frank Mahovlich.
Bottom: Leafs vs. Canadiens: a war every Wednesday night.

Hockey Hall of Fame

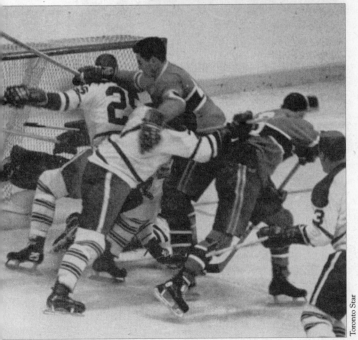

Toronto Star

The superstar, Bobby Hull.

The superpest, Bryan "Bugsy" Watson.

*Opposite page, top: John Ferguson (right) confronts Tim Horton.
The irresistible force meets the immovable object.*

Bottom: Another Shack attack. This time, Terry Harper's the victim.

The Globe and Mail

Strikebreaker Eddie Shore. At sixty-four, he had a handshake that could crack walnuts.

Hockey Hall of Fame

Yvan Cournoyer beats Suitcase Smith, Christmas 1966.

J.C. Tremblay asks Santa for an end to the Habs' 1966 slump.

Glory was never enough. A subdued Terry Sawchuk immediately after his 100th shutout.

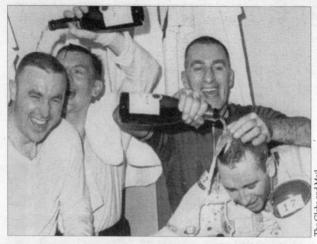

The Globe and Mail

Graphic Artists / Hockey Hall of Fame

Frank Prazak / Hockey Hall of Fame

The turning point: Bob Pulford beats Rogie Vachon, second overtime, game three, 1967 finals.

Graphic Artists / Hockey Hall of Fame

The goaltending tag team that beat Montreal: Terry Sawchuk (left) and Johnny Bower.

Opposite page, top: Had men gone mad? (left to right) Hawks' Dennis DeJordy, Stan Mikita, equipment manager Socko Uren and Kenny Wharram celebrate Chicago's first regular season championship.

Bottom: Brian Conacher kills the Black Hawks, game six, 1967 semi-finals.

To the victor…Punch with 1967 Cup.

The last long walk. Toe retires after winning the 1968 Cup.

Crowd noise
Paradise lost

Orr's 1966–67 hockey card is worth $1,800. Esposito's
rookie card goes for $600. This hockey fan had both—in
traders! Back then, you couldn't get a set of 100 without
buying 500 cards. That's because O-Pee-Chee cravenly held
back cards; for every Béliveau they issued five bloody
Toppazzinis. Now even Jerry's card is worth dough. Mint
66–67 sets are worth $3,500. Doesn't matter how much
they're worth because no one hung on to them, except fussy,
stamp-collector types. Where'd they all go? Tell you where
mine went: In 1965, I customized my table-hockey game by
cutting heads off cards and then gluing them on figurines.
No Ingarfields or Hebentons were used here, just future
hall-of-famers; I lost $5,000 that day. Kid brothers
destroyed, oh, another $10,000 worth. Brother Bill
clothespinned cards onto the spokes of his banana bike just
to hear them go ft-ft-ft-ft. My parents got rid of still more.
Dad crammed cards in shoeboxes in the basement. Then
Mom threw the shoeboxes out. Those boxes were stuffed
with $10 bills. Not that I'd sell a single card if I still had
any. In fact, I still buy the old cards at collector shops.
No big stars. Can't afford 'em. Today, I specialize in
obscure players. Warren Godfrey. Val Fonteyne.
Last year I spent four dollars on a Jerry Toppazzini.

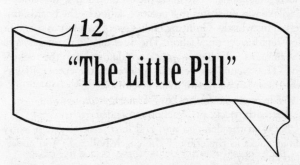

12

"The Little Pill"

On Valentine's Day, Toe Blake got his first look at the kid who was supposed to help down the stretch. Blake was skeptical of rookies. Minor-league coaches taught, NHL coaches coached, he believed. Still, watching his team work out this morning, Toe realized the Canadiens needed help. Montreal was still buried deep in the pack, twelve points behind New York, nineteen back of Chicago. Offense was the problem, critics agreed. Hodge made the first half All Star squad, but the Habs remained last in scoring. The team had fifty-seven fewer goals than Chicago. Thirty fewer than Detroit.

While GM Pollock scoured the empire for help, newspapers speculated on which minor-league forward was NHL-bound: Mickey Redmond, who had recently scored five in one game in Peterborough, and Danny Grant, the best sniper in Houston, were prime candidates, with Gary Peters (Houston) and Gary Monahan (Peterborough) having outside shots. To everyone's surprise, Pollock didn't return with a forward, or even one of the organization's fine young offensive defensemen, like Carol Vadnais or Serge Savard.

"When I went down to our top farm club [Houston], I saw three games," recalls Pollock. "And our young goalie, Rogatien Vachon was sensational all three nights. The best player on the ice. It wasn't a difficult choice really. Vachon was the guy who looked like he could help the most. You can never have too much goaltending, so we made the decision and up he came."

Blake was on skates this practice, idling by the boards, fingering his whistle. Grunting bodies swept past fast as cars, but Toe kept his eye on Vachon. The intersquad scrimmage was a few minutes old when the puck was dumped into the rookie's end. The twenty-one-year-old sprinted to the corner. Blake's whistle was in his mouth in an instant.

"Where you going, my boy?" Blake roared.

"After the puck, sir," Vachon responded.

"Stay in the damned net, and let the defensemen worry about pucks in the corner," the coach hollered. "You understand me, boy?"

The last-place Bruins were at the Forum two days later—a perfect game to test a rookie. But Toe went with Hodge. Maybe Vachon's wandering convinced him the youngster wasn't ready. More likely Blake figured his team needed a win and Hodge was his best bet to deliver a victory. Whatever, Toe probably spent much of the previous evening wrestling with the decision. The Montreal coach was having as much trouble as Imlach sleeping these days.

"[I ask myself] 'how could we be where we are with the personnel we have?'" Toe told Red Fisher. "With the centremen we've got…with the four or five right wingers…with the left wingers and defenders? I haven't slept for nights thinking about it. I'll go to bed and I'll sit straight up in the middle of the night and start wondering and worrying all over again. Hell, it's reached the point where it isn't first place any more, it's making the playoffs. I know what my players can do, but they're not doing it. Some of them come back to the bench without a drop of sweat on them. How can a player be relaxed about defeat. Tell me—how can they?"

The games since Christmas had been agony for Blake. The team would win one, though never easily, lose the next, often on a late goal, win two more, then get blown out in Detroit and head off on a bad streak.

Christmas Eve was typical of the torture the coach endured. New York was in town. It should've been an easy win. The Rangers were practically Montreal's junior varsity team—Boomer, Goyette, Marshall, MacNeil, Fleming, Maniago, Berenson, and Hickie were all players Habs had deemed expendable. Not that Blake took them lightly. "For Christ sake pay attention to those ex-Canadiens," Toe told players before Ranger games. "They'd love nothing more than to come in here and make us look bad."

So what happened? Goyette set up Nevin in the first, and the Boomer notched two in the middle frame, the second on a breakaway. The Habs fought to even the score. A tie seemed imminent when, with a minute left, Montreal lost the puck and Marshall popped one over Hodge.

Montreal rebounded the next night, beating the Wings 4–0 in Detroit. The following Wednesday, in Montreal, Hodge seemed ready to collect another shut-out, against Boston, but after Roberts beat Cheevers to break a scoreless game, Montreal fell into a fugue-like trance, managing seven shots the last period and a half. "You knew they were going to tie it up, the way we were playing," sighed Blake. Sure enough, Wayne Connelly steered a pass over Hodge's shoulder with two minutes left. The Forum crowd rained boos on the Canadiens as they departed. Blake sympathized. "I don't understand how our team can play so poorly in front of their own fans. Just doesn't figure," he said.

The Habs were sluggish early against New York on New Year's Eve. The Marshall-Goyette-Nevin line played handball against Hodge for ten minutes. Spurred by their little goalie's spectacular play, Montreal eventually came to life. Cournoyer scored a power play goal. Then Backstrom's line won a series of hand-to-hand battles along the boards, with Fergy ramming a clear-out past Giacomin. A second period tip-in by Provost, the culmination of one of Henri's twisting "where's he going now?" dashes, sealed a 3–0 Hab win.

It figured Habs would have trouble next game. The team had followed the logic of a pendulum all season: good as they were one night, that's how bad they'd be the next. And so Sunday in Detroit, the Habs went down 4–1, losing by the same three-goal margin they'd enjoyed the evening previous.

On Wednesday, at home against Chicago, the Canadiens were on again. After a scoreless first, the Habs jumped ahead in the middle period. Henri scooted in on Stapleton, then skimmed a screen shot past Hall. Provost had a breakaway. Hall made the save, but Duff leaped on the rebound to make it 2–0. Hodge was "clutching pucks in his fists like a man gathering loose dollar bills," in Red Fisher's words, and the team seemed on the verge of a big win. Then Bobby Hull happened.

With time running out, number nine bore down on J.C. and Laperrière. First, he wheeled outside, taking number three with him, then hopped back, splitting the defense with a quicksilver move that drew a gasp from Forum fans. Now he was in alone. He shifted left, drawing Hodge, then lifted the puck to the far corner. Charlie strained, but momentum carried him the wrong way. Suddenly it was a one-goal game. Seconds later the Hawks were back, with Maki swooping in. Hodge held his ground, taking the shot on his pads. The rebound got away. Maki grabbed the puck, swung around the net, and backhanded a pass between the circles to a streaking Hull. Tie game.

The next match was more of the same. Montreal started slowly against Detroit. Howe scored two early. The Habs came back in the second. Duff notched a pair, and Yvan and Fergy added singles. Then came the inevitable jittery finish. Prentice made it 4–3 with three minutes left. Seconds later, Parker MacDonald missed on a breakaway. With Crozier pulled, Detroit forced three face-offs in Montreal's zone, but the Wings never managed to bang one through the thick forest of limbs in front of the Montreal net. "Why do you have to make everything look so hard? Why do we always let the other guy back in the game?" Blake moaned afterwards. He'd be asking the same question all next week.

In New York, Montreal let a 1–0 lead vanish in the second, then saw a tie disappear in the last minute when Goyette beat Richard on a draw, sweeping the puck to Nevin, who banged a shot off the post by Hodge. On Wednesday, in Montreal, Hodge misplayed Ellis's harmless shot to hand the Leafs a 2–1 win. But all that was a grim foreshadowing of what would happen three nights later.

The Bruins were in Montreal that Saturday. First period seemed like old times. The Habs were firing; the Bruins, cannon fodder. Duff notched two, and Ferguson tallied late to make it 3–1. The teams traded scores in the second. In the third period the Habs opened with a furious siege. Then Bucyk slipped behind Montreal's defense and it was 4–3. The Canadiens rallied, battering Cheevers, only to have Orr grab a loose puck and fly coast to coast to set up Martin for the tying goal. Fans were still slapping their foreheads when Bob Woytowich intercepted a Laperrière clearing pass. Two relays later it was 5–4 and game, Bruins. The Canadiens had been outscored 3–0 in a period in which they outshot Boston, 18–6.

With rookie Gary Bauman in net, the Canadiens took the Bruins 3–1 the next night in Boston. Then came the All Star game. Although Fergy had the opposition showing the white flag by the second period, Montreal's 3–0 victory didn't impress Blake. "Nice, but we don't get any points. Let's see how we do this weekend against Chicago," the coach said.

Saturday's game was heralded as the biggest game this season at the Forum. Chicago was poised to overtake New York. Mikita's line was hot. Hull had fifteen goals in nine games. For Montreal, Béliveau was back after missing a month with an eye injury. And the second half was underway. "We still have half a season," Henri told Jacques Beauchamp, "and there's still the Stanley Cup. We can still make this a good year."

Then the Habs went out and dropped a three spot to the Hawks in the new season's very first period. Mikita slipped a pass into the slot that Hull redirected with a blur of the wrists past Hodge. Minutes later, Bobby darted around a scrambling J.C. and leaned into a wrist shot from sixty feet out. Hodge never moved until the puck slingshot back out of the net.

After Esposito scored to close the first, the Habs rallied. Midway in the second, Rousseau stole the puck and flew into the Hawk zone, throwing himself into a balletic twirl to escape Pilote and Jarrett. Landing awkwardly on his right skate, he tottered, regaining his balance in time to feint a sprawling Dejordy, then slipped the puck into the net. The crowd leapt to its feet, cheering. Fans would've thrown roses if they had 'em.

The final period featured a variety of rough, frantic action. Tremblay, on a pass from Rousseau, drilled one over DeJordy's shoulder to bring Montreal close. As Gilles circled the net, arms high, Matt Ravlich threw out a hip, sending him into the boards, which brought a snarling Duff into the fray. Oaths, then punches, were exchanged. Soon Fergy, Larose, Harris, Van Impe, Ken Hodge, and Nesterenko had all tossed their gloves.

The best match was between Larose and Hodge. Claude looked good early, yanking his opponent's jersey over his head and pumping away. Then Hodge stripped off his sweater, shoulder and elbow pads and waded into the Montreal winger, drilling him to the ice. The rest of the card was uneventful. Van Impe and Ferguson yanked each other's blouses, and Harris easily took Nesterenko, pushing the big forward around like a broom.

Half an hour later, referee John Ashley untangled the penalty mess and teams returned to hockey. The Habs were flying now. At twelve minutes, Henri snaked into the Chicago zone and found Duff creeping inside the blueline. The winger stalled at the circle, lateralling to Rousseau, who stepped into a slapshot from the high slot, sending a scorcher under DeJordy's glove to tie the game.

The Forum crowd was still standing, cheering, when Backstrom's line stormed in. Ferguson, his eyes bulging, had the puck in the corner. Larose came free in the slot. Fergy feathered a perfect pass. Claude fired—just wide of the open net.

The game ended 3–3. Although his team had staged an impressive comeback, Toe refused to get excited. "Yes, we fought back nicely. But I was disappointed we weren't ready to play in the first period," he said. Two periods of good hockey meant nothing. Blake wanted to see if his club could put two good games together.

On Sunday in Chicago, however, the Habs couldn't rub two good shifts together. Ferguson hustled. Bauman made some nice saves. Otherwise, the team was lifeless in a 4–1 loss. Even the power play lacked a pulse. "During three Chicago penalties…[Montreal] failed to get a shot," wrote the *Gazette*'s Pat Curran. "Twice while shorthanded, Mohns and Mikita broke away and forced Bauman to make great saves."

Blake was a volcano whose time had come.

"Either they're quitters or they haven't got it anymore," he said after the game, his voice hoarse with emotion. "I never thought I'd have a team that would quit."

A reporter asked if Blake thought Chicago was worried about Montreal. "What for?" he screamed. "The only team that should be worried about us is us. But all we get is alibis and excuses. I've been accused of not playing everybody. All I know is I have eighteen guys on the bench, and they all played—or should I say they were all on the ice."

Blake's comments were headline stuff in Montreal. The coach had accused his team of dropping the flag. Did he mean it? Was it true?

"Oh, I remember that," Cournoyer says today, adopting a grave tone. "Toe was pretty mad. I guess we were playing bad for a long time. What was our record? Under 500 after Christmas, oh boy! yes, he woulda been mad." A frightened giggle. "All I can remember is the frustration. When a good team plays bad for a long time, you start asking yourself questions. Lot of times, it's no good to ask questions. You have to play, you know. Maybe we were questioning ourselves more than Toe. Maybe that was our problem.

"But that was a big thing in Montreal, Blake calling us 'quitters' like that," Cournoyer continues. "Toe, he never said things like that. So everybody woke up when he said it. I think it helped us, maybe."

"At the end of his career, Toe had more problems with the pressure," Béliveau says today. "He had very high standards, and it became harder for him to deal with players, when they did not care as much as he did." Béliveau thinks for a moment. "But nobody cared as much as Toe."

At the time, the Captain did his best to explain away the furor. "[Toe] says a lot of things when he's angry," Béliveau said. "I'm sure that he did not mean it [calling the team 'quitters'] in the strict sense of the word. Let us say that he was carried away by the excitement."

Blake was unrepentant. "If they beat the Leafs Wednesday, I'll call them quitters again," he said. "I'll use it for the rest of the season. I'll do anything to get this team to win."

The team grabbed a 3–1 win in Toronto. The Leafs were in such a tumble, however, that a victory, even in their rink, meant no more than two points. "Leafs are a team on the way down," Pollock told players. "But watch out for Boston— they're a team on the way up." Sam was fibbing. Bruins had won four of fourteen since Christmas. But the GM figured his team couldn't take anyone for granted these days. As usual, Pollock was right, although he undoubtedly gained little satisfaction watching his team stumble to a 4–1 loss in Boston.

Then, finally, the team tore off a nice string, trimming the Rangers and Bruins by identical 3–2 scores to end January. The following Wednesday, the Habs bombed the Leafs 7–1. Best part of the streak was Béliveau's play. A new line— Ferguson-Béliveau-Cournoyer—counted eight goals in three games. Jean was carrying the puck with energy; Fergy ruled the corners; and Cournoyer, on a regular shift at last, gave the line speed and a touch around the net. The line looked good. The team looked good.

"Geez, I hope we're out of it," Toe said after the Toronto game. "That's three good ones in a row. That hasn't happened for a while. I'm encouraged. Hopefully, they'll keep it up."

Then the pendulum swung back. Saturday, February 4, Chicago invaded the Forum. Béliveau scored. And the Larose-Backstrom-Tremblay unit was superb, scoring twice and holding the Scooters to a few chances. That was the good news. The bad news was the Habs blew another late lead when Hodge waved at a long shot from Nesterenko. And Harper suffered a shoulder separation. Cournoyer also had to return to the shop after getting caught with his head down by Jarrett. Although the game ended 3–3, the Hawks did all the hugging and smiling as teams left the ice.

The loss of Harper was costly. Terry was the club's top rear-guard so far this season, with a plus five on-ice grade. Everyone else was in the minus category. J.C. and Laperrière shared an identical minus five. After a swing to Detroit and Chicago, where the team was embarrassed 6–1 and 5–0, Jacques dipped into the minus teens, which sounded more like an overnight low in Winnipeg than the work of the reigning Norris Trophy winner. Against the Wings, Jacques was victimized for four goals; in Chicago, he was on ice for three more. He'd also failed to score a goal and had contributed only fifteen assists to date.

"When Laperrière is playing well, he's the best defenseman around," Montreal Canadien Junior coach, Claude Ruel, once observed. "But when he has a bad game, you get scared, because he can lose his confidence and then he has a bad bunch in a row."

Number two was now in the midst of a bad bunch. So was partner, Tremblay. With Harper gone and Harris playing with a broken finger, the Canadiens were in trouble at the blue-line. (In Chicago, Toe gave Jean Gauthier and Noel Price regular shifts.) Worse still, for the first time this season, the Habs experienced goaltending problems. Bauman was injured, so Hodge was seeing more ice time. Too much, Blake figured. The tiny (5'5", 150 lb.) goaltender was a dependable sub, but wilted from overwork. "Charlie looked tired," was Blake's tart observation after a one loss.

In Chicago, Blake tried the Imlach-like gimmick of switching goalies every five minutes. Hodge was tired and Gump hadn't fully recovered from knee surgery, but Toe figured they could both play a little. It didn't work. Hodge was beaten by Mikita on the first shot one shift, and Gump gave up a quick goal to Jarrett on another turn. "I wanted to surprise them, but Charlie wasn't ready," a glum Blake said after the game. "A few other players weren't ready and the surprise was on me."

The Canadiens were courageous the following weekend. Still, things kept going wrong. With the score tied in a Saturday away game in Boston, Bucyk cut in on the Montreal net with Laperrière lassoed around his shoulders. Worsley, in his first start in two months, was buried in an avalanche of falling, twisting bodies. All three men and the puck ended up in the net. The Bruins were ahead 3–2, but the Canadiens cared little about the goal. Bucyk and Laperrière landed on Worsley's bad knee. The Gumper passed out in pain as soon as he hit the ice.

"All I know is that when I went down the first thing I thought was the knee was broken," Worsley said later. "Then the lights went out. Next thing I know, I'm looking up at the lights and they're looking back at me and then mouths are opening and closing and I guess they're saying something, but I don't hear nothing."

The Canadiens rallied in the third. At seven minutes, Backstrom drew a posse of Bruins behind the net before slipping a pass in front to Larose, who knotted the game. Ten minutes of hard scrabble later, Rousseau flew down the boards, around Watson, forcing Bernie Parent into a toe save. Balon chipped the rebound home to give the Canadiens a 4–3 win. But the victory came at enormous cost. Afterwards, players were told that Worsley would miss the remainder of the season.

The team picked right up next night in New York. Backstrom beat Maniago with a short backhand before the game was a minute old. And Ferguson scored a goal in every period to register his first hat trick. Despite playing their fourth consecutive game on the road, and missing Worsley, Harper, Richard, and Provost (the latter pair crissed when they should've crossed, knocking each other out in a frightening mid-ice collision in Detroit), the Habs took a 4–3 lead into the last minute.

Francis pulled Maniago, replacing him with Fleming. The Rangers were pressing when Béliveau and Goyette took a face-off to the right of Hodge. Jean won the draw to Laperrière. For the next half-minute Jacques and J.C. played piggy-in-the-middle with Geoffrion. With thirty seconds left, J.C. had the puck outside centre. Looking up, he saw the empty net and figured he'd give it a shot, lobbing a flip shot into the lights. When it became clear his effort was wide, the defender realized he was about to commit the sin of icing the puck with a goal lead and less then a minute to go. Off he went after the puck. So, inexplicably, did Béliveau and two other teammates.

The Rangers got to the puck before icing was called. Two passes later, Goyette, Geoffrion, and Fleming were coming the other way, with Laperrière back. Goyette waited, faked two passes, then found Geoffrion in the clear. Boomer fired. Charlie slid, making the save, but Fleming lifted the rebound high into the net to tie the game with a few seconds remaining.

After the game, Blake was spitting carpet tacks: "I sent out my four best checkers…and four of them get caught up the ice…in the last minute…when we're leading by one." He just shook his head.

Vachon was on the bench for the Rangers' comeback, and had two practices with the team before its February 16 contest with Boston. The Canadien players weren't panicking, but there was tension at the executive level upon his arrival, he says.

"Guys were very loose," Vachon remembers. "Everybody was good to me. Béliveau and Richard helped my first practices, telling me when I wasn't cutting the angle, or if I was giving too much corner, stuff like that. Blake seemed very nervous, tense. Béliveau and Ferguson, they knew when to talk to him. The rest of the players tried to keep out of his way. Pollock looked nervous, too. Both those guys walked around looking uptight. I remember thinking, boy, these guys worry about hockey twenty-four hours a day, seven days a week."

Blake and Pollock would need a few days fretting to figure out what happened to the Canadiens this night. After putting in a heroic weekend's work on the road, the team once again fell apart in front of home fans. The Bruins scored on their second and third shots, with Tommy Williams sneaking a twenty-footer past Hodge, then banging in a Watson rebound seconds later. Late in the period, Orr set up Bob Dillabough, who clubbed a long slapshot past Charlie to make it 3–1. In the second, Hodge was out of position on a shot from Ron Schock, and fell to the ice too soon on a Martin drive. After the fifth Boston goal, fans offered a cynical hurrah every time the little goalie touched the puck.

Blake sealed off the dressing-room at the end of a lopsided 5–1 Bruin win, so it was left to reporters to put into words just how purposeless the Canadiens looked. Red Fisher came close to defining the club's disorganization. "Canadiens," he wrote, "milled around all evening like ladies at a fire sale."

The following Saturday the Red Wings were in. As usual, Toe hadn't tipped off who was starting in nets before game time.

"I was sitting [in the dressing-room] with Charlie Hodge before the game," Vachon remembers. "Both of us were dressed, but I was sure I was going to be back-up, just like the last couple of games. Toe never told me that he was going to use me. I wasn't sure if I was ever going to get into a game. [Goalie Ernie Wakely had been brought up weeks earlier and never saw the ice.] Then the trainer comes to me and drops the puck in my glove. It was a Canadien custom. That was the way you found out which goalie was starting. I couldn't believe it. I looked at him to see if it was a joke. But he wasn't smiling. I went uh-oh and then the buzzer goes and we had to skate onto the ice."

Vachon had played with the Junior Habs when he was sixteen. "So I'd played at the Forum before," he says. But never with Les Glorieux on a Saturday night. "Oh, it was different from junior," Vachon recalls. "I remember looking up and seeing all the people in standing room. You couldn't even see the aisles, you know. There were just people everywhere. In junior, the building looked bigger because there was empty seats. With all the people somehow it looked smaller. And the noise was something. There was an electricity in the old Forum you don't have anymore. It was the same as in Chicago. There was, I don't know, an exciting feeling when you stepped over the boards.

"When I look up the ice, I remember being surprised to see the Red Wings. Isn't that funny? Maybe, I don't know, I hadn't thought about who I was playing. But I remember being shocked to see Howe and Delvecchio skating at centre. You know people said I looked very cool when I was a rookie. What was it that they said? I had ice in my veins. But that night, oh, I had the butterflies bad.

"At first the game seemed far away," Vachon continues. "The puck was way up ice. I skated around, waiting." Then at four minutes, Detroit's big number nine kicked the puck free at the blueline and hopped free. The Forum crowd rose as one, understanding instantly the dramatic implications of the situation: the immortal Howe, hockey's best player for twenty-one winters, versus The Kid, a gum-chewing rookie seven months shy of his twenty-second birthday.

"As he came in he was looking right at me," Vachon recalls. "When he was forty feet away I came out to cut down the angle. He skated in some more, then, and I remember this clearly, he lowered his head to shoot, and when he did I skated out fast. Then I felt the puck bounce off my pads and there was a scramble. Somehow I got the puck. When I stood up people were hitting me on the pads and the crowd was screaming. Me, I was thinking, thank God he shot, if Gordie fakes, he scores easy for sure, and maybe, who knows? there goes my thirteen-year career."

A few shifts later, the youngster faced another test when Harris was chased for tripping. In an ensuing goalmouth scramble, Howe threw one off Vachon's arm. Seconds later the goalie fell to his knees to block a Delvecchio screen shot. The Habs seemed to have the penalty killed when Ullman picked J.C.'s pocket at the blueline and stole in. The young goalie came out, squared himself. Ullman waited for the rookie to move. He didn't. Suddenly, Normie was in too close. He fired. Vachon shifted slightly and the puck kicked off his pad wide.

Howie Young, a recovering alcoholic who'd found work on Detroit's defense after spending the previous season hanging out with Frank Sinatra,* made a nice move to finally put Detroit on the board. The Wing defender stepped in from the blueline, twirled away from a forechecker, then threw a low shot to the corner of the net. Vachon snaked a pad out, but the rebound came to Howe, who tucked the puck into the top corner.

---

* *Howie even had a small part in Sinatra's 1965 film,* None But the Brave.

The Canadiens finally got rolling after Howe's goal. The Backstrom and Béliveau lines forced the acrobatic Crozier into a series of dives and somersaults. But the makeshift Balon-Peters-Provost line got the team's first goal. Gary Peters, subbing for Henri, took what appeared to be a harmless shot at the Detroit net. Crozier, who seemed to be expecting a pass, bobbled the rebound. Provost hopped on the puck and it was 1–1.

Detroit controlled a frantic middle period. The Wings might've had five goals but for bad shooting. Smith and Prentice missed open nets. Henderson had Vachon deked on a breakaway, but shot wide. At twelve minutes, the Canadiens gave Detroit a two-man advantage for ninety seconds. Vachon robbed Delvecchio twice. Ullman hit the post. And a pass to Henderson, parked alone by the side of the net, hopped his stick.

"Vachon appeared to have horseshoes in his pants," was the euphemism the *Gazette*'s Pat Curran employed to describe the young goalie's good fortune.

As unlucky as the Wings were with Vachon, that's how fortunate the Canadiens were at the other end. Early in the second, Larose tried to catch Crozier napping with a blueline slapshot. The blast was wide, but shot thirty feet straight up in the air. Roger skated to the side of his net, looked around, then felt a tickle down the back of his jersey. When he heard the crowd's roar, he didn't bother to look behind. "I've played hockey a long time, but I've never seen a puck do anything like that," Howe would say later of the pop-up that rolled in off his goalie's back.

Late in the period, the Habs scored on another trick shot, when Balon threw a backhand across the crease. Crozier rushed to the other side of the net in anticipation of a shot from Rousseau, but the puck struck Léo Boivin's skate, slicing over the goalie's shoulder into the net.

Suddenly, the other team was having pucks hop sticks and hit the post. And Montreal was getting the odd goofy goal. It had been a long time since the Canadiens caught any breaks. Now, in one game, they received close to a dozen.

"Before Rogie comes along, we had been playing like a sick

team," says Cournoyer. "But when he joined the team, he seemed to change our luck real fast. It was like, you know when you're sick, the doctor gives you the pill. Well, Vachon was our little pill. When he came along, we felt better all of a sudden."

Pollock agrees. "Sometimes a single player can change a team's chemistry when he arrives," he says. "Who knows why this happens, but it does. Dryden did that for us in 1971. Vachon this season. But sometimes I've seen even a small change get a team going — like when we put Rochefort together with Richard and Balon in the 1966 spring playoffs. A small change, but it won us a Stanley Cup. There's no explaining it."

Rogie permitted a bad goal late in the second, on a long shot by Prentice that caught him backed too far in the net. But "The Kid From Palmarolle," as papers would call him on Monday, looked cool in the third period, steering aside thirteen Detroit chances. After the Habs' 3–2 win, Rogie even kidded with reporters. "After the [Howe] save I figured I could stop them all," he said, winking. The easy laughter in the Montreal clubhouse was dramatic proof of the little pill's effectiveness.

FIRST PERIOD
1. Detroit, Howe 18th (Young, Hampson) 8:50
2. Montreal, Provost 10th (Peters) 14:14
Penalties—Harris 5:28

SECOND PERIOD
3. Montreal, Larose 15th (Backstrom, J.C. Tremblay) 0:11
4. Montreal, Balon 7th (J.C. Tremblay) 17:27
5. Detroit, Prentice 18th (Marshall) 18:54
Penalties—Bergman 2:01; Young 7:34; Peters 11:00;
Laperrière 11:48

THIRD PERIOD
No scoring
Penalties—Talbot 10:10

Shots on goal
Detroit   16   14   13 — 43
Montreal   11   15   8 — 34

FEBRUARY 20 STANDINGS

	P	W	L	T	F	A	Pts
Chicago	52	31	13	8	190	124	70
New York	52	25	19	8	145	133	58
Montreal	51	22	22	7	130	136	51
Toronto	50	20	21	9	131	151	49
Detroit	53	22	28	3	164	171	47
Boston	54	15	32	7	137	182	37

LEAGUE LEADERS

	P	G	A	Pts	PIM
Mikita, Chi.	52	28	48	76	12
R. Hull, Chi.	51	36	18	56	27
Ullman, Det.	52	22	33	55	26
Wharram, Chi.	52	26	28	54	17
Goyette, N.Y.	52	10	38	48	4
Howe, Det.	53	18	29	47	31
Rousseau, Mont.	51	12	34	46	38
Mohns, Chi.	44	19	26	45	50
Esposito, Chi.	51	14	26	40	25
Delvecchio, Det.	53	13	26	39	6

Crowd noise

Invocations of Expo

As Expo drew close, Canadians fell into a patriotic
swoon. Advertisers were quick to pounce,
invoking the world's fair to sell:

adhesive tape:
"Join the Expo Celebration, get your flag NOW! A full
54x27 Canadian flag complete with sewn in rope and
toggle can be yours for only $3.75 and the plaid tab
from any roll of "Scotch" brand tape. Simply mail…"

women's underwear:
"I dreamed I went to Expo in my Maidenform bra."

fertilizer:
"Here comes the Green Machine to give you
a lush, green lawn just in time for Expo 67."

—ads from Montreal papers, spring 1967

smoked meat:
"A tip of our Stetson to Moishe's, which, in a period
when many restaurants appear to be wondering how high
they can jack prices for Expo, is stockpiling thousands
of pounds of frozen meat (it uses four tons in a normal
week) for when meat will be in huge demand, and
accordingly, more expensive, during the Fair."

**—from Bruce Taylor's Montreal *Star*
"Montreal Days and Nights" column.**

13

"We buried Muldoon!"

"A key has been the young guys back of the blueline: DeJordy in nets, and Stapleton, Jarrett, and Van Impe on defense. We finally have some real depth to go along with the big guns."

—Black Hawk coach Billy Reay after his team clobbered Toronto 6–1 in early November.

"Hall was key for us in nets tonight. I can't say enough about the Mikita line, they're the best in the business."

—Reay after his team shut out the Habs 5–0 in late November.

"Everybody is pitching in, that's the key. We've got three lines, and four solid defensemen. And our bench, guys like Hodge and Angotti, have come through. We're playing as a team like never before."

—Reay after his Hawks drubbed Detroit 6–1, mid January.

"Well, Bobby is really starting to skate now, that's a big key. When he's going like this, he's unstoppable."

—Reay after Chicago thumped Boston 6–1 in early February.

Any more keys and Reay would've been running a hotel. Not that the Hawk coach wasn't justified in handing out plaudits. If his team swept March 11–12 dates with Montreal and Toronto, Chicago was guaranteed the league championship three weeks before season's end. Better still, the curse of Muldoon would be lifted forever.

Pete Muldoon was Hawks' first coach, back in 1926. The next year he was out the door. "This team will never finish first," was his alleged parting shot. Actually, the Muldoon curse was fabricated by Toronto *Star* sportswriter Jim Coleman on a slow news day. The myth took because Hawks laboured as if under a crippling hex. Between 1946 and 1957, the team finished last eight times, compiling a woeful 207–428–105 record.

After taking the Cup in 1961, the Hawks flamed out in consecutive post-seasons. Sports writers, even some players, said the team succumbed to the "Pilous plague." Rudy Pilous was a Spartan disciplinarian, it was said. His practices were gruelling and endless. "The result was disastrous [late season] collapses that reduced talent to zombies on the ice," concluded the Chicago *Tribune*'s Ted Damata. The team rebelled in the spring of 1963. Pilous was fired, and Reay, a more affable sort, brought in.

This season, the Hawks prospered under Reay's relaxed hand. After compiling a fifteen-game unbeaten streak to jet into first, the players were flown to Florida for an all-expenses-paid three-day vacation in mid-February. Compared to the Leafs and Canadiens, the Hawks had it soft. Practices were often optional, especially for team stars. Hull and Mikita were double-shifted games. If they needed a day off after a match, let 'em take it, Reay figured. The coach's faith in his superstars was boundless. "I don't coach Mikita's line," he said in February, "Stan does."

Who could argue with Reay's tactics? The Scooters were poised to break the NHL point record for a line.* Hull seemed sure to top his fifty-four-goal season mark. DeJordy and Hall had the League's best goals-against average. These new Black Hawks were the complete package, experts said—a team finally, not merely an assortment of stars.

"This team could…win the Stanley Cup in no more than ten or eleven games," Scott Young wrote. "This team is as good as the overpowering Canadiens in the late fifties; as good as the Leafs were in their prime years in the early sixties."

At least one Hawk didn't believe Chicago's dominance had much to do with improved depth or a change in team philosophy. "We were the same team," recalls Glenn Hall. "We had an explosive offense, and we tried to outscore you. Thing is, we were just better, probably because the core of the team—Bobby, Stan, Kenny, and Pierre—were at their peak, in their late twenties, early thirties. They could all move and throw the puck around."

A skeptic in a sport dominated by holler guys, Hall once declared that at the end of every season, "All I want to do is stand out in the middle of my 180 acres and scream, 'Fuck you!' until I'm good and hoarse and hear the 'you, you, you,' echo back across the field." Predictably, he shared few of his teammates' sentiments on how the Hawks were run in the 1960s.

"Personally, I got along well with Rudy," he says. "He was a good hockey man. That stuff about him working us too hard…oh, I don't know; what he did different was give us a noon skate, game day. But that's all it was, a skate. Guys got out there, tested their blades and sticks for that night. A half-hour later they were in the dressing-room. Wasn't a big deal. Maybe some guys were upset because they couldn't sleep in."

Not that Hall didn't get along with Reay.

"No, Billy was a good hockey man, too. Course, he was quieter than Rudy, or Scotty [Bowman, Hall's coach later in

---

* *The Detroit trio of Lindsay, Ullman, and Howe compiled a record 216 points in 1956–57.*

St. Louis]. Scotty, he'd yell if the guys were doing something. If they didn't stop, he'd yell louder. Never took more than two times for something to sink in. Billy, he'd quietly tell a guy something fourteen times and hope it got through."

Hall does agree that the 1966–67 edition of the Chicago Black Hawks was a superb offensive team. "Oh sure, Bobby and Stan and some of the other guys were wonderful with the puck," he says. "Some nights I felt sorry for the fellow at the other end. We had more shooters than any other team. When Bobby, Dennis, Stan, or Kenny wound up you were afraid sometimes. No doubt about it, if you liked offensive hockey, with goals piling up, you would've loved that team. It was the best offensive team going." (It should be noted that Hall says all of this with the cramped enthusiasm of a marine talking about the air force.)

Despite Vachon's medicinal qualities, the Canadiens continued their desultory lurch through the season into March. After Rogie stared Howe down in his debut, the Habs travelled to Detroit, where they managed a single goal, an early power play marker by Cournoyer. The game was tied late in the third when Boivin's slapshot banked off Laperrière's skate into an empty corner. Delvecchio added an empty-netter for a 3–1 Detroit win.

The next Wednesday, Habs were in Toronto. Hodge got the start. Although he was a first-half All Star, little Charlie was fighting for his job. "Goaltending in Montreal is like centre field in Yankee Stadium," Bugsy Watson says. "Since the 50s, you've got Plante, Worsley, Dryden, and Roy—Hall-of-Famers. There's a level of excellence fans are used to. That coaches are used to. Two bad games in a row and a goalie is out of there." Charlie had given up five goals in eighteen shots against Boston a week earlier. This would be his fatal second bad game in a row.

Montreal owned the Leafs early as the fast-flying Hab forwards forced Toronto into a string of interference calls. Bower was resolute, however, while Hodge—well, Charlie was having a bad night. At ten minutes, Mahovlich bulled past Harris and found Shack in front. Eddie dispensed with Hodge with a "psychedelic move," according to Rex MacLeod, then slammed the puck into the empty net. A minute later, Keon flipped a shot on goal. The puck hopped off Price's skate, landed for the briefest moment on Charlie's pad, then jumped backwards into the net.

The Habs got a break in the second when Hillman forgot what decade it was and sent Duff in alone. "I thought I was still playing [with Duff] back in Kirkland Lake," Hillman joked later. "We've been playing together since we were kids. Duffy and I lived on the same street together."

Montreal dominated the third, but were outscored 3–1, the result of nifty work by Bower and a brief Hodge nap. A minute in, Mahovlich thrilled fans with a frantic dash down the boards. At the circle, he lateralled to Ellis, who misfired, but managed to send a looping field goal over Hodge's shoulder. Then Pappin slapped a Walton draw off Price's skate past Charlie and the game was over, even though, this being a Hab-Leaf game, there was lots of action left, including two more goals (Larose, Conacher) and Ferguson and Shack's ritual bumping of heads.

The next two games, both in Montreal, provided further evidence of the decline of the league's best defense pairing. Thursday, J.C. and Laperrière were on for both Bruin scores in a 2–2 tie. Saturday, the duo were out for four goals in an embarrassing 5–0 loss to New York. Orland Kurtenbach, a forward as long as his name, slipped by the defensemen for four breakaways and two goals.

The players were booed unmercifully both games. J.C. still remembers the crowd's sting. "A Montreal fan forgets good plays, the bad plays he remembers forever," he says. "One year [1970–71] I made a record for scoring for Montreal defensemen [eleven goals, fifty-two assists], and I was first-team All Star. Next year, first game I make a mistake—fans start booing. First game! Doug Harvey, he used to joke about scoring on his own net in the play-offs. If I do that or Harper, someone would shoot us, I'm not joking."

J.C. has a theory about why the Canadiens faced increased fan pressure in the 1960s: "Before, you had only newspaper and radio. Every Canadien was a hero [on radio]," he says.

"On TV you see every mistake. Then you get five replays. Next game the fans all boo."

Billy Harris says the same thing happened in Toronto. "Listening to Foster Hewitt, the Leafs never played a bad game in the 50s. It was always luck that beat 'em—puck bouncing over a stick or something. When TV came along, fans realized that sometimes the team just wasn't that good."

After the New York game, Blake muttered he might "pull an Imlach" and let someone else coach. Losing was getting to him. That night he forgot to line up transportation for when the Habs arrived in Chicago next afternoon.

"That was funny," J.C. remembers. "Our train comes late into Chicago and there was no bus. We need police to bring us to the rink. It felt like we were going to jail. They had to use the big police trucks with sirens and everything. Everybody thought it was funny, eh? Except Toe. We don't laugh when he's around. But when he was away we were kidding pretty good."

The Habs were sensational that evening. Toe finally split up J.C. and Laperrière. Carol Vadnais, a call-up from Houston, played with Jacques, while J.C. was teamed with Harris. J.C. turned in his best performance in months, collecting a goal. Henri ended a long scoring slump and Vachon was steady. Still, a bad break cost the team when a Hull shot ricocheted off Laperrière's traitorous boot to give the Hawks a 2–2 tie.

"After the game, boy, did Fergy give it to Toe on the train," J.C. remembers. "Making noise like a siren, like the police were coming for us again. Toe just laughed because we'd played well."

The Habs were flying in their next game, a classic Wednesday night encounter against Toronto. Clancy's Leafs had won eight straight and were playing with the coltish enthusiasm they had displayed earlier in the decade. Back and forth the game went, with Montreal enjoying the best chances. Bower was unbeatable, however. So was Vachon. Breaks would decide this one. Montreal got the first, when Laperrière, playing beautifully again, blurred a slapshot off Henri's leg past Bower.

For two periods, Canadiens worked to swell their lead, but couldn't force another puck past Bower. The Leafs had chances, too, especially in the second with a two-man advantage, but J.C., Harris, and Roberts did the skating of five to turn Toronto aside. With three minutes to go, Béliveau had the clincher. J.C. found him at the side of the net during a power play. Jean shot, raised his stick—but Bower, diving, got his stick on the puck. Seconds later, Leafs caught what had to be the game's last break when J.C. fumbled a blueline pass. Kelly threw the puck ahead and took off. The Forum crowd jumped up. This was the game. Vachon came out when Kelly hit the blueline. At the circle, Red looked, saw an open corner, then lowered his head to fire. Vachon sprawled before Kelly released his shot, deflecting the puck wide.

Sawchuk, back for a week now, turned to Pappin on the Leaf bench. "Shoulda deked," Ukie said.

With seconds left, Clancy pulled Bower and threw on Pappin. The Habs turned away a Leaf rush. The crowd edged to the aisles. From his blueline, Keon found the Big M in full sail. Frank cut to the middle, taking J.C. with him, then back-handed a pass to the exploding Pappin, sneaking up on his wrong wing. The right winger swept in alone on Vachon. Twenty-five feet from the net, Pappin lowered his head. Rogie sprawled. Pappin faked, shifted, then tucked a backhand into the empty net.

Afterwards, newsmen circled Blake. What was wrong with Montreal? they asked. Toe studied the floor and whispered "I don't know" three times.

Next weekend, the Habs tantalized Blake again. On Saturday, the team rolled to a 6–0 lead over Detroit before coasting to a 6–2 win. Sunday, in New York, Vachon threw a 2–0 shut-out. "We've played four good games and could have won all of them," Toe said after Vachon closed the door on the Rangers. "Defense seems solid again and we should have Harper back soon. Vachon has really helped. He looks like he could be a good one."

The Toronto papers were full of features on Rogie when Montreal visited on Wednesday, March 8. In eight games, the rookie had allowed sixteen goals; a record all the more

impressive when you consider how many had gone in off
Laperrière's big feet. Tonight, however, Rogie proved there
was no figuring this crazy Montreal season, as the rookie followed his best game in the pros with the worst period of his
career.

Montreal hopped to a quick 1–0 lead. Vachon made a nifty
save on Ellis. After that, however, the goalie who was a closed
door in New York turned into an open window. First, Pulford
lobbed one from centre to end a shift. He was at the bench
when the puck sailed past Vachon's mitt. Two minutes later,
Stemkowski slapped a draw in off the post with Rogie out of
position. Then the Palmarolee Kid mishandled a Horton shot
and watched Keon rap in the rebound. He was out of the net
when Pappin scored at nine minutes, and too far back twenty
seconds later when Horton banged in a blueline slapshot.
Baun ended the Leaf scoring early in the second with a 70-
foot change-up Rogie lunged at and missed.

Down 6–1 with thirty minutes to go, the Habs rallied.
Fergy scored and bloodied Hillman's nose. Henri set up three
goals. J.C. performed a blueline twirl to escape a checker then
zipped one over Sawchuk's shoulder. But the hole was too big.
At the end of the 6–4 Leaf win, an unhappy Canadien club
flew back to Montreal for a Saturday game against the first-
place Hawks. With eleven games left in the season the
Stanley Cup champs were still not a 500 team (24–25–10).

"Our games with Chicago were how hockey was meant to
be played," remembers Béliveau. "The fans they would say the
same thing. I know any time the Black Hawks came to the
Forum there was an exciting, clean game. They had the scorers and of course Glenn Hall. We were a skating club ourselves. It was always good hockey."

"Canadiens were the best for a simple reason," says Hall.
"They could do something no one else could. Their fellas
played offense and defense equally well. We were an offensive
club. Same with Detroit. Toronto was defensive. Fellas like
Béliveau, Backstrom and Richard could play offense and
defense. So could the other forwards. That's why they won so
many Stanley Cups."

Hall agrees with Béliveau about the level of skill evident in Chicago-Montreal battles at the old Forum.

"Sure, it was good hockey," he says. "Montreal had the best ice in the NHL. Fast ice. Detroit was also good. Other rinks were all bad. Come playoffs, our rink was terrible, and you had to wonder why, considering we were a skating team. But they were all bad, except Montreal and Detroit. And Montreal's was best. When we came in you had two fast-skating teams going at it; you were going to see good hockey."

So far this season, the Hawk games here had all been dashing, eventful affairs...good to the last drop of the puck. The last three matches had ended in ties. Overall, however, the Hawks had killed Montreal. "Anybody who wants to know why Chicago is in first place...just has to look at their games with us this year," Blake said. "Eleven games and we've won one."

Tonight, the Habs roared out as if intent on evening their record in the first period. Backstrom won the opening draw. Fergy barged over the Hawk line, then flipped a pass to Backstrom, who traded off to Larose, cruising the slot. Claude's backhand flew through a tangle of bodies (Ferguson had crashed the net) past a reeling DeJordy. On the next shift the trio were back: Backstrom swirled from the Hawk defense, spotted Larose, his eyes bright as headlights, alone in the crease, then threaded a forty-foot pass through a maze of sticks and skates. Two-nothing Montreal. Minutes later, Rousseau took a Richard pass to the left of DeJordy, faked, waited for the goalie to teeter, then tucked one inside the post.

Down 3–0 before they'd tested Worsley (miraculously back after missing just a month with his wounded knee), the Hawks hung on for the rest of the period, clinching and holding in the manner of a wobbly boxer trying to make it to the bell.

After a sniff of smelling salts—Hawks reminded themselves with a win they could clinch the championship on Sunday against Toronto—Chicago snapped to life in the second. As was so often the case, Mikita's line led the way. A few days earlier, the Scooters had invited a *Sports Illustrated* writer up to Mikita's hotel room for a chat over a tub of beer.

"You know," Mikita offered, "everybody thinks we're magicians or something, when all we really do is make the obvious plays. We don't do anything unorthodox or surprising, we just keep skating, and each of us knows where the other guy will be."

The line did have one trick, Wharram allowed. The trio used nicknames on ice: Mikita, "the Czech who looks like a Chinaman," in Nesterenko's words, was "Kita." Wharram, the brushcut whippet, was "Whip." Doug Mohns was "Mohnsie." If a Scooter broke free he'd shout the nickname of the man with the puck. Simple enough. But how the name was pronounced offered clues to a player's predicament. "If you shout once—'Kita!'—it means you think you have a little time," Whip explained. "But if you're in a scramble you yell twice—'Kita, Kita!'—then he knows he has to rush."

The second period of tonight's game, Gump must've felt like a spooked settler squirming by a campfire listening to Apaches creeping in.

"Kita!"

"Whip, Whip!"

First, Mohns danced over the blueline to the left of the Montreal net, faked, then threw a no-look pass to the blueline. Mikita was three-quarters into a slapshot when the puck reached his hooked blade. The shot was in the top right corner past Worsley, some fifty-five feet away, that second. Up a man, the Scooters struck again. Mikita drifted over the blueline. Hull peeled to the left. Stan turned to him, then feathered a pass the other way. The galloping Wharram swung past Harris. Gump came out to block the angle. The little winger shifted past, backhanding the puck into the net.

Chicago was on the scoreboard again before the third period was a minute old. With J.C. off, Mikita slipped into the Montreal zone, circled to the right of Worsley, then waited.

"Kita, Kita."

Mohns, parked on the edge of crease, received the pass before the second "Kita" and slapped in the equalizer. Later in the same shift, Mikita found Mohns behind Montreal's defense. The winger deked and shot quickly, beating Worsley, but banging the puck off the post.

The Habs woke up five minutes into the third period. Backstrom split Pilote and Jarrett, deked DeJordy, but threw the puck wide. Henri, playing with Tremblay and Roberts, had a few good shifts. And Ferguson decisioned Dennis Hull in a punch-up. (His record was now 973 wins and one draw, according to Red Fisher.) Sensing the tide about to turn, the new, improved Hawks shifted to defense the final ten minutes and cruised to a 3–3 tie. In Toronto, the Leafs tied the Rangers. Now all Chicago had to do to capture their first league championship was win tomorrow at home.

FIRST PERIOD
1. Montreal, Larose 18th (Ferguson, Backstrom) 0:36
2. Montreal, Larose 19th (Backstrom) 3:42
3. Montreal, Rousseau 15th (Duff, Richard) 7:37
Penalties—Duff 9:13; Harper 14:14; Angotti 19:29

SECOND PERIOD
4. Chicago, Mikita 32nd (Mohns, Pilote) 1:47
5. Chicago, Wharram 28th (Mikita, Pilote) 16:28
Penalties—Nesterenko 0:46; Harper 15:22; J.C. Tremblay 19:47

THIRD PERIOD
6. Chicago, Mohns 22nd (Mikita, B. Hull) 0:58
Penalties—None

Shots on goal
Chicago   7   11   5 — 23
Montreal   7   7   10 — 24

"If Punch was a ten as far as being difficult to get along with, Clancy was…" Conacher thinks about that one. "Well, he wouldn't be on the scale. He was the easiest guy to get along with in the world. He laughed, told jokes, gave pep talks. I don't know if he could bring you to the Cup, but he did provide us with a nice breather in the middle of a tough season."

Red Kelly leans back twenty-seven years to recall life under Clancy.

"That was an odd year. We lost a bunch in a row. It looked

like we might miss the play-offs, or at least that's what the papers said. Finally, we won a few. Then Punch got sick. Was that the year he had the gall thing or the hernia? Anyway, King comes along…" He stops, sorts through a tangle of forty hockey winters. "Then we went on a hot streak, right? Ten in a row? Well, hockey's like that. When you're losing it feels like you're pushing uphill. Then you win one—all of a sudden you're going downhill. Everything's easy.

"Yeah, Clancy, sure I remember him coaching. Kept the boys loose. Younger guys played better, if I remember right. Oh, Clancy he was a character, no doubt about it." Kelly chuckles. "You never saw a fella talk more in all your life. He'd chew your ear off behind the bench. But he was always encouraging. Real, real encouraging. King was the biggest holler guy you're ever gonna meet. As different from Punch as night is day."

The *Globe*'s Dick Beddoes captured Clancy's antic charm at an informal press conference in early March. The King had been to the doctor's and was keen to share test results with the world:

> "A number one, they found me. Lights in my nose and up my ears like they think I got something hiding in there. Two hours they got me and they find I'm suffering from nothing except numbpluck!"
>
> Students of Clancyese, which is a live language only superficially resembling Swahili, are alert to the rich, crunchy nouns the King constantly inserts in his speech. Numbpluck, sir?
>
> His map-of-Ireland mug wore his perpetual high-beam grin. "Yep, I'm suffering from numbpluck. That means," he said approximately, "that I'm full of flap-doodle."
>
> Leafs had finished their daily exertions and Clancy was meeting the press in an exercise of amusing double talk. He was keeping all hands loose, like everybody's benign uncle who shows up at a family anniversary a little bombed.
>
> "How's Imlach?" a guy asked in reference to the

Leafs' ailing curator, who has been horizontal in hospital for two weeks.

"A number one," Clancy recited. "Hunnert per cent, six-two-and-even."

"So when they going to spring him?"

"Saturday. One more test and he's going to walk out of jail, laughing."

"What's the test they're giving Imlach?" Rex MacLeod wondered, in comic ignorance. "An algebra test?"

Mr. Clancy closed one eye in an elaborate wink, which with him can mean anything from a football prediction to a declaration of war on the Viet Cong. Then, having felt for an apt Punch line, replied: "Oh, Imlach'd pass algebra, all right. A geometry test, too. He knows, ho, ho, all the angles."

....They are odd blocks of wood, Imlach and Clancy, tempermentally as far apart as two humans can be. Clancy is the original good humour man with the built-in public relations of Francis of Assisi. Imlach is a different saucepan of shad—perverse, profane, loyal, often a cussed martinet who refuses to accept less from any player than his absolute best every day. There seldom appears to be any warm camaraderie between Imlach and his players.

A born sidekick, Clancy idolized Imlach ("finest man in hockey," he called him). Nevertheless, he ran the team as he pleased. Shack was benched. Walton took a regular shift. Horton, the best defenseman in the league now, played forty minutes a game. Mahovlich received extra time, too, taking a turn at point on the power play. ("Got something to say to you," Clancy told Frank upon taking over. "Shoot," Mahovlich said. "That's it! I want you t'shoot more," King cried.) Practices were giddy affairs. One scrimmage, Clancy rotated Keon, Conacher, and Shack in net.

Clancy did share one trait with Imlach. Both men were superstitious. King was wearing a blue-striped shirt when Leafs ended their long losing streak. He wore the same shirt a week later pinch hitting for Punch in Toronto's 5–3 win over Boston. Pronouncing the jersey good luck, he refused to change shirts for two weeks.

On February 22, Clancy's team ended Hodge's season with a 5–2 crunching of the Habs. The next night, the Leafs were in Detroit. Sawchuk, in his first game back in two months, kept Toronto alive early. Leafs were down 2–1 in the second when Walton flew around Boivin and fired a bullet over Crozier's shoulder. Same shift, the rookie freelanced into the Wing zone and passed to Mahovlich. Crozier handled Frank's shot, but missed Ellis's tap in. Minutes later, Armstrong set up Mahovlich for the game's final goal. The Big M played with four different centres that evening. That might've been by accident, Kelly says today, laughing.

"Sometimes, I wasn't sure King had a clear idea what he was doing back there," Red says. "He'd be behind the bench, cheering, y'know: 'C'mon this guy! C'mon that guy!'" A laugh. "Dang, if he didn't get people's name wrong. And every now and then he'd get all balled up calling out lines. Sometimes the wrong guy got out onto the ice, I'm sure. But we kept winning."

The streak rolled to seven the following weekend, with decisive 4–0 and 4–2 wins over Detroit and New York. Saturday, Horton gathered two assists and dominated play. Call-up Jim McKenny scored his first NHL goal, slapping a Mahovlich rebound past George Gardner. And Sawchuk recorded his ninety-ninth career shut-out. Sunday, Bower killed the Rangers, making thirty-four stops in the first two periods. But the big news this weekend was the play of what was now the team's best line: Pulford, Stemkowski, and Pappin. Pulford collected three goals. Pappin scored the winner on Sunday. And Stemkowski left Red Wing and Ranger tattoos all over the boards.

"Yeah, that was a big line of ours down the stretch," remembers Kelly. "Funny thing was at first all we did was talk about how they looked. They all had the big noses, y'see. So the joke was if we could only get them to turn sideways, nobody could get past them. But they were a good line for us. Pappin was good around the net. Pulford was a good all-around player. And Stemkowski was a big physical forward."

Clancy had about rubbed the stripes off his lucky shirt by the time Pappin beat Vachon to preserve the streak in Montreal. Three days later, the Hawks were in Toronto. "You gotta stop Mikita, he's the best in the business," King told players. To stop the Scooters, Clancy shuffled his winning hand, starting Pulford, Keon at centre, and Stemkowski. Three centres on one line! Imlach, still holed up at Toronto General, must've kicked his bed sheets when he heard that line-up; it was just the kind of stunt he'd pull.

The line worked while it lasted (a period). Stemkowski scored the game's first goal, muscling a backhand over DeJordy. All Leaf lines played well, in fact. Through two periods, Toronto outshot Chicago 31–14. If not for DeJordy, who made fine saves on Keon, Pulford, and Mahovlich, it would've been a rout.

When the puck was dropped to begin the third, Keon tore into the Hawk zone, setting up Conacher. DeJordy made the save, but seconds later the centre was back, slipping the Hawk defense, then backhanding to Armstrong, who flashed the webbing above DeJordy's arm with a wrist shot. On the next shift, Pulford made Van Impe ("the Belgian Basher") look like a minor leaguer, faking a shot to collapse the defender, then slipping the puck between his skates, circling around to collect his own pass before snapping a shot over DeJordy's blocker. After that it was just a question of whether Sawchuk would achieve his record shut-out. Incredibly, he'd been tested only once by the Hull and Mikita lines all night.

"When Leafs put their mind to it," remembers Hall, "they could play the tightest hockey you ever saw. What got me was their defense. Most goals don't come from pretty plays. Usually someone's man is loose and they knock in a rebound. Some nights watching Toronto I could swear the defense never gave up a rebound. Not one."

In the third, getting the puck away from Leaf defense was like pulling a bone from a snarling dog. With twenty seconds left and the puck buried deep in the Hawk end, Sawchuk lifted his arms in a wide V to celebrate his hundredth shut-out. "Man, were they coming back tonight. They were really checking for me," he said later. Then he offered a rare smile and said, "First 100 are the toughest."

The next night, in Chicago, Leafs continued to work, outplaying the Hawks the first twenty minutes to grab a 1–0 lead. But Hull and Mikita could only be contained for so long. In the second, Bobby beat Bower on a blueline scorcher. Then Mikita set up Angotti. Late in the period, Stapleton, on a great rush, made it 3–1. The Tasmanian Forward, Shack brought Toronto close, scoring a goal and banging what would've been the tying marker off the post. With a few minutes remaining, Leafs were called for a penalty. DeJordy hurried to the bench. Hull jumped on. Bobby and the Scooters put on a spellbinding display, controlling the puck for forty-five seconds before Hull tapped in a Mikita pass. After the goal, Horton and Baun dragged themselves to the bench, bent with exhaustion. The Leafs' ten-game joyride, a journey that had taken them from oblivion to striking distance of second place, was finally over.

Punch was out of hospital pj's and back in the Gardens for the Leafs' next game, the 6–4 massacre of Vachon. After the game, Imlach strode into the dressing-room, pretending to be upset over the way his club had let the Canadiens back in the game. "Nice going, Shorty," he said to Clancy, "but any more of those and you'll put me back in the hospital." Imlach then met the players and took some ribbing from Shack. "Hey-hey, that's what happens when you burn the candle at both ends, eh Punch," Eddie said, pumping his coach's hand. Across the room, Clancy advised reporters this was his next-to-last game as coach. "We're gonna beat them Rangers Saturday night, and that'll be it for me, yes sir. We'll be in second. Then I'll hand it over to Punch and tell him, 'Listen you, I got us into second, all you have to do is keep us there.'"

King didn't quite deliver, as Leafs had to come back on a third period goal by Keon to tie the Rangers, 2–2. But his contribution to the 1966–67 season remains enormous.

"Through any season every team is going to have ups and downs," Stanley says. "People are gonna get on each other's nerves. King helped out, I think, just by being who he was—a fun-loving Irishman who loved to talk, and talked to everyone. Look, we knew we were always Punch's team. We all knew he was coming back. But while [Clancy] coached he made the game fun again, you could say. He helped team morale. He was a rare character; a man who saw the best in everybody."

Although the old Chicago Stadium crammed 20,000 spectators, even fans in the back row were right in the game. The outer walls of the snug, three-tiered box were 100 feet from the ice. The building was so small, Hull could fire a puck through the building onto the street. "What we used to do was line [a puck] up so that you could shoot it out one of the Stadium's exit ramps," Bobby said. "Hit it right, and it could go over the glass, through the doors, break the window and wind up somewhere on West Madison Street."

More than anything, the Stadium was noisy. "I never forget going for the first time into that building," recalls Vachon. "All the fans were screaming and the organ was going. You got tingles." Tingles, indeed. The building's massive-sounding Barton organ was built into the rafters. At full volume, the organ had the decibel level of twenty-five brass bands. When the Hawks scored, a foghorn blared just as the organ reached full cry. On Sunday afternoon, when the Hawks hit the ice in search of their first league championship, organs and foghorns joined together for a five-minute salute.

The Stadium was still throbbing when the puck was dropped thirty minutes later. Reay started the Scooters. Punch countered with Stemkowski's line. Within seconds, Pulford was free inside the Hawk blueline. Pilote took a penalty for bringing him down. The Leafs looked disorganized on the power play. Maybe the noise bothered them. "You couldn't think in that place," Kelly says. "Heck, it was loud." Then Nesterenko tripped Horton. Ravlich tore up ice, beating Sawchuk. The goal was nullified, however. Vern Buffy had called a penalty that no one heard. Stadium fans didn't mind. They kept cheering, confident this was their night.

After a ragged start, teams settled into tight-checking hockey. At eleven minutes, the Hawks caught a break. Stapleton, under pressure from Stemkowski, cleared. Pappin was about to intercept, but stepped on Hull's stick, falling. The Toronto winger was arguing with Buffy when Bobby stole inside the Leaf line and fed Esposito. Phil looked to return the pass, but Bobby was tied up by two defenders—which meant Ken Hodge must be free. Sure enough, the curly-headed winger appeared alone in the high slot. One pass later, the Hawks had a lead.

While the organ and foghorns joined in a noise that sounded like two ships passing in a canyon, Pappin went zebra hunting. "He called me everything under the sun," Buffy said later. "In fact he used a couple of expressions I'd never heard before. That's when I gave him the misconduct." When Pappin refused to enter the penalty box, he received a game misconduct.

The coronation became official late in the first when Hull's line scored on consecutive shifts. First, Espo swept around the Leaf defense and slipped a pass in front. The Golden Jet lost the puck in his feet, but Hodge slapped a croquet shot past Sawchuk. Two minutes later, Stapleton joined the line on left wing, allowing Bobby to lag behind. Three relays later, the little defenseman dropped a pass to number nine, alone at the blueline. Hull stepped in, recoiled, then fell into a shot that Sawchuk could only flinch at.

The next periods must've been confusing to hockey newcomers who stumbled on CBS's Sunday afternoon game. The action slowed to a crawl—the ice was slow, the contest over—but Stadium fans responded as if on a thrilling roller-coaster ride. "Louuu, Louuuu," they shrieked whenever Angotti touched the puck. Hall's clearing of a dump-in excited more delirium. The Leafs played like they were in a hurry to leave town, especially after Keon drew a face-off into his net early in the third. "Didn't touch it at all," grinned Angotti, who was credited with the goal. "All I was trying to do was get the puck to Wally Boyer, but Davey beat me cleanly. I guess he got too much wood on it."

With Angotti's goal, fans began throwing everything but car keys. Balloons and unfurling toilet paper floated down even while work crews tried to gather up discarded hats and gloves. Late in the period, Angotti scored again, signaling more bedlam. The last minutes of the game were played in a rain of confetti. Finally there was the inevitable countdown: "...three, two, one." The organ wailed. Foghorns sounded. The crowd, which included his Honour, Mayor Daley, danced and hugged. On the ice players fell into an excited mob.

"We buried Muldoon!" Reay shouted entering the dressing-room. Tubs of champagne were wheeled in, then ravaged. Hull and Esposito, stripped to their shorts, tumbled about like playful cubs. "Tough guy now, eh?" Hull hollered, alluding to Esposito's fight in the Forum the previous evening with Larose. "So who'd you ever handle?" Phil shot back. "A shrimp like Bugsy Watson. Big deal."

Mikita and Ken Hodge deposited GM Tommy Ivan in the shower. "Soon the room was a scene out of Marat/Sade," reported the Chicago *Tribune*. "Had men gone mad?"

Yes, and probably a little prematurely, thought Glenn Hall. The goaltender changed quickly after the team's win. "Nine more games," he said, smiling, then disappeared into the night. Mr. Goalie was long gone when Reay cried, "This first place business has been a monkey on our back. Every year people accuse us of having the best team and losing. Well, maybe we weren't the best team then. Maybe we didn't have the balance or all-around ability to finish first. But now we are the best, and we've finally proven to everybody that we can win the championship."

While the party raged, a cab swung through Chicago's South Side for O'Hare. The cabbie was eager to talk about today's contest. His passenger, a stranger, allowed that he'd been at the game. "I suppose they'll start talking about the Toronto players putting out more for Clancy," the cabbie concluded.

"Ah, that's nuts," Punch Imlach replied unhappily, dipping his trademark fedora over his eyes. "The Hawks won because they were too good for the Leafs."

FIRST PERIOD
1. Chicago, Hodge 6th (Esposito, B. Hull) 11:54
2. Chicago, Hodge 7th (Esposito, Stapleton) 15:12
3. Chicago, B. Hull 48th (Stapleton, Hodge) 19:31
Penalties—Pilote (hooking) 0:07; Nesterenko (holding) 1:28;
Horton (tripping) 2:35; Pappin (misconduct and game misconduct)
11:54

SECOND PERIOD
No scoring
Penalties—Hillman (boarding) 2:33; Pilote (holding) 11:37

THIRD PERIOD
4. Chicago, Angotti 3rd 5:57
5. Chicago, Angotti 4th (Wharram, Mohns) 18:06
Penalties—Stemkowski (tripping) 17:08

Shots on goal
Toronto   14   15   10 — 39
Chicago   14   7   18 — 39

MARCH 13 STANDINGS

	P	W	L	T	F	A	Pts
Chicago:	61	37	14	10	225	141	84
New York:	61	27	23	11	163	155	65
Toronto:	60	26	23	11	162	174	62
Montreal:	61	24	25	12	154	164	60
Detroit:	61	24	33	4	182	200	52
Boston:	62	16	36	10	162	213	42

LEAGUE LEADERS

	P	G	A	Pts	PIM
Mikita, Chi.	61	32	56	88	12
R. Hull, Chi.	60	48	22	70	29
Wharram, Chi.	61	28	31	59	19
Ullman, Det.	59	24	34	58	26
Goyette, N.Y.	61	11	45	56	6
Howe, Det.	61	21	34	55	41
Rousseau, Mont.	59	15	39	54	52
Mohns, Chi.	53	23	30	53	56
Esposito, Chi.	60	16	35	51	38
Pilote, Chi.	61	6	41	47	78

Crowd noise
Canadian philosophers define the summer of love

[Love] means encounter, in the sense of both impact and response. There has to be feedback. And perhaps what was suspect about the old 19th century liberal love for mankind was that it went out, as it were, toward mankind, but wasn't too interested in any feedback or response, or able to take account of the feedback response. One of the effects of speedup in information of all kinds—pictorial or verbal or personal—is that the moment of impact and the moment of response are the same. There's no gap, no time lagging any more. That's what's wrong with the Vietnam war...

—Marshall McLuhan in *Saturday Night*'s "Love" issue.

Only a go-go girl in love with someone who didn't care.
Only 21 she was a young girl just in from somewhere.

—Gordon Lightfoot, from "Go Go Round"

14

Habs Run the Table

Worsley rejoined the Habs none too soon, Blake figured. It was mid-March. There were nine games left. Just enough time to get ready for the play-offs. Vachon? Well, Rogie was a fine prospect, but those five goals in ten minutes in Toronto, hoo boy! That was the kind of break-down that could sink a team in the post-season. The Gumper was playoff-tested. The man to go to in a big game. So Toe went with Worsley again in New York, Sunday, March 12, the night after the Habs and Hawks battled to a 3–3 tie.

Two minutes in, Ratelle stole the puck and scored. A little later, Gump was in his crease, studying play at the other end, when a nimbus explosion went off in his head. He staggered and fell. Teammates rushed back. What was in his hair? "An egg," trainer Eddie Pelchak replied tersely. Some moron from the upper deck had beaned the Gumper with an egg. The goalie was OK, but woozy, unable to play. Suddenly, the Canadien clubhouse was a burlesque dressing-room. Worsley stripped and back-up Hodge flew into his gear. What next? Toe must've wondered, watching Vachon warm up on the ice.

What was immediately forthcoming was Eddie Giacomin,

and plenty of him, as for forty minutes the Canadiens outskated and outperformed every Ranger on the ice. Except Giacomin. Time and again the Backstrom and Richard lines hurled themselves at New York's net. Once Backstrom redirected a pass at a wide, empty corner, only to have Eddie shoot out a leg, switchblade quick, kicking the puck wide.

"In boxing, you hear people talk about sweet hands, they're quick with their mitts," Emile Francis says. "Well, Giacomin had sweet feet. Oh, he was fast with those feet. That year he was fantastic. Night after night he made saves no other goalie could make."

After Montreal had been held scoreless for eighty minutes (including two periods against Chicago), Toe shuffled lines, throwing out Balon, Peters and Roberts to open the third. But it was the reformation of the Ferguson-Béliveau-Cournoyer unit, a grouping that had worked well after Christmas, that led to Montreal's first score. It was an odd goal for a hot goalie to allow, a fifty-footer from Ferguson. But then Fergy had Giacomin's number. Of the fourteen goals he'd scored this season, half had come against New York. "Don't know why," Giacomin recalls. "Fergy just seemed to beat me early in my career, although I stoned him a few times later on."

The Canadiens continued pressing. Giacomin did the splits to stop Gilles Tremblay, and was up in an instant to snatch Richard's rebound try, exciting a chorus of "Eddie, Eddie" from the Garden faithful. Then came the kind of mix-up that had led to so many Hab defeats this season: two Montrealers chased Geoffrion, leaving the Earl of Ingarfield (as New York tabloids called him) in front. Ingarfield made it 2–1, New York, with eight minutes left. At the rate Montreal was scoring, that seemed enough. But seconds later, Rousseau stole in on Giacomin and Howell, faked a shot, dropping both men to their knees in prayer, then tossed a pass to Gilles Tremblay, who tied the game for good. Toe made sure of that, replacing Cournoyer and Larose with Roberts and Talbot, a sure sign he was willing to settle for a tie, and a resounding non-confidence vote against the team's offense.

Going into the club's next game with Boston, the Habs were still last in goals with 154, 69 fewer than Chicago. In six previous seasons, Canadiens had finished first in scoring four times. The year before, they were second, one back of Chicago. Now this.

GM emeritus Frank Selke suggested injuries to the team's centres was the problem. Béliveau had missed two months; Richard, a couple of weeks; and Backstrom had groin problems early on, Selke pointed out. "Without our centres we're just not the same team," he said. Selke was astute—but kind. The cold truth was Montreal's centres weren't performing. Canadien middlemen had fewer goals than Mikita (32–30). Backstrom, after a terrible start (twelve points at Christmas), had been solid. Henri was fine early, but slumped from December to March. Béliveau—well, he hadn't scored in eighteen games.

When asked to define Canadien hockey, Blake once said, "Get the puck the hell out fast as we can." How? the questioner continued. Toe smiled. "Give it to Richard." He could've as easily said Béliveau or Backstrom.

"Our game was built around our centres," Harper explains. "Toe was a genius because he made the game simple. At the beginning of the season, everybody talked about our centres, who was going to do what that year. Toe knew players liked to score, but he only had one goal every season. Just one. 'Win the Vezina,' he'd say. Never 'I want Béliveau to score this many goals, or even for us to finish first or win the Stanley Cup.' He knew with our centres, we'd score, but if we managed to allow fewer than anyone else, everything else would fall into place.

"On defense, one man stayed in front, the other went in the corner. Simple, but if you screwed up, you didn't play. Today, I laugh when I see defensemen throwing the puck back and forth behind the net, then carry the puck out. Toe would've died. We kept a defenseman in front. What we did was bring the centre back in the corner. And he'd bring the puck up. Or he and one defenseman would bring it out. The other defenseman stayed back. We made our centres work the entire rink, all game. No floating at the blueline. Our centres started and finished everything. And we only used three. Man, if they weren't playing well at both ends we were in trouble."

Only rarely this season did the team have two centres going. Three? never. The result was a stalled offense.

At first, the Wednesday, March 15 Boston-Montreal game seemed a repeat of every Forum contest between the clubs this season. The Bruins, who hadn't lost here since October, scored first shot, with Pie McKenzie sweeping a Bucyk rebound past Vachon (Gump was still out with a concussion). The fans grew restless, booing Béliveau during a power play. Then Toe threw out Backstrom, Ferguson, and Cournoyer. The trio hit the ice churning. Fergy carried Gary Doak to the net. Before crashing he knocked a pass to Backstrom, who muscled one past Johnston.

The Backstrom line played the rest of the period at a ferocious pace. At ten minutes, Ralph held up in the corner, watched Fergy, Johnston, and Marotte merge in the crease, then lobbed one at the heaving tangle, sure his man would emerge with the puck. He did, breaking his stick whacking in the go-ahead marker. Five minutes later, Backstrom flew down the boards and idled in the corner, while Ferguson shed tacklers Oliver and Skip Krake moving to the crease. Ralph shot just as Fergy arrived, banking a shot off his winger past Johnston.

Backstrom continued his brilliant play in the second. No shock here, number six had been performing well for months. But Henri also contributed a superb twenty minutes, skating a mile every shift and setting up goals by Balon and Rochefort. Béliveau also put in a compelling stretch, skating hard and moving to the net with assurance. He also orchestrated the evening's best goal, swinging wide of Marotte before cutting in on Parent, yanking the goalie, then slipping a smart pass to Rousseau, who scored easily.

In the third, Montreal's centres played with even greater purpose. Béliveau set up Rousseau again. Richard scored twice. Backstrom tallied and helped on Cournoyer's power play marker. Finally, Henri, in what seemed like a vaudeville trick from "The Ed Sullivan Show," sent five Bruins spinning before passing off to J.C., who scored Montreal's eleventh goal.

Eleven goals? Montreal had scored twelve in the six previous games. What happened? "Our centremen put together their best game of the season," a relieved Blake commented. "At the same time, that is." The last part was no throwaway line. Without the centres performing well, the team frayed at the edges: Stress fractures appeared on defense. Wingers slipped into slumps. But when the big three were flying, everyone fell into all star form. With this game Richard, Backstrom and Béliveau were finally back "at the same time."

The next weekend, Henri spearheaded the attack, leading his line to seven goals. On Saturday, the Habs spotted the Rangers two quick ones. Ferguson beat Giacomin late in the first period. Then the nimble Richard took over, winning every shift—skating, hustling, always pressing. For two periods, whenever Henri was on, the puck was in the Ranger end. Midway in the second, number 16 tipped a Harris shot past Giacomin. On the next shift, linemate Balon rapped in the winner. Late in the third, Richard exhausted defensemen MacNeil and Neilson with a whirlpool dash, then threw a pass back to the blueline. Rochefort banged in Harper's rebound to give the Canadiens a 4–2 win.

In Chicago, Henri was even better, firing a hat trick and setting up Rochefort in the first forty minutes. "Montreal dominated play through two periods like no visiting team this year, outshooting Reay's Hawks by a wide margin [31–15]," the *Tribune* reported. "That was as fine a game as I've seen the little Richard play," Reay remarked. Canadiens would've won easily, except for the brilliant work of DeJordy, and some fine shooting by Hawk forwards, including a vintage fifty-foot slapshot by Hull. "Never saw the puck," Vachon said at the conclusion of the 4–4 game.

After the Leaf unbeaten streak ended in Chicago, the team faced the Wings at home the following Wednesday. As well as marking Punch's return to coaching at the Gardens, March 15 was Imlach's forty-ninth birthday. Safe to say he had passed happier anniversaries. Toronto squandered a 2–1 second period lead (on goals by Pulford and Pappin) to fall behind 3–2 late in the third. With six minutes left, Detroit took a penalty. Leafs huddled at the bench during a break. Punch talked. The players nodded. Seconds later, Vern Buffy dropped the puck to the right of Crozier. Keon won the draw, but barely. Horton and Ullman raced for the squibbed puck. Normie arrived first, flicking the puck up the boards. Suddenly, Detroit had three clear, as Ullman, Henderson and Young chased down ice in formation, with a pack of red-faced blue shirts trailing. Sawchuk made a save on Young and got a pad on Ullman's shot. Henderson, however, rapped in the second rebound to salt away a 4–2 Detroit win.

A three-man break the other way when you're up a man? Punch took a day off to figure that one out, leaving Clancy to handle practice. After scrimmage, players faced reporters and the question every amateur hockey expert in Toronto, from sportscasters to cabdrivers, was now asking: You win seven straight with Clancy, then lose as soon as Punch comes back—why won't Leafs put out for Imlach?

"People ask me the same question," Armstrong confirmed. "Of course when I say we play as hard for Punch as for King, they always say, 'You have to say that.'" He shook his head. "Fans were saying the same thing when we were winning Stanley Cups—that we didn't like Imlach."

"It's nothing to do with Punch," Baun asserted, "it's just a natural let down after the winning streak."

The Leafs still weren't themselves the following weekend, at least not defensively. On Saturday, the club let Hull roam free, and the muscled meteor, as Dick Beddoes called him, participated in five goals. On Sunday in Detroit, Howe played superstar, firing two goals and setting up a third, leading the Wings to a five-goal afternoon. But the Leafs made it clear in these games that they were far from the droopy bunch who lost ten in a row at mid-season. Those Leafs counted fifteen goals in a month. This new team scored fifteen goals in less than twenty-four hours, winning by margins of 9–5 and 6–5.

"I hope this shuts up a few people who say we won't play for Punch," Armstrong said after the Chicago win. Imlach was beaming after his club overcame a late 5–3 deficit to win 6–5 on Sunday afternoon in Detroit. "They were great and I'm quite pleased with all of them. They refused to quit," he said.

The next day Punch warned his players not to relax. "I told them we're facing our most important games so far this

season," he informed reporters. "Montreal's in here
Wednesday night, and we're back in their building the following week. Those two games are for second place. I hope
they're ready, because I know we are."

"Oh, I loved going in there to play against Toronto," Ferguson
remembers. "Those games were wars. They hated us. We
hated them. Ever hear the story about Toe in Maple Leaf
Gardens? Well, one night we were in there. Toe was changing
after a game, it was winter, he couldn't find anything to wear
on his feet. It was cold out, so he says, 'Bring me a pair of
socks.' Someone brings him back a pair of white socks with
blue leafs up the side. Toe flipped. 'I'd rather freeze,' he says,
throwing them away. Then he goes outside in the freezing
winter with no socks.

"That's the kind of rivalry it was," Fergy continues. "And
what emotion! Everybody was up for those games. You could
tell the fans felt it, too. They'd boo and cheer a little louder.
Which was perfect for me, because my game was emotion.
Against Toronto, I was an animal. I played as hard as I possibly could. I never played better than I did against them.
Couldn't. Every shift I gave it every ounce I had.

"And I was cocky, eh? Punch, he always brought some
hired gun up from the farm to handle me—Kent Douglas or
Jim Dorey, somebody like that. I'd skate by first shift, look
over at the Toronto bench and holler, 'Send 'em out now,
Punch, cause I'm ready.'"

Stanley also remembers the rivalry as something special.
"To win the Stanley Cup we had to beat Montreal, and we'd
been playing each other, basically the same teams, for a while,
so there was quite a competition between us. But it was more
than just players going at it. We knew the fans were watching,
too. Not just in Montreal and Toronto, but across the country. And the fans never let you forget when you won or lost
against Montreal. To this day, I still have people talk to me
about the old games with Canadiens. So you can see that
those games stayed with people."

The games stayed with referee Art Skov, who handled the
Wednesday, March 22 battle between Montreal and Toronto.

"Games between Canadiens and Leafs were a problem for a simple reason," he remembers. "Imlach and Blake were hot-heads. Complained all the time, trying to get an edge. They were the worst in the league by far. Usually, I'd pretend I did-n't hear them. If Montreal was playing Detroit, I'd skate down Detroit's side so I didn't have to listen to Blake. But that was no good if Montreal was playing Toronto, because then I'd get it from Imlach. So I was stuck. The only thing I could do was skate down the middle with the players. And even that wasn't much good because [Imlach and Blake] were so loud that I could hear both them."

Tonight, Skov heard it from Imlach. The first two goals, both by Montreal, sent Punch into orbit. "We were given the works," he said later. "First goal, Harper trips Stemkowski, then he skates down and sets up a score [a tip-in by Backstrom]. Next period, big Béliveau skates right through our crease, practically knocks down Gamble [an emergency replacement for the ailing Sawchuk]; Christ, that's another penalty right there, and they score again [J.C. stepped in quickly to convert a Rousseau pass]. They shouldn't have had any fuckin' goals, instead they've got two. Hell, what happens if we score a goal or two on a power play we should've received from those penalties? Instead of being up one or two, we're down two…right behind the fuckin' eight-ball."

"Punch was a typical coach," Skov says. "Expected every-one to see the game his way. According to him, it was always the other guy who started it. Always the other team that should get the penalty. I just let him talk. Unless the language got bad, then, hey, there were kids around, I'd have to give him a two minutes for unsportsmanlike."

Montreal extended its 2–0 lead in the second period. At seven minutes, J.C. took advantage of a clumsy Toronto line change and skated in alone, outwaited a flopping Gamble and tossed the puck high into the open net.

Then Leafs took over, outshooting Montreal 22–9 the rest of the game. Ellis made it 3–1 midway through the second, backhanding a Kelly pass beyond a lunging Vachon. For the next three minutes, Toronto pressed, testing Vachon from every angle. At times the rookie appeared out of position—

"kid was lucky, we missed so many fuckin' open nets," Punch grumbled later—but Rogie got in front of everything directed between the pipes.

At the other end, this wasn't one of Gamble's better games. The netminder had kept his team in many games earlier this season, but couldn't make the one save required of him this period, failing to close his legs in time to smother a Richard backhand.

Down 4–1, the Leafs refused to surrender. Pulford solved Vachon with a zinger off the post. Ellis brought the Leafs to within one at nine minutes into the third, banging a Mahovlich set-up through Rogie's pads. Finally, it was a game. For seven delicious minutes, the Leafs lay siege on Vachon. Stemkowski steered a Pulford pass wide. The Big M burst over the blueline with room to manoeuvre, wound up—the Gardens crowd joined in a shriek of anticipation—then pounded one off the boards.

"Oooooohhh."

Keon slapped at a loose puck in a goalmouth scramble. Vachon sprawled, taking the puck in his chest. Then Ferguson collected a rebound and was off the other way. Grimacing, hunched over—Fergy always skated as if his boots were a half-size too small—number 22 stole down the left side. Béliveau was with him. Hillman and Pronovost back. At the blueline, he flipped a pass back to Big Jean, who, without looking, took a short slapshot that exploded off his stick sixty feet past a startled Gamble.

"Uuuuhhhhhhh."

"I shoot a slapshot different from a lot of other player," Béliveau explains. "I found that if you take a big wind-up, you get a hard shot. But what was the sense? The defenseman, he would get his stick in the way and the puck would go into the crowd. Or the goalie would have time to come out. Me, I would pull the stick back six inches then shoot. I believe it is easier to surprise a goalie than to try to beat his reflexes."

After scoring, Béliveau skated to the net, head down, to collect the puck. Not in celebration of his first goal in twenty-one games. Or because he might be retiring, as the Montreal press feared (seven springs earlier, Maurice Richard fished his last goal out of a Toronto net before retiring). In a scene out of a Hollywood sports bio, Jean retrieved the puck for a youngster back in hospital in Montreal.

The Canadiens won this evening because their centres played well. Béliveau, Richard, and Backstrom all scored. Vachon and J.C. also made important contributions. But maybe the team's most valuable player was Ferguson. He set up the opening and closing goals, and fought "like an animal" every shift in between. Fergy scuffled with Pulford early; tangled with Hillman and Baun in the middle period; and flattened Pappin twice in the closing minutes. But when the three stars were announced, he was in the dressing room, passing out "well dones" to teammates.

"You know all those games I played in Toronto I was never named one of the three stars," he says, laughing. "I guess Foster Hewitt hated me. Not once was I named a star. It got to be a joke in the dressing-room with Backstrom and me. 'Comb up your hair tonight, Ralphie-boy, because Foster's going to be calling you at the end of the game,' I'd tell him. Sure enough, I'd get a goal, maybe a couple of assists, work my butt off. Ralph, he'd have a puck go in off his leg or something," Ferguson chuckles again, "and what do you know? Ralph would be named second star. Me, never."

FIRST PERIOD

1. Montreal, Backstrom 13th (Harper, Ferguson) 15:11
Penalties—Stemkowski (high sticking) 3:12; Hillman (major—fighting), Pappin (major—fighting), Ferguson (major—fighting), Harper (major—fighting) 6:27; Horton (interference) 8:08; Rousseau (tripping) 9:53; Stemkowski (holding) 11:57; Balon (boarding) 17:47

SECOND PERIOD

2. Montreal, J.C. Tremblay 6th (Rousseau, G. Tremblay) 0:58
3. Montreal, J.C. Tremblay 7th (Rochefort, Talbot) 6:55
4. Toronto, Ellis 20th (Kelly, Pronovost) 11:25
5. Montreal, Richard 18th (Balon, Harris) 14:56
6. Toronto, Pulford 15th (Stemkowski, Ellis) 16:09
Penalties—Vadnais (hooking) 4:48

THIRD PERIOD
7. Toronto, Ellis 21st (Mahovlich, Hillman) 9:23
8. Montreal, Béliveau 9th (Ferguson) 16:54
Penalties—None

Shots on goal
Montreal   16   12   7 — 35
Toronto   12   17   12 — 41

Montreal's unbeaten streak stood at six. The first sixty games seemed a bad dream. The team was playing well. Second place was within grasp. Everything was as it should be at the Forum. On Saturday night, the Habs were again in top form, taking Detroit 4–1. "Could've been 10–1 if Crozier hadn't been so hot," Toe said. Canadiens won every period, outshooting Detroit 42–27. Vachon was sharp. Harper and J.C. were efficient in both ends. Béliveau and Richard each chipped in a goal and an assist. And Blake? well, Toe was in top form, too.

Early in the game, the coach reminded players this was March; October mistakes were no longer allowed. At three minutes, Rousseau lost the puck behind Detroit's net. Instead of giving chase, he threw out his stick. Up went Vern Buffy's arm. Two minutes, hooking. Blake wasn't so forgiving. For taking a penalty in the offensive zone, the team's top scorer sat out the rest the game.

"Toe would never scream at you on the bench, eh?" Cournoyer remembers. "You did something stupid, you go to the end of the bench. You don't have to ask why. Someone else was out there next time."

"That was Toe. He didn't allow you to make mental mistakes," Harper says. "Winning isn't a problem if you play mistake-free hockey."

Blake now had a problem. A nice problem, but a problem. His team was playing too well to fit in players he might need in the play-offs. "I'd like to get Duff in there and Worsley, too. But how can I?" he said after the Detroit game. Gump was OK again. Toe wanted to play him against the Wings, but Worsley's wife, Doreen, delivered a baby girl that Saturday.

"I never felt like the number one goalie," Vachon recalls. "Every game, Gump and I would show up before the game, get dressed, then wait until game time. Then the trainer put the puck in my glove, so I'd know I was playing that night."

"Rogie was our good luck charm," Cournoyer remembers. "End of that year it seem when we play him we knew, no matter what, we'd win. So how can Toe not play him?"

Vachon was sturdy on Sunday against the Bruins, but the rest of the team took most of the afternoon off. The game was 1–0 Boston at the end of two. In the first minute of the third, Orr grabbed a puck in his end and navigated the left boards, swung behind the Hab net, then slipped a pass out to Martin, who doubled Boston's lead.

"That Canadien club, we just knew we were gonna win every game we played," Ferguson recalls. "Didn't matter if we were down five goals in the third period, we just knew we were gonna win. We had that confidence."

The Habs really could have overcome a five-goal deficit this afternoon, as they threw a touchdown on the board in a furious ten-minute span in the third period. Gilles Tremblay, Ferguson, Rochefort, Rousseau, Backstrom, and Béliveau all beat Parent. Vachon just stood back and watched. "Some nights it was incredible," he says today. "Something would happen and the team would catch fire. It was unbelievable. Every guy would be skating as fast as he could. All of a sudden, I wouldn't have anything to do. The puck was always at the other end—and the goals, they never seemed to stop."

After their home loss to Montreal, the Leafs tore off two wins. On Thursday in Boston, Toronto scored four unanswered goals in the last period to dig out of a 3–1 hole. Stemkowski's line led the comeback: Pete recorded a hat trick, his first, and Pappin counted the winner. Two days later, the Bruins were in Toronto and up to their old tricks, playing fiercely for forty minutes, then falling through the ice. With an exhausted Orr faced the wrong way, Keon found Armstrong alone in front with seconds left to give Toronto a 4–3 win.

On Sunday in New York, the Leafs were victims of Sweet Feet's ninth shut-out. The loss dropped Toronto into a tie with Montreal, and brought the Rangers to within a point of second. Punch pretended not to care. "We're gonna finish second, don't worry," he said after the game.

On the eve of his team's crucial Wednesday match in Montreal, Punch repeated his mantra. "We're going to finish second," he told Red Fisher. "Canadiens can't win 'em all. They'll find some way to fuck up." The quote, delivered in enemy territory, was typical Imlach. Punch loved antagonizing Blake and the Canadiens.

"With the team they've got right now, I don't think Montreal is going to make the play-offs," Imlach predicted at the start of the 63–64 season. Montreal finished first and Toronto third, but Punch was as cocky as ever going into the post-season, telling everyone, "We can take Chicago in spades and Montreal in hearts. The Canadiens—ha, they're nothing but a bunch of singers' midgets."

"It was a game Punch played, certainly not our style," comments Pollock without humour. "It bugged me something awful," Ferguson says. "That's one of the reasons I worked so hard against Toronto. I know some of the other boys felt that way, too. We wanted to throw those words right back in his face. Geez, who knew why he did it? Our games with the Leafs didn't need anybody to be building them up. Both teams were always ready to go."

In fact, the Leafs were ready to go the day before the showdown with Montreal. Fights broke out during an inter-squad workout on Tuesday. Imlach, upset at what he perceived to be his club's delicate play in New York, stripped defensemen of their sticks, insisting they use the body during the work-out. That led to ugly bashing along the boards. The third time they collided, Jeffrey, who had a stick, took a Willie Mays cut at Hillman's head. "We're gonna finish in second place," a satisfied Imlach predicted after practice.

Both Montreal and Toronto were nervous early on in their last big Wednesday-night encounter this season. The Leaf passers were colourblind and Sawchuk coughed up fat rebounds. The Habs enjoyed an edge in play but were overexcited. With open nets, Rousseau and Richard hurried shots wide. Béliveau rang one off the post. Ferguson put Backstrom offside on a two-on-one. Toronto scored first, with Hillman, working with a stick now, banging a Mahovlich set-up past a falling Vachon. Still, it seemed inevitable the Canadiens would take over. The Leafs were sloppy and Sawchuk just looked beatable, flopping about his crease as if in a malarial daze.

Laperrière took a penalty at nine minutes, but it was the Canadiens who jumped to the attack. Provost, wound taut from two weeks on the bench, sped around pointman Pappin and dashed in on Sawchuk. Terry made the save, but never located the rebound 15,374 screaming Forum fans, along with Jean-Guy Talbot, saw settling like a dropped coin in the crease. After Jean-Guy's goal, with Leafs still on the power play, Provost sent Talbot in free. The penalty killer had the puck alone with Sawchuk dead on the ice, but hit the crossbar.

For the next ten minutes, the Habs were all over Toronto. "Those first periods with Montreal in the Forum were murder," Kelly remembers. "Fans were screaming and the Canadiens were skating. Well, you felt like you were riding a bronco in a rodeo. But if you could just ride that horse for a while, get through the first period in decent shape, then you had a chance. Cause then they would settle down. But you couldn't make a mistake ever. If you did, back they'd come again."

It seemed the Leafs might escape without further damage, but with a minute left, Rousseau swung into Toronto's zone, dipsying past one Leaf, doodling by another, always on the verge of collapse, but continuing somehow on top of Sawchuk, before lateralling to Gilles Tremblay, who chipped one in the empty net.

The Forum crowd was savouring the announcement—"avec l'aide de numero quinze, R-r-r-rober-r-r-t R-r-r-ousseau" when Kelly and Mahovlich broke out, with Harris and Harper back. The Big M got ahead of Harper. Red slowed, brought his stick back as if to pass, then whipped a shot along the ice past a motionless Vachon. The old-pro move allowed the Leafs to escape the first period with a tie.

But not the wrath of experts. Milt Schmidt, assistant GM of the Bruins, mentioned to a reporter, "Leafs gave the puck away twenty-one times that period. I thought only our club played that way." Jacques Plante, here doing TV analysis, was scathing about his old rival. "[Sawchuk's] fighting the puck," he said. "Something is the matter with him. He's not sharp. He's fumbling the puck. Funny, this place was the spot he used to be terrific."

Having survived the bronco ride, Leafs looked confident early in the second. Then came the mistake Kelly warned against: Baun took a bad penalty. Out skated the Hab power play—Rousseau and J.C. back, with Gilles Tremblay, Béliveau, and Cournoyer up front. Leafs still hadn't figured out what to do with Cournoyer.

"He was so fast," Conacher recalls. "Both as a skater and a shooter. And the other guys on the power play were all great playmakers. You had to watch them. Cournoyer would get loose when you were chasing the puck. Béliveau would find him and it was in the net before you could do anything."

It took thirty seconds for Yvan to score his eleventh power play goal against Toronto this season. It happened as Conacher remembered. Habs moved the puck. Leafs chased. Then Béliveau slapped one to the breaking Cournoyer, who lashed the puck past Sawchuk, giving the Canadiens a 3–2 lead.

The goal sparked Montreal. The Forum was all "ooohs" and "ahhhs" as the Béliveau, Richard, Backstrom lines conducted a relay around the Leaf net, testing the wobbly Sawchuk from everywhere. Terry was a boxer out on his feet waiting for the finishing blow. That came when J.C. intercepted a pass at the blueline and leaned into a high shot at the heart of the Toronto net. Another game, Sawchuk would've steered the puck wide. Tonight, he took the puck in the chest, falling away from the rebound, which Rochefort knocked in to make it 4–2.

Imlach pulled Sawchuk. When action resumed, the Habs swooped in for the kill, testing Bower. The Canadiens might've put Leafs away, except Fergy was more interested in literal destruction of the enemy. Number 22 took three straight penalties, for high sticking, hooking, and tripping (John now had 171 total penalty minutes, shattering Lou Fontinato's club record).

If they were playing football, Punch might've declined the penalties. His team had given up three goals with a man advantage in four games. Leafs looked bad again first two power plays, but a new combination—Walton-Kelly-Ellis—pressed Vachon after Fergy's third infraction. Red emerged from the corner, danced free of Harris, then slipped a pass to Walton, who skimmed a shot past Rogie. Two minutes later, Fergy tried to atone for his sins, rushing furiously out from behind his net, only to have Stemkowski strip him and walk in alone. The centre lifted a backhand to an open corner that Vachon grabbed just under the crossbar. Fergy shuffled head down to the bench, where Toe let him cool for the next half-period.

Up one, Canadiens played carefully, shortening passes, taking fewer chances in Toronto's end. The Leafs collapsed into a familiar counter-attack mode. For twenty minutes the game was classic Montreal-Toronto hockey: fast, hard-hitting, with the Habs in control, but the imperturbable Leafs never more than a chance away from swinging the game around.

An old Leaf nemesis decided the game midway through the final period.

"I played a mental game," J.C. says. "Making the right anticipation. Maybe that's why I play well against Leafs. All the play-off and all the games we play, I knew them pretty well. If Pulford was centre, I could pinch because he was not so fast. I was not afraid of being beaten if I lost the puck. If Keon was centre, I would stay back, because he was so fast if something goes wrong he was away. Also, I know Bower and Sawchuk. Sawchuk comes out more, so maybe I fake a shot then pass. Bower, I shoot right away. Stuff like that. I don't know if I would be as good today. You see a team once a year, how are you suppose to know what to do?"

As Backstrom circled with the puck in the Leaf end, J.C. appraised the situation in a glance—Keon was off, Bower in nets—and stole in from the blueline. Ralph found the defenseman coasting at the circle. Tremblay skated into a low slapshot that flew between Bower's stick and glove. The perfect shot made it 5–3 Montreal.

It was all over but Imlach's shouting. Although Montreal had taken the majority of the penalties, Punch figured his team was jobbed. "A schoolboy could've done better," he hissed when asked about officiating afterwards. Punch was hot about a play late in the second. Pulford and Harris collided chasing a puck in front of Vachon. Pulford fell. Harris cleared. "My man is goin' in and he gets hooked," Imlach complained. "In Toronto [referee Bill Friday] calls a penalty shot on my side [an arcane reference to Nevin's penalty shot in early November]. Against Canadiens? Nothing! If my man isn't hooked, it's a 4–4 game. OK, let's say it could've been a 4–4 game. Canadiens were ready to be taken."

Punch had one more thing to say:

"We're still going to finish in second place, easy. Who's to say the Canadiens won't lose to Chicago, Saturday night? Or against Detroit, Sunday? Hell, they might lose both of them. All they have to do is screw up one and we're in. They didn't show me much tonight."

FIRST PERIOD

1. Toronto, Hillman 4th (Mahovlich) 8:15
2. Montreal, Talbot 3rd (Provost, Harris) 9:41
3. Montreal, G. Tremblay 13th (Rousseau) 19:08
4. Toronto, Kelly 14th (Ellis, Mahovlich) 19:38

Penalties—Pronovost (tripping) 2:43; Laperrière (charging) 9:01

SECOND PERIOD

5. Montreal, Cournoyer 24th (J.C. Tremblay, Béliveau) 4:34
6. Montreal, Rochefort 8th (J.C. Tremblay) 7:25
7. Toronto, Walton 6th (Ellis, Kelly) 13:21

Penalties—Laperrière (holding) 1:08; Baun (cross-checking) 3:59; Ferguson (high-sticking) 5:59; Ferguson (hooking) 9:09; Ferguson (tripping) 11:34; Stemkowski (boarding) 14:11

THIRD PERIOD

8. Montreal, J.C. Tremblay 8th (Backstrom, Ferguson) 8:33

Penalties—Baun (fighting) 10:01; Backstrom (fighting and high-sticking) 10:01

Shots on goal

Toronto	10	14	8 — 32
Montreal	25	18	12 — 55

Going into the final weekend, the streaking Habs could still finish second or (gulp!) fourth. But they controlled their destiny, being one up on New York, and two ahead of Toronto. The Hawks were in Montreal on Saturday, without Hull, who'd banged up a knee earlier in the week. Chicago was also, it could be argued, without motivation, having taken the season title weeks ago. Reay felt otherwise. "We've played well here all season; we don't want to give anything back now," he said. This wasn't press agentry. Everyone predicted a Montreal-Chicago final. The Hawks had lost once to the Habs all year. A blow-out tonight could erase that momentum.

It was clear early there'd be no blow-out. After Henri set up Balon at three minutes, both teams fell back and the game turned into a mid-ice scrum. Chicago found itself late in the second, with Esposito passing to Dennis Hull, who blew the equalizer past Vachon. Then the Scooter Line paralyzed J.C. and Harris with a bewildering weave of passes that left both defenders and Vachon out of position, and Mikita alone in front with the puck.

Down 2–1 with twenty minutes to go, Toe rallied the troops. "You're not shooting enough. Give me twenty shots this period and we'll be OK." This was Blake's great talent as a coach: to reduce dressing-room strategy to simple workable concepts. "He didn't fool around between period," Béliveau recalls. "The lesson was always short and sweet."

The Habs went out and pelted DeJordy with nineteen shots; the Hawks responded with nine of their own, all of them choice, in a superior period of shinny. First it was Montreal, with Backstrom's line winning scraps in the corner, moving inexorably toward DeJordy, forcing one...two shots on net. Esposito then drifted over Montreal's blueline and found Hodge free. The muscular winger bowled Vachon over with a windmill blast. Hodge and Harper raced for the rebound. Esposito moved to the slot. Laperrière pursued the big centre, whittling away with his stick, but it was like whacking a statue with a broom. The pass was on Esposito's stick briefly, then behind Vachon.

Three-one, Chicago.

A minute later, Cournoyer caught Henri at mid-ice. The little centre took a hopping stride to move into high gear, flew around Pilote, drew DeJordy, then slid a backhand in off the post.

Three-two, Chicago.

Stapleton was tossed a minute later. Béliveau won the draw. Gilles Tremblay shot. DeJordy got a pad out, but Yvan whipped in the rebound. Seven seconds. All it took was seven seconds.

Three-all.

Béliveau and Cournoyer were in on DeJordy again. The defense pinched. A shot went wide. Chicago had the puck and in two long passes, Nesterenko was in alone on Vachon, faking, deking, scoring.

Four-three, Chicago.

Montreal forced the play, digging, skating. Midway through the period, Rousseau peddled through the Hawk zone, swooped, circled, then ripped an off-balance shot, which DeJordy stopped, but Fergy, bursting between defenders, got a fast stick on the rebound.

Four-all.

Cournoyer, Béliveau, and J.C. enjoyed consecutive chances. Then Mikita had the puck, with time to scheme inside the Hab blueline, but Harper deflected a pass that would've freed Wharram. Seconds later, with the Scooters up ice, Backstrom's line broke in on Pilote and Jarrett. Ralph veered to the middle, drawing the defenders tight, then threw a pass outside to Larose. The racing winger cut around Jarrett, locked eyes with DeJordy, then slipped a pass to Ferguson, who was steaming through the middle, wearing Pilote around him like a robe. Before falling, Fergy steered in his twentieth goal of the season.

Five-four, and game, Montreal.

What an ending! These are the best clubs in hockey—what a Stanley Cup finals a Hawks-Canadiens series would make, fans remarked as they quit the Forum for the cool Montreal night. Inside the old building, however, Blake had another message for his team. "We haven't got second place yet. There's still a game left. Let's not forget about those Red Wings. Detroit scares me most of all," the always-cautious coach lied.

On the eve of the final weekend of the season, Baun and Keon got into a stick-swinging duel at practice. At scrimmage's end, Imlach blew his whistle. "OK, stops and starts for anybody who thinks they need them. Do as many as you think are necessary. If you don't think you need any, get the hell off the ice." Although the team had worked hard for six months, nobody left the rink for another half-hour.

The next night, the Leafs pounded New York 5–1. The team banged, checked and played tenacious defense, while maintaining their offensive edge. Pappin scored two, and Mahovlich, Walton and Horton contributed singles. Sunday, in Boston, the goals continued: Pulford, the Big M, and Ellis scored in the first twenty minutes, and Pulford and Keon added third-period markers on the way to an easy 5–2 win over the Bruins.

"I'm satisfied where we are right now," Imlach said at game's end. Why not? The Leafs hadn't put together better games back-to-back all season. Especially encouraging was Bower's play. Johnny was the China Wall, his old nickname in Cleveland, both evenings. Leafs hadn't received this kind of goaltending since back when Clancy was in charge.

After Saturday's match, Bower bumped into Rudy Pilous, manager of the expansion Oakland Golden Seals, in the runway. "God, but you made it look easy," Pilous said, slapping Bower on the back. "You think it's easy?" the forty-two-year-old goalie moaned. It had reached seventy degrees in Toronto that day, a record, and the Gardens was a sauna. Bower was a river of sweat. "Sure. You're playing from memory," Pilous joked, alluding to the team's glory years of the early sixties.

Would his teammates also be able to recapture the old magic? They'd find out soon. The Leafs would open the play-offs in Chicago on Thursday night.

The Leafs were playing the Hawks because the Habs had dumped the Red Wings 4–2 Sunday in Detroit. (The win meant Montreal would open at home against New York in four days.) Béliveau had played his best game this season, scoring, setting up another goal, and firing nine shots on net. Henri also scored. The centres were ready. The team was ready. Even Blake was pleased. "[The Canadiens] played a ter-rific third period," the coach beamed.

The Black Hawks also indicated they had lots of hockey left, drubbing the Rangers 8–0 Sunday in New York. "We're number one!" a band of visiting Hawk fans chanted at one point (before being drowned out by a long chorus of "We're number four!" from Ranger partisans). The Hawks were number one. Seventeen points and sixty-two goals better than second-place Montreal. The team's eight-goal explosion gave them 262 for the season, three more than Montreal's record total in the 1961–62 season. The Scooter Line tallied seven points to establish a new season record for a line (232). And DeJordy's shutout lowered Chicago's league-leading goals against average to 2.42. "We're ready," said Mikita after the game.

Everybody was ready. Now came the play-offs—two quick sprints after the marathon regular season.

1966–67 FINAL STANDINGS

	P	W	L	T	F	A	Pts
Chicago	70	41	17	12	264	170	94
Montreal	70	32	25	13	202	188	77
Toronto	70	32	27	11	204	211	75
New York	70	30	28	12	188	189	72
Detroit	70	27	39	4	212	241	58
Boston	70	17	43	10	182	253	44

LEAGUE LEADERS

	GP	G	A	Pts	PIM
Mikita, Chi.	70	35	62	97	12
R. Hull, Chi.	66	52	28	80	52
Ullman, Det.	68	26	42	68	26
Wharram, Chi.	70	31	34	65	21
Howe, Det.	68	25	40	65	53
Rousseau, Mont.	68	19	44	63	58
Goyette, N.Y.	70	12	49	61	6
Esposito, Chi.	69	21	40	61	40
Mohns, Chi.	62	25	35	60	58
Richard, Mont.	65	21	34	55	28
Delvecchio, Det.	70	17	38	55	10
Keon, Tor.	66	19	33	52	2
Pilote, Chi.	70	6	46	52	90
Bucyk, Bos.	59	18	30	48	12
Hampson, Det.	65	13	35	48	4
MacGregor, Det.	70	28	19	47	14
Gilbert, N.Y.	64	28	18	46	12
D. Marshall, N.Y.	70	24	22	46	4
Mahovlich, Tor.	63	18	28	46	44
Prentice, Det.	68	23	22	45	18
Ellis, Tor.	67	22	23	45	14
Pulford, Tor.	67	17	28	45	28
Geoffrion, N.Y.	58	17	28	45	42
Nevin, N.Y.	67	20	24	44	6
Martin, Bos.	70	20	23	43	40
D. Hull, Chi.	70	25	17	42	33
Ferguson, Mont.	67	20	22	42	173
Backstrom, Mont.	68	14	27	41	39
Orr, Bos.	61	13	28	41	102
Cournoyer, Mont.	69	25	15	40	14
Howell, N.Y.	70	12	28	40	54
Béliveau, Mont.	52	12	26	38	22
Maki, Chi.	56	9	29	38	14
Nesterenko, Chi.	68	14	23	37	38
Kelly, Tor.	61	13	24	37	4
McKenzie, Bos.	69	17	19	36	98
Kurtenbach, N.Y.	60	11	25	36	58
Larose, Mont.	69	19	16	35	82
K. Hodge, Chi.	68	10	25	35	59
Oliver, Bos.	65	9	26	35	16
Stemkowski, Tor.	68	13	22	35	75
Bergman, Det.	70	5	30	35	121
J.C. Tremblay, Mont.	60	8	26	34	14

LEAGUE LEADERS (*continued*)

Stapleton, Chi.	70	3	31	34	54
Hadfield, N.Y.	69	13	20	33	80
Armstrong, Tor.	70	9	24	33	26
Pappin, Tor.	64	21	11	32	89
G. Tremblay, Mont.	62	13	19	32	16
Fleming, N.Y.	61	15	16	31	146
Bathgate, Det.	60	8	23	31	24
Shock, Bos.	66	10	20	30	8
Connelly, Bos.	64	13	16	29	12
Jeffrey, Tor.	57	11	17	28	27
Conacher, Tor.	66	14	13	27	47
Murphy, Bos.	39	11	16	27	6
Jarrett, Chi.	70	5	21	26	76
Shack, Tor.	63	11	14	25	58
F. Smith, Det.	54	11	14	25	8
Horton, Tor.	70	8	17	25	70
Stewart, Bos.	56	14	10	24	31
Provost, Mont.	64	11	13	24	16
Duff, Mont.	51	12	11	23	23
L. Hillman, Tor.	55	4	18	22	40
Williams, Bos.	29	8	13	21	2
Boivin, Det.	68	4	17	21	78
Hay, Chi.	36	7	13	20	12
Laperrière, Mont.	61	0	20	20	48
Balon, Mont.	48	11	8	19	31
Van Impe, Chi.	61	8	11	19	111
Dillabough, Bos.	60	6	12	18	14
Angotti, Chi.	63	6	12	18	21
Harris, Mont.	65	2	16	18	86
Walton, Tor.	31	7	10	17	13
Young, Det.	44	3	14	17	100
Rochefort, Mont.	27	9	7	16	6
Cullen, Det.	28	8	8	16	8
Green, Bos.	47	6	10	16	67
Harper, Mont.	55	0	16	16	99
Marotte, Bos.	67	7	8	15	112
Neilson, N.Y.	61	4	11	15	65
Watson, Bos.	69	2	13	15	38
Pronovost, Tor.	58	2	12	14	28
W. Hillman, N.Y.	67	2	12	14	43
Stanley, Tor.	53	1	12	13	20
Brown, N.Y.	69	2	10	12	61
Ratelle, N.Y.	41	6	5	11	4
Boyer, Chi.	42	5	6	11	15

LEAGUE LEADERS (*continued*)

Baun, Tor.	56	2	8	10	83
B. Marshall, Det.	57	0	10	10	48
Schinkel, N.Y.	20	6	3	9	0
Woytowich, Det.	64	2	7	9	43
Krake, Bos.	15	6	2	8	4
Goldsworthy, Bos.	18	3	5	8	21
Talbot, Mont.	69	3	5	8	51
D. Roberts, Det.	12	3	2	5	0
Berenson, N.Y.	29	0	5	5	2
Wall, Det.	31	2	2	4	26
MacNeil, N.Y.	57	0	4	4	44
Rivers, Bos.	8	2	1	3	6
J. Roberts, Mont.	63	3	0	3	44
Ravlich, Chi.	62	0	3	3	39
Vadnais, Mont.	11	0	3	3	35
W. Smith, Chi.	2	1	1	2	2
Awrey, Bos.	4	1	0	1	6
B. Watson, Det.	48	0	1	1	62
Lonsberry, Bos.	8	0	1	1	2
Doak, Bos.	30	0	1	1	50
Carleton, Tor.	5	1	0	1	14
Peters, Mont.	4	0	1	1	2
McKenny, Tor.	2	1	0	1	2

GOALKEEPERS' RECORDS

	GP	GA	SO	AVG.
Chicago				
DeJordy	44	104	4	2.46
Hall	32	66	2	2.38
(Chicago totals)	70	170	6	2.43
New York				
Giacomin	68	175	9	2.61
Maniago	6	14	0	3.70
(New York totals)	70	189	9	2.70

GOALKEEPERS' RECORDS (*continued*)

Montreal				
Hodge	37	88	3	2.60
Vachon	20	48	1	2.48
Worsley	18	47	1	3.18
Bauman	2	5	0	2.50
(Montreal totals)	70	188	5	2.66
Toronto				
Sawchuk	27	66	2	2.81
Bower	27	65	2	2.66
Gamble	23	68	0	3.39
G. Smith	2	7	0	3.63
A. Smith	1	5	0	5.00
(Toronto totals)	70	211	4	3.01
Detroit				
Crozier	58	183	4	3.35
Gardner	11	36	0	3.85
Bassen	8	22	0	3.44
(Detroit totals)	70	241	4	3.44
Boston				
Johnston	34	112	0	3.70
Cheevers	22	72	1	3.33
Parent	18	61	0	3.71
(Boston totals)	70	245	1	3.61

Crowd noise
Firecracker Day

May 21 was Victoria Day. But no kid spoke of the great
grey governess of the pink dominion. It was Firecracker
Day. You bought the explosives at corner stores. Tiny,
harmless lady-fingers came in two-inch skirts and were
perfect for dropping into the windbreakers of dopey
cousins—*fft-ptt-fft-ptt-ftt*! Red firecrackers made great
joke-cigars for bullfrogs emerging from winter comas.
A cannon cracker could blow an empty can thirty feet high.
Yes, they were dangerous. Especially when you got a dud.
What you'd do then is break the cracker in half and light
the wounded middle. Out shot a flame three inches long.
Except sometimes the explosion would bazooka backwards
into your hand and then you had to go to the hospital.
Which is why Firecracker Day was banned. Once upon a
time, spring was the Stanley Cup and Firecracker Day.
Now the former is in summer and the latter doesn't exist.
Robins tell us when winter is over.

15
Ten O'Clock Galoshes

There's a smile in Vachon's voice when he remembers how management prepared the Canadiens for the Stanley Cup play-offs. "Before a series, Toe would come in and tell us how good the other team was," Vachon recalls. "We could beat them, but we'd have to play our best. Then he'd tell us not to say anything but positive things about the opposing team in the newspaper. 'Make yourselves the underdog,' he'd say. After that, Sam Pollock would come in the dressing-room and tell us all the same thing."

Prior to the Thursday, April 6 Hab-Ranger opener, Blake even lobbied bookies to shift the series odds, which were 13–5 Canadiens, more in favour of the Rangers. "Thirteen to five?" he cried. "Hell, odds should be 6–5—pick 'em!" Toe skated smooth as Béliveau around the Rangers' record (9–16–5 since the All Star game). "They beat us three times in our building this year," he pointed out. "Look at the year Giacomin's having. If he's hot…" Toe also said he was worried about all the ex-Canadiens who would be returning to the Forum.

Blake wasn't the only one concerned about the eight ex-Montrealers in the Ranger line-up. "We tried to instill pride in our players," Pollock says. "I think over the years we did a good job. But that became a problem, I suppose, when we traded a player. They had that pride...you worried about them coming back to haunt you."

Hours before game one, Toe did his best to mollify one ex-Canadien. The summer previous, Geoffrion returned to Montreal after being fired as coach of Quebec Aces. He understood he'd replace Blake some day. Toe's not ready to go, owner David Molson told him. Geoffrion was offered a job coaching the Junior Habs at $6,000. Bernie took the salary offer as a slap in the face.

"Put my name in the waiver draft. You may not want me, but somebody will," Boomer said. "I'm coming back to the Forum, and I'm going to whip your butt, Molson."

The last thing Blake wanted was a hot-eyed Geoffrion tearing down on his rookie goalie. So he made a point of bumping into Boom Boom before New York took the ice for afternoon practice.

"What the hell has Francis got that I didn't have," Toe said, patting Boomer's flat tummy. "When he says take it off, you take it off." After chuckling it up with his old right winger a while, Blake returned to his office to fret.

Emile Francis also worked the press prior to game one. In fact, he said the same thing as Blake: Forget New York's recent record, especially the 13-1 thrashing at the hands of Chicago and Toronto the last games of the season. "Going into the final weekend, [Montreal, Toronto, and New York] were so close you could've covered the three of us with a dime," he told New York reporters, lighting a cigarette. "In the play-offs, goaltending is half the battle. And we've got the best in the business. We can win those low-scoring games. We won four games 1–0 this year with Giacomin. Eight points on four goals. That's play-off hockey."

Ranger forwards were hot, Francis insisted. Marshall and Gilbert counted hat tricks in the same game recently. Hadfield had six goals in five contests since going to a curved stick. More important, everyone was healthy. The Cat lit another cigarette and imitated Jack Kennedy: "Few expected us to get into the play-offs—but we did. Few expect us to win the Stanley Cup—but we will."

Although he sounded confident, Francis was chain-smoking for a reason.

"We were a tired team going into the play-offs," he says today. "I had to play Goyette, Gilbert, Howell and Giacomin way too much the last half. Geez, I felt for Harry. What was he, thirty-five? and I'm playing him forty minutes a game down the stretch. He looked half-dead skating off some nights. But what could we do? We didn't have depth, eh? We had to do that just to make the play-offs."

But Francis thought the Rangers could win.

"Could? Oh sure," he says. "It wouldn't be easy but it could be done. Sure it could. What I wanted was for the defense to keep cool and for the forwards to hit them every turn. We wanted to slow 'em down, see. Now to do that we had to be skating ourselves. Cause if you weren't skating and tried to hit those Canadiens you'd take penalties, and they had the dandy power play. But if we could slow them to our speed, we figured we could take 'em. We had the better goaltending and some veterans who knew their way around the net. Slow 'em down, sure we could beat them."

First period, opening game went pretty much as both coaches hoped. Montreal's centres controlled play, and the defense was unyielding, holding Rangers to a few long shots. As promised, New York forwards hit, and blueliners Howell-Brown and MacNeil-Neilson kept their cool. Montreal had few real chances, just an occasional wrist shot from the circle, or a slapshot from well out, nothing the league's best goalie couldn't handle. Both teams returned to the dressing-room figuring they were right where they wanted to be.

In the second twenty minutes, Rangers found their early-season form. So did the Canadiens, unfortunately. At two minutes, Laperrière was tossed for cross-checking. New York turned to the attack. Berenson found room inside the blueline. Harper fell to block his shot. Gilbert jumped on the rebound, swung around, then spotted Geoffrion loose at the point. Boom Boom's low screamer threaded a dozen legs and sticks past Vachon.

Take that, David Molson.

Montreal rallied. Béliveau sent Gilles Tremblay in. Giacomin hugged the post until the winger shifted in front, then lunged, spearing the puck wide. A minute later, Larose had a clear path to the goal. Eddie moved out quickly, making the net disappear behind him. A few minutes later, New York suffered a perilous moment during a Hab power play, but Giacomin, then a diving Howell made saves.

"Harry was the best defenseman I ever saw blocking shots," Giacomin remembers. "He just seemed to know when a guy was shooting and when he was faking. He was another goalie out there. When he went down on the short side, you knew it was covered. He wouldn't give a foot inside the post like some guys. So I knew I could swing over to the other post. Some nights we blocked the whole net."

Howell was off when Canadiens finally struck. Harper went on a dangling adventure down the right boards, veered in at centre, backhanding to Larose, who cut around Neilson, driving to the net. Again, Giacomin came out. Claude leaned into a shot—stopped, lifted his head, then lobbed a pass to the middle for Backstrom, who smacked in the tying goal.

Canadiens had the game in hand when a scrap broke out in front of Montreal's net. Ingarfield pushed Laperrière. The defenseman shoved back, letting an elbow ride high. Earl threw his hands to his face and dropped to one knee. After the whistle, the Ranger centre eagerly offered a bloody mitt to Art Skov. He nodded gravely, then signalled a major penalty. Blake exploded at the Montreal bench. Skov pretended not to hear.

"I'd deal with Béliveau," the referee says. "Blake didn't want to talk, just scream. Béliveau, he never hollered. He'd look at you very closely and say, 'Are you sure?' Once, I made a call, Jean kept following me around, asking, 'Are you sure?' 'Yeah, I'm sure.' 'You're really sure?' This went on a long time. After a while, cripes I wasn't sure. Intermission, I went in and got the rulebook, brought it out next period when players were skating around. I see Béliveau, I yell over, 'Jean, I'll show you.' He just laughed and waved me away."

New York conducted themselves with admirable cool during the five-minute advantage. There was no greedy rush to fill the net. The Rangers were cautious in their end, deliberate in Montreal's zone. Three minutes into the power play, Gilbert took a pass wide of the circle and let a low slapshot go at the crowded bus stop that was the Montreal crease. Vachon, spreadeagled, took the shot on his pad, but the short rebound hit Harris's stick and disappeared between his legs.

"If we were down going into the third, Toe wouldn't get mad in the dressing-room," Harper recalls. "He'd focus on what was wrong. If Jacques took a couple of bad penalties, he'd say, 'Listen, penalties are killing us.' Other guys made mistakes, he'd point 'em out, but in a general way. Saying positions, not names. Then he'd leave. Nothing fancy, eh? But he'd done a job on team psyche. Like saying 'defense.' If he yelled 'Laperrière, you son-of-a—' Jacques'd be mad. By saying 'defense' you could say he let him off the hook. And Jacques would've appreciated that. Except everybody knew who Blake meant. I was in Jacques' position many times. You felt eighteen guys looking at you like you let 'em down. That got you more than being yelled at directly. He drops two, three messages like that going into the third, maybe he's got ten players feeling they've let the team down, and out we go, as a team, ready to really work."

With the start of the third, Montreal raced to the attack. Béliveau's line put in a minute of determined labour. Richard's trio pressed hard. Too hard, in fact; Balon picked up a penalty (maybe he was in the loo during Toe's speech). A minute later, Gilbert intercepted a clearing pass. His rising backhand was wide of the goal, but not poor Laperrière. The puck struck Jacques' arm, bouncing past Vachon.

Next Rogie made a mistake. Kurtenbach grabbed the puck inside the blueline, and let go a shot Vachon stopped easily, then left to the side for J.C. Except J.C. wasn't there. Hadfield was. Now the score was 4–1.

With Hadfield's goal the anger that had simmered through the Forum since Laperrière's major finally boiled over. Whenever Jacques touched the puck, the crowd turned ugly. Vachon's saves were greeted with derisive cheers. A raw, hostile energy crackled through the overpacked rink. Even the Canadien players bristled.

"When we were down all those goals, we saw some Rangers laughing at us on the ice," Cournoyer remembers. "I can't remember which ones, but I remember they were, and, oh boy, we were mad on the bench."

The lowly Rangers laughing at the champion Canadiens in the first game of a seven-game series?

"Geez, if I saw any of our guys out there laughing I think I would've walked out on the ice and strangled them," Francis says, groaning. "No way. Absolutely no way."

Perhaps not. Probably not. But Canadiens perceived some slight. Sometimes it didn't take much. In the 1966 play-offs, a few Red Wings leaving the Forum with White Owls wagging from their jaws was deemed a mortal insult. What Habs were most upset about, of course, was the score. So were the fans. The atmosphere in the Forum, both in the stands and on the rink, was charged.

One Canadien partisan did manage to keep his cool. "No matter how hot things got, Toe was calm," Harper remembers. "The crowd would be roaring, and the players would be flying back and forth, but Toe never panicked. Funny, sometimes it seemed like he became calmer."

In the middle of the furor, down three with fifteen minutes to go, Toe calmly re-arranged his line-up: Duff and Provost were dusted off and thrown out with Rousseau at centre. Gilles Tremblay replaced Ferguson on Backstrom's line. Béliveau now centred Ferguson and Cournoyer. The changes picked the team up instantly. The return of the hustling Provost in particular ignited the fans. Soon the Canadiens were flying. But with eleven minutes left they were still down three. And Giacomin was hot.

"That night I felt great," Eddie remembers. "Even though we were ahead 4–1, we weren't killing them. We just managed to get some good bounces and I was having a good game. Midway into the period I was loose, focussed. Everything was automatic."

Then the young goalie made a mistake.

"Geez, I can still remember that play," he says. "Provost had the puck in the corner. I was looking for him to pass and he shot. I moved my leg, but the puck caught the corner. He had no business scoring. I thought I had the side covered, but I guess I gave him a couple of inches. Give him credit, though, he made the shot."

Provost's goal "was like a blazing torch thrown into an open case of fireworks," Red Fisher wrote. A wild, excited roar raced the building. The crowd was still on its feet, cheering, when Richard won the centre face-off. The Habs rushed back. Henri took a pass inside the Ranger blueline and swung in on Giacomin. Three Rangers converged. The centreman swooped wide to the boards, turned, and passed to J.C. between the circles. Giacomin stiffened upon seeing Tremblay, as if he'd turned on a light and found a stranger in his room. J.C.'s quick shot sailed under the crossbar to make the score 4–3.

Down came rubber footwear from the stands—hundreds of toe rubbers and floppy galoshes. "This might hurt the Canadiens," TV play-by-play man Danny Gallivan would say. "Montreal might cool off in the length of time it takes for maintenace staff to clear the ice."

Harper disagrees.

"When those rubber galoshes came down in the Forum it meant the other team was dead," he says. "That was our fans intimidating the opposition, telling them that they were going to lose. The other team would sit there on the bench and have to think about what just happened while the galoshes came pouring down. Some nights, you'd look out there and the galoshes were so thick they looked like leaves under a tree in the fall."

In baseball, the Yankees referred to swift late afternoon rallies as "five o'clock lightning." Canadiens had the same thing. Only it happened at ten o'clock. And instead of lightning, you had galoshes.

"I never saw a team get back into the game after those galoshes came pouring down," Harper says.

With the ice cleared, the Habs resumed their frenzied assault. A minute after J.C. scored, Béliveau bulled through two defenders and fired a low shot Ferguson deflected past Giacomin. Then Larose found Backstrom in front and Montreal suddenly had the lead. Finally, Provost scooted down the right side, bringing the crowd to its feet (and the Ranger defense back into Giacomin's face), before dropping to Béliveau, who ripped a short slapshot in off the post to make it 6–4 Montreal.

Béliveau's goal provoked another shower of footwear. But the gesture was lost on New York. They knew they were beaten when J.C. scored the third goal.

"I wasn't too worried when Provost scored," Giacomin says. "We were up two, there was ten minutes left. But when they got the third one quickly we were in trouble. Emile told us to try and keep the fans out of the game. That goal they just went crazy. The noise for the next ten minutes was simply incredible. Suddenly, we were uptight. And the Canadiens just kept coming. They were a fantastic team."

Francis groans remembering the long-ago battle.

"Man, I tried everything I could think of to slow them down that third period," he says. "I told the guys to ice the puck. I took extra long with my line changes. Asked to speak to the ref a couple of times. Nothing worked. Heck, when those Canadiens started coming at you like that, only thing you could do was go out there and turn the net backwards."

FIRST PERIOD
No scoring
Penalties—Fleming, Harper, 9:27; Hadfield 16:03

SECOND PERIOD
1. New York, Geoffrion 1st (Berenson, Gilbert) 3:46
2. Montreal, Backstrom 1st (Larose, Harper) 9:34
3. New York, Gilbert 1st (Schinkel) 16:06
Penalties—Laperrière 2:32; Brown 5:51; Laperrière (major) 13:07

THIRD PERIOD
4. New York, Gilbert 2nd, 1:49
5. New York, Hadfield 1st (Kurtenbach) 5:18
6. Montreal, Provost 1st (Duff, Rousseau) 9:12
7. Montreal, J.C. Tremblay 1st (Richard) 9:34
8. Montreal, Ferguson 1st (Béliveau, Laperrière) 11:03
9. Montreal, Backstrom 2nd (Larose) 14:55

10. Montreal, Béliveau 1st (Provost, J.C. Tremblay) 18:07
Penalties—Balon 1:24; Hadfield 2:19; Hadfield 18:27

Shots on goal
New York   6   14   6 — 26
Montreal   10   11   15 — 36

The second game of the series was a miniature of the first. The same ingredients were all there, except on a smaller scale and in a slightly different order.

Habs attacked quickly. Rangers responded with a stern show of defense. Once again, Giacomin was in top form early. New York caught the game's first break when Marshall jumped in free during a sloppy Hab line change. Vachon kicked his low shot wide, earning a shout of approval from fans. The teams then settled into a cautious defensive game. Toe got restless early this day, however, and when Henri and Rochefort failed to force the issue on a power play, out came Duff for a rare (these days) shift alongside Béliveau. Seconds later, Rousseau, behind the net, played peek-a-boo with Neilson in front. The defenseman lost sight of Duff. Rousseau made a short, sharp pass. Dick shot quickly. One-nothing, Montreal.

Giacomin made a beautiful save on a Talbot breakaway early in the second, skating swiftly out to cut the angle, then dancing backwards, steering the shooter wide. The stop seemed to inspire teammates. New York fell into a comfortable rhythm: skating hard and hitting often, slowing Montreal down. When Béliveau took a penalty, the Rangers finally got their offense in gear. Vachon was sharp on a Hadfield deflection. Canadiens cleared. Now Geoffrion had the puck. At centre, he found an ancient forward gear, dipping around Harris. Rogie hung back, waiting to jump out quickly when Geoffrion wound up for his trademark slapshot. Boom Boom peered up from the top of the circle, saw a sliver of net to Vachon's long side, then snapped a forty-foot wrist shot in off the post to tie the game.

Montreal played fierce hockey to open the third, squeezing the game inside the Ranger blueline. Still, the match was tied when MacNeil made like Angelo Mosca at centre, tackling Rochefort. Half a minute into the ensuing power play there was a face-off in Ranger end. Blake sized up his line-up—J.C. and Rousseau back, Gilles Tremblay, Béliveau, and Cournoyer up front—chewed his lip, then tapped Ferguson on the shoulder. Number 22 hopped the boards and Gilles skated off.

"Where do you want me?" Fergy asked Béliveau at the circle.

"Front of the net, between the circles," Jean replied.

Referee Bill Friday dropped the puck. Marshall beat Béliveau on the draw. Brown turned to fire the puck. Cournoyer jumped in front of the defenseman. The puck hit Yvan on the shin and shot over to Ferguson, still in place between the circles. Fergy banged the puck into the empty net to give his team the lead.

Down came the galoshes. (The match was played Saturday afternoon to accommodate U.S. television, but any match in the Forum seemed like an evening game, which meant it felt like ten o'clock when Fergy scored.) Five minutes later, Backstrom finished off the Rangers by ripping a Larose pass over the sprawling Giacomin.

At the end of every game, reporters gather around the big scorer or defensive hero. This afternoon they surrounded Blake. On Thursday, his line tinkering had led to five goals. Today, Blake moves resulted in two more goals.

"Sometime we think Toe had a crystal ball," J.C. recalls. "So many times, I can't remember, he made a little move— put Billy Hickie, or Danny Grant out there, someone off the bench, the guy hadn't played all game. Oops, right away he scored. This happened year after year. It was incredible."

Toe accepted the reporters' kudos with weary resignation. "I'm a great goal-scorer alright," he harrumphed. "I'm a genius—until the next game." In fact, Toe didn't want to dwell at all on the Forum triumphs. There were at least two more games to worry about.

"This isn't a three-game series, you know," he told reporters in a voice loud enough for players to hear.

"Toe, he always worried," Harper remembers. "Especially in the play-offs. If we lost a game he worried we were going into a bad streak, maybe on our way to losing the series. But then if we won two or three games in a row, he'd worry about us letting down for a moment. The day after we won the Stanley Cup, that's the day he stopped worrying."

FIRST PERIOD
1. Montreal, Duff 1st (Rousseau, Béliveau) 8:55
Penalties—Harris 1:23; Hadfield 3:20; Cournoyer 4:50; Howell 7:17; Hadfield 11:37; Brown 12:24; Ferguson 13:40

SECOND PERIOD
2. New York, Geoffrion 2nd (Kurtenbach, Gilbert) 12:03
Penalties—Vadnais 2:41; Béliveau minor and 10-minute misconduct 10:24; Gilbert 12:39; Balon 15:14; Ferguson 17:37

THIRD PERIOD
3. Montreal, Ferguson 2nd (Cournoyer, Béliveau) 7:46
4. Montreal, Backstrom 3rd (Larose) 13:25
Penalties—Ratelle (bench minor) 2:50; McNeil 6:55

Shots on goal
New York   11   8   8 — 27
Montreal   10   9   12 — 31

"As soon as the series swung to New York, I brung my guys together," Emile Francis recalls. "I reminded 'em how close we come to winning in the Forum. And that wasn't a bit of exaggeration. Heck, they don't get that funny goal in the third period, first game, we win for sure. Second game was close, too. Now I tell 'em, 'This is a whole different ball of wax— we're in our rink, with our fans behind us, and we know they'll be hopping. All we gotta do is turn it up a little and we got 'em. Skate and hit a little harder, play a little tougher, we win.'"

The Cat was right about one thing: the playoff-starved Ranger crowd was primed for Tuesday's third game. They'd started "hopping" two weeks earlier, when tickets went on sale. Seven o'clock that Monday morning, nine thousand fans were in line at 49th and Eighth, when someone yelled, 'Doors

open!' They weren't. The line rushed forward, exploding sideways in both directions, carrying fans 100 yards from spots
they'd secured twenty hours earlier. Fights broke out. People
were trampled. It took police five hours to restore order.

Now those fans were in Madison Square Garden,* waiting
to pounce on the Canadiens.

Tonight, the Garden crowd started making noise during the
opening bars of the American anthem. By the time referee
John Ashley dropped the puck it sounded like a jet was taking
off. The first hit occurred before the contest was a second old,
when Fleming banged Backstrom during the opening draw.

"In the play-offs, we were use to other teams trying to
intimidate us on the road," Béliveau says. "It was natural. We
were a better skating team, so they would try and hit us to
slow us down. Maybe their fans would get excited and make
them play better. It was always that way when I was on the
Canadiens. What would we do? Score goals. If we got a lead,
we would quiet down the crowd and take away [the opposition's] aggressiveness."

After taking a jolt from Fleming, Backstrom directed a
short pass to Ferguson, who circled then threw a pass back to
his breaking centre. Backstrom worked into the Ranger end,
falling into a slapshot from a sharp angle near the boards. The
blast surprised Giacomin, hitting him high in the chest.
Larose got the rebound and it was 1–0 Montreal. The
Canadiens had removed the crowd in thirteen seconds.

A minute later, Fleming ran Harper, who retaliated. Both
were tossed. At five a side, Canadiens showed off their skating
game. Béliveau flew down the middle and beat Giacomin
with a short, deadly slapshot from outside the circle.

---

* From 1925 to 1968, Madison Square Garden was located on Eighth Ave.
and 50th St. This was actually the Garden's second location. The original
building, which was located at Madison Ave. and 26th St., was constructed in
1879, then torn down and rebuilt further uptown (by architect Stanford
White) in 1890. "It was a funny old barn, but we called it home," Francis
said of the old Garden. The rink was small and the ice surface substandard.
After the Zamboni returned to its lair, pigeons swooped down and drank from
small glacial pools in corners of the rink. One game this season, Francis complained, "I've seen better ice on Saskatchewan roads in winter."

The Habs might've cruised from there, except for a call that seemed, at first, in their favour. Béliveau was nicked for roughing. Goyette hopped on as the extra attacker and flipped a backhand past Rogie. Ashley disallowed the goal, claiming Montreal touched the puck. The Cat leapt snarling to the boards, one paw on the glass, to get at the official. Fans emptied lungs and pockets, showering the referee with fruit, chocolate bars, and an angry chorus of "Ashley's a bum!"

The crowd was back. Soon so were the Rangers. For the rest of the period, New York played with wounded rage, winning fights for pucks all over the ice. Vachon was superb here, attacking shooters like the ghost of Jacques Plante. Finally, late in the period, Rangers got one back on a power play when Neilson sneaked into the slot and threw a fifteen-footer between Rogie's pads.

The Canadiens regrouped in the intermission and scored quickly in the second, with Rousseau tipping a Richard shot over Giacomin's shoulder. The Rangers wouldn't give up, however, and three minutes later, after New York put on a robust display of forechecking, exciting a wild, glass-thumping ovation along the boards, Fleming found Ingarfield free in the slot to make it 3–2 Montreal.

The Rangers had momentum and the support of an untamable crowd. But after Ingarfield's goal, the Canadiens proved they had the better team, raising the game's tempo to a speed the Rangers couldn't match. In the last half of the period, New York managed two shots on Vachon. The Habs tested Giacomin repeatedly. Duff, on a sweet Béliveau set-up, picked the top corner, only to have Giacomin, falling backwards, snatch the puck from the mouth of the net. Then the goalie swept across the crease to turn away Richard. Late in the period, Gilles Tremblay, again on a Béliveau pass, had an open net. Shot. But somehow Giacomin materialized, kicking the puck wide.

The Rangers knew their seasons were on the line in the third period and threw themselves recklessly into battle. The first ten minutes raced at the pace of a "metronome gone haywire," according to Gerald Eskenazi of the New York *Times*. After that, Béliveau, Richard, and Backstrom took over. Time

and again, Rangers lobbed the puck in and gave chase. But a
Hab defenseman would get there first. A pass later, Béliveau
or Richard was swinging the other way. One rinkside fan grew
so frustrated he reached over the glass and tried to wrestle
away Henri's stick.

In the game's last minutes, Toe finished off New York by
double-shifting Béliveau, his best player this evening, on a
new line with Talbot and Provost. Francis responded a minute
later by pulling Giacomin. It didn't help. Playing six skaters,
New York still looked undermanned. The match ended with
Béliveau ragging the puck in New York's end, ringing a last-
second shot off the goalpost.

After the game, Red Fisher caught up with a reflective
Béliveau on the way back to the hotel:

> We walked on the street of lights that is Broadway
> and talked about the evening's work. As usual there
> was a slight shrug of the shoulders when his part in
> the production was mentioned. He looked at the peo-
> ple as the reflections of neon played on their faces and
> then he touched on some of the other grand nights
> and why, in his view, he enjoyed them.
>
> "You go back...I think about the nights when I knew
> I could go on the ice and skate and skate. It is some-
> thing you cannot explain. You feel good and then you
> know how good it is when you skate and skate.
>
> "Tonight...maybe it was not as good as the other
> years, but I cannot think of another night when I felt
> so good...so strong. I think about it, but I cannot
> explain it."

The Habs were now just a game away.

FIRST PERIOD
1. Montreal, Larose 1st (Backstrom, Ferguson) 0:13
2. Montreal, Béliveau 2nd (Rousseau) 3:09
3. New York, Neilson 1st (Fleming, Nevin) 16:51
Penalties—Harper, Fleming 1:26; Béliveau 4:27; Rousseau 15:48

SECOND PERIOD
4. Montreal, Rousseau 1st (Richard, J.C. Tremblay) 2:05
5. New York, Ingarfield 1st (Fleming, Nevin) 4:34
Penalties—Hillman 0:06; Berenson 7:13

THIRD PERIOD
No scoring
Penalties—Howell 11:19

Shots on goal
Montreal   11   13   14 — 38
New York   15   9   6 — 30

Blake, who never liked a satisfied club, managed to find something to rile his team during the Wednesday off-day in New
York. The circus was at the Garden, which meant the
Canadiens practiced in Iceland. Not the country. Iceland was
what Rangers called their practice rink, located on the fifth
floor of the Garden. Twenty yards wide, thirty-five, maybe
forty yards long, the rink was egg-shaped at one end and had
metal boards. Blake hated it.

"I think it's a disgrace," Toe fumed one practice. "I mean
here we are in the middle of the hockey playoffs and we have
to play second fiddle to a bunch of clowns. Pretty soon, they'll
ask us to dress with the elephants."

Later that night, Blake tossed in bed, trying to decide
whether to start Gump next game. If he needed Worsley in
the finals, he'd be cold. Then again, Vachon had strung
together six good periods. The team was winning. By morning, he'd decided to stick with Rogie.

"I figured that if the kid was going to have a bad night it
would be in New York," he said before game four. "After all,
it's quite a lot of pressure to come into a strange rink with all
those people yelling. But I just kicked it around in my head
for a while. When it came right down to it, I couldn't see
myself doing it."

Toe felt game three featured "more checking and body con-
tact than the other two [in Montreal] put together." Thursday
night, the pounding was doubled again, as the cornered

Blueshirts fought to leave New York alive. In the first period, Ranger players popped Canadiens at every turn. In corners. At mid-ice. Face-offs turned into wrestling matches. Fans cheered every hit, especially the one Fleming laid on Harper at five minutes: a piston jab that sent Terry to one knee.

The Canadiens hung on, mainly because of their blueliners. In the first period, Rangers had dozens of chances, but only six shots got to the net, and only a third of those, in-close efforts by Nevin and Hadfield, tested Vachon. The remaining shots ended up in Harper and Laperrière's legs, or Harris's stomach. Maybe the best Hab defender was J.C. Despite all the mayhem, number three calmly went about his business, slipping vicious checks as he picked his way out of danger. Tremblay also made the period's best offensive play, taking a pass from Henri at the blueline and nailing a perfect screen shot along the ice inside the right post past Giacomin.

The second period was more of the same. The Cat's plan was working. Ranger hitting turned the contest into a series of battles along the boards, taking Montreal's centres out of the game. But Vachon and the Hab defense remained unbeaten. Montreal had the contest's only goal. And the ardour of the stomping, screaming fans could only survive so long on Kurtenbach and Fleming's crunching checks. Then, for the fifth time this series, the Habs were burned on a penalty. Fergy was chased for charging Howell. Goyette won the draw in Montreal's end. Marshall, from the corner, lobbed a shot into a scrum. The puck ticked off a skate onto Goyette's stick. Vachon moved quickly, but the puck trickled off his stabbing pad just inside the post.

The happy, screaming crowd threw together a quick celebratory ditty. "We're not dead yet, we're not dead yet," they sang. By the time the song reached pricey seats around the glass, the Habs were in trouble again. Another penalty, this time to Henri. Rangers stormed Vachon. Rogie made an alert toe save on a shot from a scramble ("kick save and a beauty!" Ranger radio announcer Marv Albert would say). With thirty seconds left, Howell moved in from the point, circled wide of an argument in front of Vachon, then, looking up, found Marshall alone at the opposite circle. The ex-Canadien sent a screamer toward the open net that J.C., appearing from nowhere, slid across to kick wide. Jumping up at the boards, Tremblay raced to the corner, knifed between two Rangers to get the puck, then lobbed a high shot down the ice to kill the remaining seconds.

The Rangers were greeted with a standing ovation and another chorus of "We're not dead yet!" to begin the third. No, not dead, but dying. Both teams were. Rangers seemed to abandon hope of scoring and lost themselves in a full-scale physical assault. Gilbert banged like Fleming. Fleming hit like a dropped anvil. The Montreal big men, Ferguson, Harris, Harper, and Béliveau, retaliated. By the end of the scoreless period, only the crowd was upright. In fact they were standing, screaming for more. This was the play-offs. No ties allowed. Overtime loomed.

"I don't think we were nervous in overtime," Francis remembers. "Not after the game we had played. Everyone was right in there scrapping. We always wanted [Montreal] in that position, where the next goal wins. You see, we had to play 'em close and hope we scored the last goal. We knew we weren't gonna win shoot-outs. No, I would've taken overtime every night."

"Me, I know I was only a rookie, but I wasn't nervous in overtime," Vachon says. "Really, there is no difference between overtime and the third period of a tie game in the play-offs. Oh, maybe you get a little nervous at first. But as a goalie, you have to concentrate so much, you forget you are nervous."

The Rangers tried to replay the third period in overtime. Hadfield even picked a fight with Harris. But the Habs were too quick to be drawn into battles. At the opening face-off, Ferguson burst in on Giacomin and fed Backstrom in the slot. Ralph's low shot was inches wide. A minute later, number six forced Giacomin into a fine stick save. Then Larose tested the Ranger goalie with a tricky slapshot.

Toe double-shifting Backstrom's line. "You have to go with your best in overtime and they had been our best line all game," he would say later. Also, Ferguson had that knack of beating Giacomin. "Everyone else saw him as an all star," Ferguson says today, "and he was having a great year. Lot of guys were seeing him for the first time; maybe they were intimidated. Me, I'd played against him a couple of years in the AHL, back when I was in Cleveland and he was with Providence. I always had pretty good luck with him. So he was no mystery to me. I was confident going up against him. That confidence always gives you an edge."

Although the Canadiens were all over New York, Francis was sure his team stole the game at five minutes.

"Oh boy, Red Berenson, who was playing cause Goyette was banged up, he takes a pass at the point. Comes in. Vachon, he was screened or something, he was lookin' the wrong way. Berenson whistles a shot past the goalie. Bing! right off the inside of the post. I thought it was in. I thought we won the game. Right off the inside of the post. I was sure that shot was goin' in."

But it didn't and a minute later Larose was hustling the other way. At the blueline he ripped a high hard shot that Giacomin gloved at the shoulder. Eddie left the net to pass off to a defenseman. "I heard the fans screaming, but I didn't know why at first. I thought I had the puck in my glove," Giacomin says. Then, his stomach sinking, Eddie whipped around to find the puck ten yards away, nestled in the middle of the crease.

"I couldn't believe the puck was there," Ferguson says. In fact, he must've blinked because he missed with his first shot. On his second try, he cracked the puck in the middle of the net just as Arnie Brown arrived. After scoring, Fergy hopped and waved. When he saw Backstrom and Larose he burst into tears. The Canadiens were in the Stanley Cup finals.

"We lost that series, but I thought we played well," Francis says today. "We took the Canadiens to the limit all four games. We showed we belonged in the league at last. And the Ranger franchise went straight up from there.

"And oh, you had to say that was a great Montreal team, eh? Those centres—Bel-ee-veau! Sometime when he come out, well, it's like when you're playin' on the pond as kids, and you're doin' OK until the big kid comes out to play. He was a great one.

"You know, it took me a long time to get over that series. Course that was my first experience in the play-offs. I'd think about that first game in Montreal. And the overtime game in our building. Games we might've won. Geez, I remember next year, I think it was, when Berenson was with St. Looie. He scored six goals one night. I remember reading that in the mornin' paper and thinking—six goals? Last year he didn't score a goal for us; no goals the whole year, play-offs included. I thought: Good for you, Red, but why oh why couldn't you have scored maybe five, and saved one for us that night in overtime."

FIRST PERIOD
1. Montreal, J.C. Tremblay 2nd (Richard) 10:46
Penalties—Fleming (high-sticking) 2:36; Harper (major, fighting), Fleming (major, fighting), Rochefort (holding) 5:10; Nevin (holding) 12:42

SECOND PERIOD
2. New York, Goyette 1st (Marshall, Nevin) 17:56
Penalties—Gilbert (elbowing), Hadfield (charging) 10:08; Marshall (roughing), Backstrom (slashing, roughing) 12:28; Ferguson (charging) 17:38; Richard (tripping) 18:29

THIRD PERIOD
No scoring
Penalties—Gilbert (tripping) 2:01; J.C. Tremblay (holding) 3:11; Ingarfield (hooking) 12:00; Brown (high-sticking), Béliveau (high-sticking) 17:14

OVERTIME
3. Montreal, Ferguson 3rd (Larose, Backstrom) 6:28
Penalties—Hadfield (major, fighting), Harris (major, high-sticking) 4:41
Shots on goal

Montreal	7	8	8	6 — 29
New York	6	12	11	5 — 34

Crowd noise
Centennial projects

Every city had a 100th anniversary project—a centennial
pool, arena, or garden. Sports franchises were called the
Centennials, 67s, and Expos. Pure Spring offered a
Centennial soft drink (carbonated chocolate). Families
planted Centennial trees and planned Expo vacations.
At school, we sang patriotic songs and donned scratchy
beards to re-enact confederation debates. Suddenly, we were
proud to be Canadians. In fact, we were worried about not
being worthy of the title. Government TV ads scolded kids
for not being as fit as an average sixty-year-old Swede.
To whip junior citizens into shape, Olympic competitions
for elementary schoolers were held late spring. Kids ran,
jumped, and hurled while teachers timed and measured.
Ribbons were handed out to everyone who didn't keel over.
At my school, winners received the ultimate icon of
contemporary Canadiana—Ook-piks. Ah, Ook-piks.
The lovably furry Eskimo trolls took the country by
storm (blizzard?) in 1967. Then disappeared forever
into the attic a year later.

16

Horatio at the Bridge

The Leafs skated onto the ice April 6 in Chicago, wearing their Centennial tribute—a remodelled blue leaf on the front of their white jerseys. Gone was the craggy, eleven-pointed emblem of yore. The brand new, five-point leaf resembled the symbol in the heart of the Canadian flag. Conn Smythe wept seeing the change. A royalist, the ex-Leaf owner called the new flag "Pearson's diaper."

"What are you complaining for, Conn, our new flag has a Maple Leaf?" the PM kidded Smythe.

"But in Detroit Red Wing colours!" Smythe thundered.

The new crest might not have craggy lines, but players inside the jerseys did. The heart of the team was still the old guard. Thirteen players had at least seven years' NHL experience. Six had turned pro in the 1940s. Bower even served in the war. ("The Boer War?" Mahovlich once asked.)

"When Red said that about young guys quitting on Imlach," Ellis muses aloud, "well in a way he could be right, you know. What Red was probably thinking was, 'Hey, we may be a veteran club, but there's young guys on the team now, too. And we veterans are getting older. It's time you young guys pull more weight.' I think it's true a lot of the young guys came on the last of the season—Stemkowski and Pappin especially. We needed to. That was probably Red's point.

"But in those play-offs," he continues, "well, it was a real comfort to look down the bench and see the old guys. There wasn't too much they hadn't seen in hockey. You need that more than ever in the play-offs."

"The veterans were an interesting mix of characters," Conacher says. "I would say what they had in common was a toughness and discipline—and a capacity for hard work. Well, how could you last under Imlach without those qualities? You could also say there was a lot of character there. Now that's a word that's overused in sports. But the Leaf veterans definitely had character—the team had character."

The evening Sawchuk earned his 100th shut-out, Armstrong scored his 250th goal. Management wanted to honour the Chief with a night. Fly the parents in. Give him a set of golf sticks. Throw in a silver tea set for the wife. Armstrong refused. The Captain felt he shouldn't be honoured when the Leafs hadn't observed Mahovlich and Kelly's 250th goals.

In the summer of 1964, Pulford was out golfing with Billy Harris when the latter said he was retiring. He couldn't agree on a contract with Imlach. "Hold off," Pulford said, then visited Imlach, hammering out a compromise. "Harris made a big contribution to our three championships," commented Pulford. "It would've been a shame to see him leave over a disagreement that could've been settled."

During the team's 1967–68 training camp, Pulford would try to sell teammates on Eagleson's new players' association. Imlach called a team meeting, excluding Pulford. "Go out there and fucking skate around until we're finished," Pulford was told. Then Punch lit into the team over "this stupid fucking association thing." Mid-rant, Horton stood up and skated out to join Pulford. Most of the others soon followed.

It's often been said Leaf veterans were loyal to Imlach. Perhaps it's more accurate to say they were faithful to the team he built. Punch shaped this Leaf club, but he never really controlled players the way Blake did the Canadiens.

"We respected Toe like a father," Ferguson says. "He respected us as grown men. There were no bed checks on the road. He didn't try and run our lives. We disciplined ourselves because we had so much respect for the man and the team."

Imlach did try to run his players' lives. After beating Boston to close the schedule, Imlach decreed the team would fly to Trenton, then bus to Peterborough (bedding down at three a.m.). After three days of boot camp, it was off to Chicago. Following Thursday's game, the Leafs would catch the red-eye to Toronto for a day of practice, then race back to Chicago for Sunday's game. No one understood the last part. Why not stay in Chicago and spare the team two 500-mile trips?

"Don't tell me how to coach my hockey club." Imlach snarled at reporters asking that very question. "If I want to fly 'em across the continent for a practice, I'll fly 'em. Besides, I don't want 'em lying around a hotel room in Chicago—two days on the loose I probably couldn't find them."

In Peterborough, the Leafs returned to army life—two practices a day, topped off by game films at night. For relaxation, Imlach had assistant John Anderson rustle up a dozen ping pong balls. After seventy-two hours of relentless competitive focus, Leafs would be whittled down to their essential conquerer selves, the coach figured.

What a disappointment Peterborough must've been for him then. Pulford arrived late for Tuesday's practice. Imlach glared at his assistant captain when he stepped on the ice.

"Why's he late?" Punch barked at trainer Bob Haggert.

"Equipment. Broken shoelace," Clancy said quickly.

"Hey, let's give Pully a hand," Shack shouted when Pulford joined the team. Players broke into mock applause, while Punch looked on, glowering. Stemkowski then led the group in calisthenics. (The team usually didn't do on-ice exercises after training camp, but Imlach had ordered his men to fall to the ice when Pulford failed to show in time.)

"Do as many [push-ups] as you can, but don't exert yourself," Stemkowski said.

"Nooo, don't do that. Don't exert yourself," Imlach echoed from the boards.

"You've got to do as many as the goals you scored this sea-son," Shack, an eleven-goal scorer this year, recommended.

"Hey Baun, how come you can't do them?" Punch shouted.

"Shoulder is sore," the defenseman replied.

"His nose will get in the way," another player suggested.

Shack was a man possessed the first ten minutes of scrim-mage, blinding everyone with ice chips. Then he faked a shoulder injury and tried to sneak back into the dressing-room for a smoke.

"Where the fuck do you think you're going?" Punch hollered.

Minutes later, Eddie clobbered Pulford. Number 20 retali-ated by rapping Shack across the wrists with his stick. Shack flung off his gloves and filled the air with punches. Punch blew the whistle and told them both to knock it off.

But they wouldn't. After scoring, Pulford raced down the boards and lanced Clancy's fedora. Shack collapsed Sawchuk with a vicious slapshot to the shoulder. "Ukey got hit by a bullet," Eddie chuckled. Punch didn't. He sometimes fined players for shooting high on goalies during practice. What made it worse was that Sawchuk had been hit on the same spot the day before.

At noon, a disgusted Imlach ordered his men off. Punch had removed his skates and was about out the door when word came that Pulford and Keon were still practicing. Punch ran back inside, fuming.

"What the fuck you doing?" he hollered from the boards.

"Don't feel like going back to the motel," Pulford replied. "Figured may as well stay here and wait for the 2:30 practice."

"Get off the ice and on the fuckin' bus or I'll fine you both $100," Imlach shouted.

If Tuesday's practice was frustrating for Punch, Wednesday's scrimmage almost brought him to tears. "I only hope nobody gets hurt," he muttered minutes before the team's sixth practice in three days. With a dozen minutes left in the last scrimmage, Stemkowski broke in on Bower, snap-ping a shot from fifteen feet out. Johnny threw up his blocker, deflecting the puck wide, then dropped his stick.

"Oh my God!" he yelled, "my hand's hurt." Throwing off

his brown practice mask, he skated off ice, moaning, "Damn—damn—damn." Blood dripped from the knuckle of his little finger. There was no kidding now. Shack skated by trainer Haggert. "Hey, Haggy—it don't look good, eh?" The trainer shook his head.

Imlach was upset ("If he holds the stick right, he doesn't get hurt!") and worried. The goalie who'd looked so good the last weekend of the season, his number-one guy in the play-offs, was hurt. Hell, both goalies were injured.

The team's behaviour in Peterborough didn't mean the Leafs weren't serious about the play-offs. Just the opposite. The night Bower was hurt, Armstrong called a meeting in his hotel room to discuss the Chicago series.

"Now that was pretty special for that Leaf team to have a players' meeting," Stanley recalls. "Boy, I couldn't tell you the last time we had one. We'd been together so long, what was there to say? Thing was we knew Chicago was a better team and we wanted to beat them." He laughs. "Maybe that's why we never had one before—didn't need it. Anyway, we had the meeting and it was quite something. We were honest with each other. We knew how good they were. They'd been clobbering us all year. Finally, somebody said, 'Well, what do we do to beat these guys?'

"That's when defensemen told forwards, 'We need help.' You know with forwards, backchecking is a four-letter word. But we told them, 'You guys are going to have to backcheck harder. We can't be giving Hull and Mikita three-on-twos or we're not going to win.' They said they understood, so it was agreed that we'd always keep a forward back to help."

Kelly had a few suggestions:

"They all had those danged curved sticks," the veteran centre observed, "and they were great shooters, no question about it. Give 'em a chance and they'd kill you. So the idea was to stay between their big guns and the net. Don't let them get the quick shot off before our goalie's ready. And make 'em go to their backhand, where it's harder to make a pass.

"Now with Mikita's line," Kelly continues, "they were all good skaters, but a little on the small size, you might say. It'd be foolish to skate with them—that was their game. We were bigger, so we'd have to hit them. We wanted to make sure Mikita knew he was in a play-off hockey game every night out."

Stanley says there was so much talk about Hull and Mikita "finally we said, 'Look, these two have beat our heads in all year. It'd be stupid to let them beat us in the play-offs.' Someone said, 'There's only two of them and five of us on ice any one time; sensible thing would be for all of us to check them.' And that's what we did. Forwards who looked after them would stay with them, of course. But any time one of 'em came into your zone, you looked after him, too. We always wanted someone banging them."

Toronto opened the play-offs with a series of bangs. Punch started Baun and Horton on defense, with Mahovlich, Keon, and Armstrong up front. All five put a lick on the Scooter Line on the first shift. Then Stemkowski's unit hit the ice like blitzing linebackers, thumping every Hawk in sight. Unfortunately, one thump, executed by Pappin, was deemed illegal.

Up a man, Chicago relaxed. With room to think, Mikita roamed the boards, waiting for a fast-orbiting Scooter to shake free. Wharram did, but Stanley, sprawling, made the save. Sawchuk smothered a Pilote try. Mohns missed a chance. Hawks had ten seconds left in their advantage when Hull danced through centre. Two Leafs rushed to greet him. Bobby paused, waiting for the speeding Mikita to near the Toronto line, then fired a corner bank-shot Stan collected wide of Sawchuk. Mikita circled the net, hitting Stapleton with a long pass the other way. The defenseman broke in, faked a shot, then lateralled to Wharram, who'd slipped his check in the flurry of seventy-foot passes. Stanley, scrambling, took away Wharram's move to the front. Number 17 had nothing to shoot at, but fired anyway. The puck was headed for Sawchuk's arm. He flinched. It struck the crook of his elbow and bent into the middle of the net.

Leafs ignored the hurricane-through-an-organ blare that greeted Wharram's goal and hurried back to work. The Kelly and Stemkowski lines won shifts, with DeJordy, a surprise starter for Chicago, making good saves on Pulford, then Stemkowski.

The Leafs had been awful on power plays recently, but were sharp tonight. After Van Impe was thrown off, Stemkowski's line worked the puck effectively for half a minute. Finally, Pilote cleared. Punch changed on the go, dispatching Keon's unit. Davey peddled down the left boards, curling around the net. DeJordy slid across. Keon swerved, waited for Mahovlich to buck Jarrett, then flipped a short pass into the crease that the Big M rapped home.

Toronto continued playing aggressively, bumping Hawks whenever possible. Sometimes even when it wasn't possible—or at least legal. At eleven minutes, Pulford hooked Pilote, then bumped Stapleton, giving his face a honk, hoping to provoke a penalty. It worked. But Leafs discovered playing Chicago four-on-four was like being down a man.

The Hawks zoomed into Toronto's end. Pilote had the puck outside the circle. Seeing Hull break to the net, the captain waited. Hull dragged an elbow across Sawchuk's face, jarring his mask, as he flew through the crease. Pilote's shot wasn't hard. But Sawchuk couldn't see. The goal put Chicago up 2–1.

Toronto kept hitting. Hull received whacks from Pulford and Pappin. Horton used an alligator-wrestling move on Esposito. Stapleton and Pilote got smacked every time they entered a corner. But the Leafs never managed to hit a puck past DeJordy, who got a glove on a Pappin bullet and made an elegant toe save on Horton late in the period.

Although Imlach warned against penalties during first intermission, Leafs continued playing brash, undisciplined hockey. Baun chopped Mikita in the ankle to open the second. With Imlach fuming, Hull scored on the power play, ripping a slapshot off Horton's stick past Sawchuk. Leafs retaliated with more thumping. Pulford nailed Nesterenko. Conacher got a chunk of Mikita, then rubbed Dennis Hull into the glass. And Baun caught Maki with a Pearl Harbour move—an elbow to the snoot when officials weren't looking.

The play of the game came midway in the second. Mahovlich swept by Jarrett, deked DeJordy, but missed the net. Pilote relayed a quick outlet pass to Mikita. Suddenly, the Scooter Line was crowding Baun and Horton. At the Leaf line, Mikita slowed, wound for a shot, pulling the defenders in, then flipped a pass to Wharram, who jumped in free. Sawchuk made the save, but couldn't reach the rebound. Mikita did. Four-one, Chicago.

Reay kept Hull and Maki on the bench in the third, instructing his troops to win the game's other battle: the contest along the boards. Hawks took three straight penalties. Although they piled up shots, Leafs never forced a puck past DeJordy. A frustrated Imlach pulled Sawchuk for an extra man with twelve minutes left.

"I fully intended to keep Sawchuk out until we scored or they did," Punch said later. "I thought it might shake things up. You gotta keep things moving."

"The experiment lasted only eleven seconds," Rex MacLeod noted next day. "Sawchuk went back in when Pulford, perhaps in an involuntary objection, incurred a slashing penalty."

Kelly doesn't believe any Leaf would even subconsciously sabotage one of Punch's showy chess moves. "Oh heaven's no—but it's hard to play without a goalie, except in that last minute when you're desperate," he says. "If you're playing with the goalie out other than that, you tend to be too worried about them scoring on you."

With Pulford gone, it was four-on-four again. Jarrett banged a slapshot into the corner. Sawchuk lumbered out. Angotti beat him to the puck, flicking a one-hander into the empty net. The goal set off every wind instrument in the building. The happy din continued the rest of the game. The crowd even cheered through Pappin's late goal, sending the home team into the dressing room on a rising note of ecstacy.

Minutes later, Reay and Imlach put game one in perspective. "I thought we got the goaltending tonight," Reay said. Imlach complained, "We just couldn't handle their power play, and we couldn't handle them on the four-on-fours either."

The papers would all say Chicago won the first game comfortably. The score, 5–2, was persuasive. But the Hawks were

anything but comfortable at game's end. Maybe the most
salient post-game quote came from Hull. "Pappin fell on me
at our blueline once and Pulford gave me a crack across the
knee with his stick that hurt," Bobby said. "I feel like an
eighty-year-old man."

FIRST PERIOD
1. Chicago, Wharram 1st (Stapleton, Mikita) 5:21
2. Toronto, Mahovlich 1st (Keon) 7:12
3. Chicago, Pilote 1st (Jarrett, B. Hull) 11:40
Penalties—Pappin 3:21; Van Impe 6:40; Horton 7:34; Pulford
(double minors), Stapleton (minor and misconduct) 11:19; Horton
(major), Esposito (major) 12:39

SECOND PERIOD
4. Chicago, B. Hull 1st (Pilote, Mohns) 1:57
5. Chicago, Mikita 1st (Wharram, Mohns) 13:46
Penalties—Baun 0:21; Jarrett 3:39; D. Hull 9:40; Pronovost
14:08

THIRD PERIOD
6. Chicago, Angotti 1st (Jarrett, Nesterenko) 9:41
7. Toronto, Pappin 1st (Stemkowski, Horton) 19:53
Penalties—Stapleton 2:29; Esposito 5:38; Mohns 8:40; Pulford
8:41; Van Impe 14:40; Armstrong 17:30; Mohns 18:43

Shots on goal
Toronto   11   17   16 — 44
Chicago   14   18   10 — 42

After game one, Leafs caught the last flight out of O'Hare,
arriving at Toronto International at three a.m. Before the
Leafs could escape to their cars, Punch declared practice that
morning optional. Players had just spent four hours racing
home for a work-out they didn't have to attend! Who could
figure Imlach?

Everybody showed next morning, however, and put in a
spirited ninety minutes of work. Back in Chicago, the Hawks
also had an optional skate that morning, but only four regulars

turned up—Hall, Hay, Van Impe and Dennis Hull. On Saturday, Toronto had another full work-out before catching the plane back to Chicago. Reay gave his team the day off.

Punch made two moves during the break: First, he absolved Sawchuk of blame for Thursday's loss. "I'm not going to criticize a goalkeeper who has 100 shut-outs," Punch said. "It says in the book how good Sawchuk is, and I feel like the book says. He been awful good a lot of times." Imlach also reunited Horton and Stanley, benching Baun, who'd taken a slashing penalty after Punch's sermon on the dangers of the Hawk power play. The last manoeuvre sent a clear message to the team about penalties.

But maybe Imlach's best move turned out to be the one for which he was so widely ridiculed. The trip back home gave the club two good practices. The Ice Capades were in the Stadium through Saturday. If his team had stayed in Chicago, they'd have worked at the Rainbow Arena, a duck pond out in the suburbs. "It's not close to a major-league facility," Reay said, explaining why he'd given his charges two days off.

In retrospect, the beginning of Sunday's game was predictable. The Hawks were sluggish, while Leafs looked like they'd never left the ice. At eight minutes, Stemkowski's line finally broke through. Pappin's digging kept the puck alive in the corner. He banked a pass behind the net to Pulford. Number 20 swung around in front, backhanding a short pass to Stemkowski, who banged a ten-footer into the open net.

Chicago snapped awake at twelve minutes, when Nesterenko caught a Pilote bomb behind the Leaf defense. The centre swept in, shifted right, left, then flipped a short backhand that Sawchuk, gliding through the crease, slapped wide with his stick. Strong work by Hull's line forced Toronto into a penalty. The Hawks pressed. Hull had two chances. Seconds later, Mikita was in alone. Finally, Sawchuk grabbed the puck. Before the face-off, the goalie left his crease to show referee Vern Buffy a loose pad strap, then dawdled to and from the bench, giving penalty killers Keon and Armstrong a rest.

They'd need that breather three minutes later when Stemkowski was tossed for molesting Stapleton. After

Sawchuk made an alert save on Mohns, Mikita won a face-off to the right of the Leaf net. The Chief managed to deflect Mohns' drop pass beyond the blueline. Armstrong then collided with point-man Hull, giving Keon a breakaway. Davey skated head down past three lines, then cruised the last fifty feet, whistling a wrist shot under DeJordy's glove to make it 2–0.

Suddenly, the Stadium was very quiet.

"Well, that was the thing about playing in Chicago," Kelly remembers. "That crowd was a little bit fickle, you know. If you could manage to get an early lead on them, the silence could be deafening, you could say. The Hawks would start pressing. Soon their own rink was a bother, not a help."

Another characteristic of the Chicago rink bothered the home side in periods two and three: bad ice. It took a week's freezing for Stadium ice to mature. With the Ice Capades in the night previous, the ice had eighteen hours to set. According to the *Tribune*, by the second period "Stadium ice looked like a frozen sewer. There was enough mud to satisfy the most finicky hippopotamus."

To make matters worse for Chicago skaters, the Leafs were hitting harder than ever. Hillman caught Mohns with a lethal hip. Horton landed heavily on Mikita's leg in a goal-mouth scramble. Toronto also capitalized on the period's best scoring chance. Mahovlich, Keon, and Armstrong shredded the Hawk defense with a precise three-way passing play that culminated with the Chief tipping a Keon pass in the open side.

By the third, Leafs had forechecked the Hawks into a damp heap. Hull, Mikita, and Mohns were limping, and the powerful Chicago offense was reduced to an occasional rush by Angotti. Sawchuk's biggest battle now was with the temperature. It had been a warm day and the Stadium held heat like a thermos. ("I think I lost ten pounds standing out there," Sawchuk said later.) Terry looked tuckered midway in the period, when Mikita beat him on a thirty-five-foot snap shot from a bad angle. For a moment it looked like Chicago might be back. The crowd was up and screaming seconds later when Espo burst in. Phil tried to deke and go to the backhand. But Sawchuk anticipated the move and steered him wide. When the play was whistled, Sawchuk skated out. Darn pad strap again. The delay allowed Toronto to catch their breath, and the team's 3–1 lead was never again threatened.

The post-game press conference was vintage Imlach. Punch put up shop outside the Leaf dressing room. Plopping in a red chair, he tilted his fedora back, crossed his arms, and snapped, "OK, let's go."

Was he surprised the Black Hawks didn't play better? a Chicago reporter inquired.

"Hell, I understood from all I read Chicago is the best hockey team in the world. I'm ready to accept that until somebody proves different.... They've got ten all stars. Count 'em if you want. All we got is a bunch of pluggers."

How did Leafs win?

"We won by check-check-check-checking!" Punch cried, wagging his head.

Was the ice a factor?

A snarl. "We both used the same ice."

Who played well for Leafs?

"Keon played well, scored a goal and killed penalties. I'd have to say he played pretty well." He gave his gum a thoughtful snap, then remembered he'd replaced Baun with Stanley. "Stanley played a helluva game also. And so did Sawchuk." Imlach lowered his voice and became mysterious. "I'd appreciate it if you didn't interview Sawchuk," he said. "I could close the dressing-room if I wanted." He would say no more. Of course every reporter then rushed Sawchuk for a story, which is probably what Punch wanted all along.

Finally, a Toronto reporter asked about the shuttle back to Toronto. It didn't look like it hurt the team, did it?

"If I let 'em loose in this town for two days I'd never find them," Punch said. Imlach stared at the questioner, who'd obviously spent the past days shuttling between bars in Chicago's downtown Loop, and shook his head. "Christ, from the looks of you, I'd never let my team stay here."

FIRST PERIOD
1. Toronto, Stemkowski 1st (Pulford, Pappin) 8:07
2. Toronto, Keon 1st (Armstrong) 18:33
Penalties—Horton (holding) 14:54; Stemkowski (hooking) 17:53

SECOND PERIOD
3. Toronto, Armstrong 1st (Keon, Mahovlich) 8:24
Penalties—Miszuk (interference) 7:53

THIRD PERIOD
4. Chicago, Mikita 2nd (Mohns) 8:45
Penalties—Pilote (interference) 18:48

Shots on goal
Toronto   8   8   8 — 24
Chicago   10   12   12 — 34

The second-game ice capades remained a story in Chicago on
the off day before the series continued in Toronto. "The ice
was just right for the Leafs checking game," Reay said. "We
didn't have a good practice for two days. The Leafs started fast
and got the jump on us."

"The ruckus was caused," the *Tribune* commented,
"because the Chicago Stadium management booked the Ice
Capades into the building at a time they knew the Hawks
would be needing the ice for the play-offs.... The situation
would be understandable were it not for the fact that the family Wirtz, which owns the Stadium, also owns the Black
Hawks. Didn't they think the Hawks would make the play-
offs? Or didn't they care?"

Good question. Harry Sinden may be right in claiming the
NHL ran a crooked table prior to expansion, and that
Canadian teams enjoyed unfair trade advantages. But it's also
clear a majority of American partners didn't care, perhaps
because their passion for sport ran second to their zeal for
business. Until this season, for instance, the Rangers occasionally played play-off home games on the road because of
the circus.

The Hawks did work out Monday in Chicago and on
Tuesday, in Toronto, as well. An incident prior to game three,
however, calls into question the value of team warm-ups. The
Hawks were in a shooting drill, when Hull, from the blueline,
lifted a slapshot over the glass into Harold Ballard's bunker,
forty feet above the ice.

"I looked up," Ballard said, "and thought I'd come down with a severe case of Hailey's squint." The puck ripped through the Leaf co-owner's program, shattering his spectacles and spreading his nose back flat to his eyes.

"[Chicago] practices were sheer terror," former Hawk Al MacNeil once said. "Bobby had the hammer out all the time and he had no compunction about trying to put it right through the guy's stomach. He just loved to hit guys with the puck."

Another pre-game ritual annoyed Hall.

"The goal judge in Chicago always held a soft drink in his hand," the goalie recalled, "and Stan and Bobby would deliberately shoot the puck off the glass in front of him to see him jump and spill the drink on himself. They thought it was funny as hell. The problem was that first it had to come over my shoulder."

Despite their cavalier practices, the Hawks looked ready the first minutes of game three. On the second shift, Hull found a lane to the net and took a windmill blast from the circle. Sawchuk, rushing out, caught the shot on the inside of his calf, deflecting the puck wide. A minute later, Angotti split Pronovost and Hillman, forcing the goalie into a quick glove grab. At eight minutes, Hull was back, levelling Sawchuk with a 100-mile-an-hour shot to the meat of the arm.

At eleven minutes, the Leafs counterattacked with Pilote stranded up ice. Jeffrey headmanned to Kelly, who tipped a pass to Ellis. The winger flew down the boards, stalling at the blueline. When Kelly caught up, the teammates broke in on Jarrett. Approaching the face-off marker, Ellis looked to Kelly—drawing Hall to the middle of the crease—then squeezed off a twenty-footer that touched Hall's pad and the post before catching the short side.

The goal deflated Chicago. For twenty minutes, the Leafs took to offense. Now it was Hall who kept his team alive, making close-in saves on Mahovlich, Conacher, and Pappin. Midway into the second, Toronto was firmly in control. Strong work by Keon's line provoked a Hawk penalty. Imlach threw Walton on. The rookie sped down the wing, making frantic spectators out of Hay and Nesterenko, then fired a fifty-foot relay across to the barging Mahovlich. The Big M shifted, then found a crack between Hall's legs. Two-nothing, Toronto.

With a comfortable lead, the Leafs concentrated on the plan devised in Armstrong's hotel room, gang-checking Hull and Mikita. Stanley then Conacher upended Mikita. Jeffrey, Horton, and Stemkowski all bashed Hull. Stemkowski was hitting everybody.

"I have this memory of Stemmer hammering Pilote into the boards this one time," Conacher remembers. "[Pilote] just fell onto the ice and you could see in his eyes he had nothing left. Next shift out the puck goes into the corner and you can see Pilote holding up to see if he was going to get hit. He just didn't want the puck anymore."

The team checking of Hull, Mikita, and Pilote left some Hawks with room to manoeuvre, but secondary stars like Esposito were unable assert themselves.

"I think Esposito was a little bewildered by what happened," Ellis says. "Hull had always carried the mail before. Now we had him covered, and Phil didn't seem to know what to do."

The next goal proved how dominant Leafs were this night. Pulford poured down on Hall, letting one go from thirty feet. The goalie snaked a pad out to block the shot, but Stemkowski, battling through the middle, smashed the rebound toward a high open corner. Hall got a shoulder on that shot, deflecting it off the crossbar back to the right circle, where Pappin calmly lifted a shot into the net. It was almost as if the Hawk defense wasn't there.

Late in the final period, Hull, after a fine rush by Angotti, banged home a rebound to ruin Sawchuk's shut-out. Bobby barely lifted his stick in celebration. Though there were three and a half minutes left, enough time to make the game interesting, but Chicago knew it was a beaten team.

FIRST PERIOD
1. Toronto, Ellis 1st (Jeffrey, Kelly) 11:10
Penalties—Jarrett 0:24; Horton 3:25; Horton 14:57; D. Hull 18:53

SECOND PERIOD
2. Toronto, Mahovlich 2nd (Walton, Pappin) 10:22
3. Toronto, Pappin 2nd (Stemkowski, Pulford) 19:15
Penalties—Hodge 9:43; Horton 12:50; Stanley 15:36

THIRD PERIOD
4. Chicago, B. Hull 2nd (Angotti, Wharram) 16:30
Penalties—Pilote 12:16; Stemkowski 15:03

Shots on goal

Chicago	16	11	9 — 36
Toronto	18	10	8 — 36

Reay lost his temper before game four. Minutes prior to the
opening face-off, Ballard grabbed a photographer and hurried
down to the ice, hailing Hull as the Hawks made their way
through the runway. "Bobby, over here," Ballard hollered, lifting his dented face in profile. "Let's show the world what
you've done. Make a helluva photo." The always accommo-
dating Hull was on his way when Reay broke back and
grabbed him.

"Get the hell out of here, Ballard," he shouted. "We've got
a hockey game to play."

Reay had been sore for two days. After game three, a
Toronto reporter asked Billy why he replaced the injured
Mohns with Dennis Hull on the Scooter Line. "Why wreck
two lines?" was how he put it. "If you know everything, why
bother asking questions," the Chicago coach exploded. "Get
the hell out of here!"

Reay wasn't taking losing to Imlach, the man who replaced
him in Toronto back in 1958, at all well. "You're embarrassing
yourselves," Reay barked at the players before game four.
"You're not skating. Not hustling. They get that first goal,
then sit back with a forward in the defensive zone and clog
the middle. And we're not skating or getting our passes off
quick. So they're murdering us when we come out."

Reay wanted his club to grab a lead, to skate hard, and to
pass quickly. He mentioned that some of the team's stars were
banged up—it was time for others to step forward. Everyone

knew he was talking about Esposito here. Reay said all this with uncharacteristic forcefulness, dipping frequently into the same longshoreman's thesaurus Imlach consulted before chats with his team.

Reay's pre-game talk threw lightning into his players' skates. Mikita slapped the opening draw up the boards. Mohns beat Horton to the puck, crossed the blueline, then lined a pass to Wharram on the opposite wing. He flashed a waist-high shot past Sawchuk. Nine seconds was all it took.

The Hawks sprinted the next ten minutes. So did the Leafs. And the game raced back and forth, fast as windshield wipers in a storm. Keon, on a Mahovlich pass, croqueted a slapshot through a cranny under the sliding Van Impe past Hall. Pilote wheeled from behind the Leaf net, waited for the cruising Hull to eclipse Sawchuk, then threw a screen shot inside the post to put Chicago back on top—only to have Horton slalom the length of the ice and beat Hall on a short wrist shot.

With the score tied, the Leafs tried to replay games two and three: gang-checking Mikita and Hull and hitting every Hawk that moved. But the Hawks were too fast. The Leafs reached, checking with sticks. Then came the penalties. Toronto drew five of six infractions from the ten-minute mark in the first through the second period.

Sawchuk kept Toronto alive in the second. The goalie out-guessed Mikita and Hay on breakaways, kicked aside a short Jarrett wrist shot, and took two more cannon blasts to the upper body from Hull. Sawchuk hadn't played more than two games a week all season, however, and by the third period of his fourth game in seven days, he began to tire. So did Stanley, who, despite a bad ankle, had put in heroic thirty-five-minute games alongside Horton in games two and three. A few minutes into the third period, Nesterenko took advantage of both, bowling Stanley over at the circle, banging a shot on goal that Sawchuk couldn't control, then knocking both goalie and puck into the net.

Five minutes later, Hull took a Pilote pass wide of the boards and wound up. Sawchuk stiffened up out of his crouch, waiting to collect more shrapnel. Only this time Hull rang a low torpedo off the post to make it 4–2.

The game that began so quickly slowed, which meant Leaf checkers could finally catch the Hawks. For ten minutes, teams traded vicious hits. Pulford flattened Pilote. Pilote sideswiped Keon. Dennis Hull made a helicopter move trying to split the defence and got a propeller in Horton's face, breaking the defenseman's nose (trainer Haggert spent four towels trying to staunch the blood). Half a minute later, Pappin wound up for a shot between the circles.

"It was late in a close game," Hall remembers, "I was trying to force myself to keep down to see the shot. Then somebody deflected it or a stick waved in front of my face. I lost the shot. And it hit me right in the mouth. Knocked me over. I was bleeding and spitting out teeth. Twenty-five stitches is what it took to fix me up. What a way to make a living, eh?"

Leafs were getting Old Testament vengence, but no closer to evening the game score. Then Imlach pulled one of those stunts that so annoyed his critics, pulling Sawchuk with three minutes left. Too early. A showy distraction. Never works, experts argued. And they were right.

Except tonight. Eight seconds after Sawchuk made it to the bench, replacement Walton shovelled a Mahovlich rebound past DeJordy to make it 4–3. Imlach threw Sawchuk back out after the goal, but kept him at the blueline. For a minute, Stemkowski's line swarmed the Hawk goal, but Chicago had the net plugged. Jarrett, Pilote and DeJordy jammed the crease, while Nesterenko and Hay crowded the slot. Leafs fed Hillman at the point. Twice the defenseman lowered his head and drove the puck at—but never through—the flailing wall.

With ninety seconds left, Punch yanked Sawchuk again, sending a pealing shriek through the Gardens. Mahovlich jumped on, joining Pulford, Keon, and Ellis up front and Pappin and Hillman at the points. A sliding Pilote blocked a Mahovlich slapshot. Pulford got a puck through that DeJordy kicked aside. The Leafs directed five shots at DeJordy in a minute. With time running out, all six Leafs stormed the crease. Pulford and Mahovlich had swings at the puck, but the Hawk net was boarded with flesh. With five seconds left,

Hillman wound up, faked, then passed off to Keon, who back-handed a shot into Jarrett's stomach as the blue light brightened to announce the end of the game.

"Holy mackerel!" Reay said afterwards.

Punch said a lot of things, few of them holy. "Ask me a million questions, but don't ask me about the refereeing. I don't want to talk about the fucking referees! It's a fucking disgrace!" he said. Then, without prompting, he started talking about the referees:

"On Nesterenko's goal, my guy (Sawchuk) had control of the puck twice. Then Nesterenko started banging away. He shoulda got a goddamn penalty, not a goal! And on that play on Horton by Dennis Hull…"

FIRST PERIOD
1. Chicago, Wharram 2nd (Mikita, Mohns) 0:09
2. Toronto, Keon 2nd (Conacher, Mahovlich) 3:42
3. Chicago, Pilote 2nd (Mohns, B. Hull) 8:32
4. Toronto, Horton 1st (Mahovlich) 10:14
Penalties—D. Hull (charging) 6:16; Jarrett (holding) 9:12; Walton (hooking) 9:33; Van Impe (elbowing) 9:49; Stemkowski (hooking) 11:25; Pronovost (holding) 16:46; Dea (served Chicago's penalty for too many men on the ice) 17:30

SECOND PERIOD
No scoring
Penalties—Mohns (high-sticking) 5:23; Jeffrey (elbowing) 5:23; Jeffrey (charging) 12:27; Conacher (hooking) 15:43; Mohns (high-sticking) 17:30

THIRD PERIOD
5. Chicago, Nesterenko 1st (D. Hull, Pilote) 2:31
6. Chicago, R. Hull 3rd (Pilote) 8:48
7. Toronto, Walton 1st (Mahovlich, Hillman) 17:37
Penalties—Jarrett (hooking) 5:14

Shots on goal
Chicago   13   7   6 — 26
Toronto   12   9   12 — 33

Punch stayed up until six a.m. moaning with Clancy after game four. The Hawks had come back! Toronto had hoped to wear down Chicago. It'd worked—for a while. Now Imlach wondered how much his guys had left. Sawchuk, who was down to 150 pounds, couldn't possibly play Saturday. Could Bower? Horton's nose was broken. Armstrong was out with a leg injury. Stanley, Pappin, and Jeffrey were hurt. The veterans looked tired.

"Punch wasn't near as cocky against Chicago as he pretended to be," George Gross remembers. "Chicago scared him. They'd beaten up on Toronto pretty good that year. They had Hull and Mikita. All the Leafs had to do was let down a second and the game was over. Punch also thought Hall was terrific. And he didn't like going into that big noisy building they played in."

With two hours' sleep, Imlach was his bouncy self next morning. After putting Leafs through a brisk drill (Reay gave his team another day off), he invited reporters into his darkened office to see a project he was working on.

"I'm sick and tired of getting hosed by referees," Punch explained. "I'm going to send this film [a compilation of alleged anti-Leaf calls] to the league office in Montreal. Newspapers can have prints Monday. They can publish them and show what kind of hosing we've been getting in this series."

Punch saw something he liked on the flickering screen.

"Hold it there. No, farther back. Go back a bit, where they're interfering with Pronovost. Yeah, that's it. Lemme see it again. Good, I want you to print that clip."

"So who you going to start next game, Bower or Sawchuk?" a reporter asked, trying to get a little work in.

Punch was helpful, as always. "You guess which one and I'll use the other guy," he said.

Bower got the call on Saturday afternoon. The Stadium was, if anything, louder and warmer than games one and two. Mayor Daley was down to short sleeves by game time. As in game three in Toronto, Reay's team started quickly, rushing Bower. Although the Hawks controlled play, their passing wasn't as precise as Thursday night. The shooters weren't sharp either. Maybe it was the ice. Or lack of practice time. The first Hawk siege passed without incident.

Then Chicago took a penalty. The Leafs couldn't seem to swing to offense, however. A minute into their advantage (and six minutes into the game), they'd yet to test DeJordy. A restless Imlach replaced Pulford with Walton. The rookie travelled in a line to the Hawk net. Pappin snared a lacrosse toss from Stemkowski, threw the puck to his feet, and flicked a short pass into the slot. Walton was there and whipped a low shot past DeJordy.

Up one, Leafs resumed hitting. Stemkowski walloped Van Impe, combing the defenseman's noggin with his stick. Both were thrown off. Playing four a side, the Hawks attacked Bower. The dependable veteran, maybe the best play-off goalie of his time, had a bad minute. First he tried to clear a puck up the boards. Pilote intercepted and slapped a shot Angotti deflected into the empty net. Seconds later the goalie misplayed a Jarrett shot. Hay got the rebound to Hull, who ripped one into the roof of the cage, giving Chicago a sudden 2–1 lead.

With Hull's goal, Imlach raced to the end of the bench.

"Ready to go in?" he asked Sawchuk.

"I'd rather go in at the beginning of the second."

Punch summoned Bower to the boards.

"Whatsa matter?"

"I don't know."

"You want to continue?"

"Sure—gimme to the end of the period."

Bower was wobbly, ready to fall, but Chicago, in the midst of a wastefully energetic first period, took consecutive bad penalties. On the Leafs second power play, Mahovlich miss-hit a Keon pass, sending an agonizingly slow roller beyond the floundering DeJordy to tie the game. After that, the Leafs clutched and grabbed to hang on to the end of the first round.

The first thing Imlach did in intermission was visit Bower.

"You look a little shaky. Are you?"

"I'm a little shook."

"Want me to make a change?"

Bower studied the floor. Around him, exhausted players loosened skates, sucked on orange quarters, and applied cold towels to their flushed faces. "Well, there's a lot at stake," he said. Imlach turned and gave Sawchuk a nod.

The teams met like charging rams to begin the second period. Stanley caught Wharram with his head down, knocking him senseless. When John Ashley, normally the most permissive of referees, called a charging penalty, Punch blew his fedora. After a brief, unsatisfying (for Imlach) argument, the Hawk power play set up to the right of Sawchuk. Mikita won the draw to Pilote, who fed the puck back into the corner. Mikita circled behind the net, looked up, and saw Hull charging in from the point.

"Hull was about thirty feet out when he took the big swing," Kelly remembers. "That puck got off the ice so high, so fast, it was like a golfer using a sand wedge. You wouldn't have thought a hockey stick could make a shot like that. Well, that was that danged curved stick. Anyway, Ukie, he'd just moved out. He probably never saw the puck, it was just a high rocket, and it caught him—I think it was high in the shoulder. Oh, he went down like someone shot him."

When Sawchuk came to, he lifted himself to one elbow and gave his head a shake.

"Stay down, Ukey," a grinning Pilote said, passing through the crease.

The goalie shot him a murderous glare.

"Where'd you get it?" trainer Bobby Haggert asked.

"My bad shoulder."

"Think you're all right?"

"I stopped the shot didn't I?"

Smelling blood, the Hawks charged in for the kill. For the rest of the Stanley penalty and on two subsequent power plays, Chicago rained rubber on Sawchuk. Always it was the same men shooting: Mikita, Wharram, Mohns, Pilote, Stapleton, and Hull. Especially Hull. Five times he tested Sawchuk with his best shot. Every time, the goalie stole out to block the angle and took a bullet somewhere to the body.

The Scooters tried to overwhelm the Leaf goalie with guile, throwing the puck around in search of their favourite equation—an open man and an empty net. A man was some-times open, but the net, never. Playing on passion and memo-ry, Sawchuk was a blur between the pipes. During one sequence, the goalie got a toe on a low Mikita screen shot, then sprang instantly to his feet for the rebound, flicking aside a high blast from Mohns with his blocker.

"Sawchuk simply put on a clinic that afternoon," recalls Milt Dunnell. "In one period the Hawks must've had fifteen quality chances to score. Hull alone could've scored three or four goals. Yes, I'd seen goaltending like that before—from Terry Sawchuk back in the early fifties. After Hull hit him with that shot, he somehow reached back fifteen years.* It was the most remarkable demonstration of goaltending I've ever seen."

By the third period, the Stadium was hotter than July. A dense cloud of curling cigarette smoke hovered above the rink. With the opening face-off, 20,000 fans leaned forward and screamed, exhorting their team on. The Hawks obliged, resuming their furious, and increasingly frantic, attack on Sawchuk. Pilote and Stapleton now routinely joined forwards deep into Leaf territory. This recklessness almost cost Chicago in the second minute, when Stemkowski and Pulford were allowed a two-on-one. Pulford put a perfect pass on his cen-tre's stick. DeJordy fell. Stemkowski had the high glove side to shoot for, but whipped the puck into the crowd.

Next came a defining moment for the Hawks. Chicago had been granted a reprieve. The game, which they controlled, was tied. The team's second-best line—Hull, Esposito, and Maki—arrived at the face-off circle. It was a time for the club to restore order in its end. But when the puck was dropped, both wingers flew up ice, ignoring their checks. Pulford beat a defenseman into the corner, wheeled, and fired to Pappin in the slot; he took two whacks at the puck. The second shot dribbled off DeJordy's pad into the crease, where Stemkowski

---

* From 1950 to 1955, Sawchuk's goals-against average never strayed as high as two goals. During those five seasons he recorded fifty-six shut-outs. In lead-ing the Wings to the 1952 Cup, his goals-against average was a microscopic 0.62.

rammed it into the empty net.

The goal put something Wharram said earlier this season into stark relief: "At first Mohnsie had a little trouble adapting to our line because he concentrated so much on the defense," the winger said. "We'd be flying down the wing and look over and he wasn't there. He was back covering his man. 'That's not the way we [Chicago] play,' we told him. 'That's play-off hockey.'"

Sensing they were about to lose this play-off match, Chicago seized the game by the throat and shook hard for ten minutes. A dozen times they seemed sure to score—but Sawchuk was always in the way. The Leaf defense took care of rebounds and rocked Hawk forwards with punishing checks. Twice Stemkowski drew penalties, driving Imlach to madness. It was after the centre's second penalty, at ten minutes, that Sawchuk was at his best.

After softening the goalie with high blasts, Hull blazed a low thirty-footer that the locked-in-a-crouch Sawchuk kicked aside. Stapleton walked into a shot between the circles. The Leaf goalie got his blocker in the way and jai alai-scooped the high rebound into the corner with his stick. Then came an unforgettable sequence: Loading up, Hull saw Mikita edge into the slot and directed a hard pass along the ice. Sawchuk saw the play developing and sprawled, catching the deflection with his stacked pads. Hodge got all his weight into a slapshot that hit the advancing Sawchuk in the arm, spinning him around. Seconds later, Mohns was in free. Sweeping across the front of the net, he tried a series of moves, but Sawchuk kept with him. For Mohns it was like trying to deke your image in a mirror. Exhausted and out of ideas, the winger finally threw a weak backhand into the goalie's pads.

With that, Chicago threw in the towel. In the last seven minutes, they managed two harmless shots. While the mute crowd looked on in astonishment, Pappin scored on a two-on-one with Pulford. Reay pulled his goalie, but it was the Leafs who continued to attack. In the last minutes, Mohns had to stop Pappin, Mahovlich, and Keon (on a breakaway) to keep the score respectable.

After the game, Punch was as gay as a thrush. "I've got the

best two fuckin' goalies in the world!" he sang, skipping into the dressing-room.

"Punch was a happy man that afternoon," remembers George Gross. "I think he knew right then and there that the Hawks were a beaten team, and that Toronto was going to be in the Stanley Cup."

Calming down, Imlach assumed the air of a pipe-smoking military strategist. "Sawchuk was like that guy on the bridge, you know, Horatio," he said. "Wouldn't let anything by. He was fantastic." Pulford was in such a good mood he didn't have the heart to point out that the Roman general Imlach was looking for was Horatius, not Horatio.

Across the dressing-room, Sawchuk sucked on a cigarette, too tired to even remove his equipment. After taking a long pull on a can of Coke, he shook his head and said softly (perhaps to himself), "I'd like to leave hockey like that. In good style." After reporters left, the goalie stripped off his t-shirt and drew a gasp from teammates.

"I'll always remember what Sawchuk looked like after that game," Ellis says. "Don't forget goalies back then didn't have near the protection they do today. Terry, he had ugly blue bruises all up and down his arms and shoulders. One shoulder was swollen up. And he could hardly move. It looked like he'd been badly beaten in a fight. Players all saw that. They knew what he had to give up to give us that win. What courage it took to rush out there in front of a Bobby Hull shot time and again. We were determined to go out that next game and give him the kind of support he deserved."

FIRST PERIOD
1. Toronto, Walton 2nd (Stemkowski, Pappin) 6:16
2. Chicago, Angotti 2nd (Pilote) 9:31
3. Chicago, B. Hull 4th (Hay, Jarrett) 11:01
4. Toronto, Mahovlich 3rd (Keon, Walton) 14:14
Penalties—Horton (interference) 2:36; D. Hull (hooking) 5:05; Stemkowski (high-sticking); Van Impe (high-sticking) 9:09; Hodge (hooking) 11:41; Hay (hooking) 13:24; Pulford (holding) 15:48; Pulford (roughing); Nesterenko (roughing) 19:28

SECOND PERIOD
No scoring
Penalties—Stanley (charging) 3:19; Wharram (slashing) 5:32;
Pappin (high sticking) 13:12; D. Hull (holding) 17:03

THIRD PERIOD
5. Toronto, Stemkowski 2nd (Pulford, Pappin) 2:11
6. Toronto, Pappin 3rd (Pulford, Horton) 17:14
Penalties—Stemkowski (tripping) 4:23; Stemkowski (tripping)
10:13; Angotti (slashing) 13:54; Pulford (high-sticking); Mikita
(high-sticking) 19:28

Shots on goal

Toronto	7	9	15 —	31
Chicago	12	15	22 —	49

"I had problems with Imlach," Billy Harris says. "And I didn't
agree with everything about his so-called system. But I'll say
this: his forcing the team to play one style of hockey meant,
come play-offs, Leafs never seemed to be bothered by injuries
like other teams; like a Chicago if one of their big guys got
hurt. If someone [on the Leafs] was hurt, Imlach had a guy on
the bench or farm he could put in. It didn't matter who was
out there, the Leafs always fit together as a team. When
Bower got hurt one spring [1962], up came Don Simmons to
help win the Cup. Another time it would be Eddie
Litzenberger."

This spring it was Conacher and Hillman. The defenseman, who'd been performing in Rochester at Christmas, was
playing the hockey of his life alongside Pronovost. And
Conacher had taken the baton from the falling Armstrong in
game three without missing stride.

"The way that series progressed was a real eye-opener,"
Conacher recalls. "I was playing [with Mahovlich and Keon]
against their big lines—the Hull and Mikita lines. Through
the season those guys had killed us, and here we were in the
play-offs going against them every second night. I had my
doubts. But by the end of series something Armstrong said in
training camp came back to me: 'You wonder why we're

working so hard now? But come the sixth or seventh game of the play-offs no one will be able to keep up with us.'" He laughs. "I thought, sure, sure. But it was true. Somewhere late in the series the tide turned. It had been a close series up to then, but then you could see Chicago run out of gas. At the end, the Hawks looked like a beaten team."

Conacher scored his first goal in twenty-three games early in the first period of game six. Keon harassed Mikita into a fumble at centre, then found Mahovlich, his shoulders pumping, motoring along the boards. The Big M took the pass at the Hawk blueline, blew past Van Impe, then passed off to the high slot. Conacher's quick shot found the tunnel between Hall's legs.

Two minutes later, Conacher was back, sweeping around a defender, then firing a low bullet that a collapsing Hall got a pad on. Mahovlich banged the rebound at the empty net, but the fallen goalie did a marine roll across the crease to steer the shot wide. On the next shift, Hall made consecutive saves on Pappin and Pulford in another torrid Leaf siege.

Horatio had a quiet period. The Hawks had plenty of shots, but from far out. Chicago had no more appetite for hard scrabble along boards and in front of the net. For Allan Stanley, this game was a joy to play.

"We were inspired now, and that's a great thing to experience," he says. "You can see it and feel it on the ice. Guys were pulling together on the bench. Any differences on the team had disappeared, and we got down to doing something we loved: playing hockey in a big game to the best of our ability. We knew they had better players, but we were proving to everybody that maybe we had the better team."

Unfortunately for Toronto, no one told Hall that the Hawks were on their way out the play-off door. He kept the Leafs to one goal in the first twenty minutes. Chicago got that goal back late in the period on a great play by Nesterenko. The Hawks' best forward this night broke up a Leaf power play and chased down the left boards, with Stapleton trailing and only Horton back. Inside the blueline, he flipped a back pass to his defenseman, who took aim at the low right corner of the net. Sawchuk moved quickly and was in position to make the save, but the puck ticked Horton's stick and flew over his shoulder.

In the second period, Leafs enjoyed a wide edge in play, but Hall remained unconquerable, stopping Mahovlich, Ellis, and Pappin close-in. Late in the frame, Keon, in free, deked the goalie, throwing a backhand at the empty net that Hall, doubled backwards, deflected wide with his stick.

A vague uneasiness settled over the Gardens as the third period began. Although the Leafs controlled play, the game was tied. One break and Chicago could do to Toronto what the Leafs had done to them game five. At three minutes, Hawks got that break. Hull took a Hay pass in front with Sawchuk out. Number nine stepped in and fired into the heart of the net—a sure goal, except Hillman popped up like a jack-in-the-box to cuff the puck wide. "I saw Terry out of the crease and I went in behind him," the defender said later, "[Hull] didn't bear down. He must've thought he'd score into the open net."

Conacher still remembers what happened next shift.

"All series every forward on our team hit people," he says. "It was contagious. When we saw a Hawk along the boards we just hit him without thinking. Ed Van Impe was trying to clear the puck, and I was on top of him, so I hit him as hard as I could. He was on the ice and the puck lay loose, and I went after it. I could see Hall preparing for me and over to my left Keon was driving to the net. I skated in, then fired the puck at an open corner behind Hall. It hit somebody's stick [Stapleton's] and rose a couple of inches. You could see Hall kind of fall back a little with the deflection. The puck hit him on the edge of his goal pad then went into the net. It took me a long time for it to sink in that I'd got the big goal. I wasn't the star of the team or anything. I was just there with a chance to do something at the right moment."

The Hawks knew they were dead after that, Conacher says.

"I remember guarding Bobby Hull, and I was skating with him, always trying to keep myself between Bobby and the puck, and their centres would look over at Hull, they'd see I had him covered, and they'd pass anyway. I'd intercept the puck and take it the other way. I couldn't believe what they were doing. It was as if they were exhausted and had run out of ideas. Hull and Mikita were plan A, and they never had a plan B."

Ten minutes later, Stemkowski beat Hall on a long screen shot to make it 3–1 Leafs. With almost three minutes to go, Reay called Hall over during a break and advised him to come off whenever the Hawks got the puck over centre. They never did. For the next 160 seconds, Leafs kept the team that had set twelve different scoring records this season pressed helplessly in its end. When the buzzer sounded, the Black Hawks almost looked relieved that it was over.

The Leaf dressing-room was subdued afterwards. There were no champagne fights, or ecstatic hugs—just the odd handshake. The Hawks were gone, but the Canadiens, their arch enemies, lay ahead. "Christ, let's enjoy this one, let's not talk about Montreal," Imlach said when someone asked about the finals. But Punch didn't look all that happy; he must've already been thinking about Blake and the Canadiens.

In the Hawk quarters, Reay was gracious. "I'm a little one-sided," he said, smiling, "so I think the best team lost. But Sawchuk stoned us and they outplayed us up the centre." (Esposito, who hadn't recorded a point this series, would be shopped the following week.) "I've got no squawks," Reay said finally. "They're champions, and I'm happy with the year they gave me. I'll be satisfied with one like it next year."

Bobby Hull patiently answered every question put to him. (Mikita hadn't stuck around to shake hands with the Leaf players.) Bobby praised Sawchuk and had kind words for Hillman, Pronovost, and Mahovlich. Only once did he acknowlege his frustration. "Just one time I'd like to play in the play-offs at top form—to be able to help the team the way I know I can," he said, shaking his head. Then he limped smiling out of the Gardens and was swallowed by autograph hunters.

Almost thirty years later, Glenn Hall says it wasn't Sawchuk that beat the Hawks in the spring of 67. Or injuries to Hull and Mikita. As usual, he says, the team beat itself.

"I never thought that we were as good as everyone else did. We just weren't built to win Stanley Cups," he says. "Everyone knows that the best defensive club wins in the end. They probably do in all sports when you think of it. And we never cared much about defense. So in the end we always lost."

In five carefully chosen words, Hall sums up the Chicago Black Hawks of the mid-60s; a compelling team that, from 1962–67, won more regular-season games than anyone else, yet only once advanced as far as the finals (losing to Montreal in the spring of 1965).

Were the Hawks concerned about personal ambitions at the expense of team goals?

"Some were."

Did the Black Hawks take advantage of Billy Reay's relaxed manner?

"Could be."

Did the team's work ethic cost them in gruelling play-off series with teams like Montreal and Toronto?

"Perhaps."

FIRST PERIOD
1. Toronto, Conacher 1st (Mahovlich, Keon) 5:06
2. Chicago, Stapleton 1st (Nesterenko) 14:38
Penalties—Stapleton (tripping) 7:05; Pilote (tripping) 12:38

SECOND PERIOD
No scoring
Penalties—D. Hull (charging) 13:32

THIRD PERIOD
3. Toronto, Conacher 2nd 4:47
4. Toronto, Stemkowski 3rd (Kelly, Stanley) 13:06
Penalties—Hay (tripping) 5:14; Stemkowski (tripping) 13:37

Shots on goal
Chicago   15   10   10 — 35
Toronto   14   14   9 — 37

Crowd noise

"The best ride I've ever been on in my life"

*I liked all the [Expo] pavillions. You learned many things
about the world. I think it would be quite interesting to live
in another land because of their different foods.
My favourite pavillions were the Czech and the American.
I also liked Ontario because of the film they showed.
It was quite interesting.... I liked the rides [at Le Ronde]
the most. The log one [Le flume] was quite good....
The best ride I've ever been on in my life was the one...
that went quite a high distance up in the air.
At the top you could see all of Expo, and all of
Montreal...and the St. Lawrence River where explorers
first came to Canada.*

**—Twelve-year-old Halifax student Tracey Fox's
school report on Expo.**

17

The Last Chess Match

As always, it had come down to Leafs and Canadiens.

"Seemed like every year back then it was Montreal and Toronto in the play-offs," remembers Red Kelly. "If we wanted to win the Cup, well, sooner or later we had to beat Montreal. And I guess they probably felt the same way, meanin' they knew they'd have to beat us."

"On the Canadiens," says Terry Harper, "we felt that we played everyone else just so we could play Toronto. That was the series. Those were the games. Ho-ho, boy-oh-boy—one half the country against the other; everybody watching! I can't describe the feeling you'd have during those series." A long pause. "It was just—well, you felt like you'd spent your whole life as an athlete preparing for those nights. It was different, special—I'm sorry I can't say it any better than that."

"Toe, he would cut off an arm to beat Toronto," J.C. Tremblay says, giggling. "Yeah, to beat Imlach, maybe two [arms]."

"Punch was just a son-of-a-bitch when it came to competition," Louis Cauz says. "Part of him hated anybody that ever beat him at anything. Blake beat him his share and I think he just grew to hate the Canadiens. Well, maybe not hate—let's just say he loved beating them. And he was a yapper. He knew where to put the needle. Blake was kind of a moody guy, so I think he figured, hey, maybe I can get this guy. So he insulted Montreal all the time, which he knew would piss Blake off."

"What Imlach did to Toe was just a chess move," Harper says. "When people ask me what happened after expansion, I say, 'There was no more chess.' Before we played Toronto fifteen or twenty times a season. And there was no turnover from year to year, so over the years, we'd played literally hundreds and hundreds of times. You wouldn't know anybody on the Leafs personally, but you knew them as hockey players— knew every move they'd make. They knew every move you made. Everything became like chess. That Cup final between Montreal and Toronto was maybe the last chess match."

Punch made his first move Wednesday, April 19, the day before the finals started. He was relaxing in the corner reds of Maple Leaf Gardens, absently watching practice. "Toronto in five or six," Imlach told reporters. Leafs would split the upcoming games in Montreal, then sweep the Canadiens at home, he predicted. Newsmen prodded Imlach for a better quote, suggesting Blake seemed to have his club in pretty good shape; what had they won, fourteen straight?

Punch knew what was up.

"What the fuck you trying to get me to say? You want me to disagree with you? To say something against Montreal. OK, Toe Blake is full of shit. If you think that it will win us the Cup if I say that, I'll say it."

Someone then asked him about Vachon's comment, "I hope Toronto beats Chicago because the Leafs would be easier to beat in the finals."

That did it.

"You can tell that Junior B goaltender he won't be playing against a bunch of pea-shooters when he plays against the Leafs," Imlach shouted. Seeing reporters scribbling hard, Punch realized he was onto something. "I just hope [Blake] doesn't disappoint me by putting someone else in besides Vachon. We'll take his head off with our first shot. Blake's been getting away with a Junior B goaltender."

By the time Red Fisher phoned Imlach for a quote that afternoon, Punch had his part memorized. After a dull prologue—"we have to take one game at a time"; "we have to win one in Montreal"—Imlach precipitated his big speech.

"Who do you think is going to take the series?"

"It'll be finished in five games," Fisher predicted.

"Who'll win?"

"Canadiens."

"There is no way that [Canadiens] can beat us with a Junior B goaltender."

"Junior B?"

"That's what I said."

"For the record?"

"Listen, you called me for a story. There it is."

Fisher reminded Imlach that Vachon was on a month-long unbeaten streak, averaging under two-and-a-half goals a game.

"I don't care about his record. He's been up against a bunch of pea-shooters. As far as I'm concerned, that goaltender is a Junior B boy."

Little did Punch know that even as he deployed his rook, he was losing a knight. After practice that afternoon, Horatio deposited himself in a Church St. bar and drank up the rest of the day. It'd been a long season for Terry Sawchuk. The goalie was down to 150 pounds (he once played at 228). Aside from the beating he'd taken from Chicago, his body ached from three decades of hard winters: 250 stitches left his face a briar patch of wrinkles; one arm was crooked (botched surgery); and his back throbbed from recent operations. Life had also left marks: there was a bad car crash in 1953; a mental breakdown in 1957; and ongoing marital problems (his wife would remarry her sister's husband in 1968).

When Sawchuk received a $2,000 signing bonus with Detroit in 1947, the chubby teenager rushed across the border to a Windsor bank to convert the cheque into 2,100 Canadian one-dollar bills. He then returned to his motel and rolled in the money as a child would a pile of leaves, dreaming of glory and happiness. There had been lots of glory, but maybe not enough happiness. Three times this season he'd tried to quit hockey.

"At the end of the season [the day after Sawchuk's grim performance in a 5–2 loss in Montreal], I interviewed Terry. He said he was through, that he wanted to go back to Detroit," Louis Cauz recalls. "Fine, I write the story, show up next day at the Gardens, he comes after me with a stick. 'You prick, what you trying to do to me?' he said. 'I wrote what you said,' I said. He kept screaming, 'You're trying to screw me— you're trying to screw me.' All the while Imlach's sitting on an exercise bike, laughing, 'Go ahead, Terry, you give it to him, take a swing at him. Fuckin' reporters never get anything right.' Sawchuk was pretty miserable most of the time, like he had the weight of the world on his shoulders."

Whether it was the mounting burden of his life or just a bad hangover, Sawchuk wasn't ready for the first game of the Stanley Cup finals. Before opening face-off, Vachon was all industry: skate-scraping the gloss off his crease and whacking posts with his stick. At the other end, Sawchuk skated slowly outside the net, head down, staring at the ice as if in search of submerged monsters.

The game started fast, with Béliveau and Gilles Tremblay trading the puck twice in a smart dash down the boards. Canadiens' momentum died, however, when Larose took a penalty. Talbot and Provost looked to have the Leaf power play controlled. Then Horton stole a clearing pass, zigged between J.C. and Harris, drew Vachon, and flipped a back-hand into the last inch of the diving goalie's glove. As a relieved Forum screamed thanks, Talbot gave Vachon a smack on the pads. The rookie had kept his head on the Leafs' first shot.

The Habs rushed back, forcing Leafs into a penalty. On the power play, Montreal showed how much jump it had this night. Béliveau beat Keon to the draw. J.C. played with the puck at the blueline, then fed Duff, who wheeled and fired a low shot that kicked off a leg wide. Horton was set to clear when Rousseau (!) knocked him reeling into the boards. Cournoyer grabbed the puck and spun in front, whipping a backhander past a stunned Sawchuk (the goalie was eyeing the slot for a pass out).

Good work by Stemkowski's line evened the score seconds later. Pappin cut around Harris, lost and found the puck in the corner, then caught Hillman steaming between the circles. The defenseman's shot zipped low past Vachon on the glove side to tie the game.

The Habs dominated the rest of the period, outskating, even outhitting the Leafs. Canadiens drew most of referee Bill Friday's penalties (five of seven), but negated Leaf advantages with fierce checking. At even strength, the rested and well-schooled Montrealers were too quick and clever for a Toronto team that was forty-eight hours removed from the murderous Chicago series.

"In the play-offs, Toe wanted us to play our game, only faster," J.C. says. "Everybody says, 'Play the man,' but most guys play the puck. Except in the play-offs. If they call every interference in the play-offs, there would be no one left [on the ice]. So our play-off practice would be fast as possible. Toronto was bad at interference, so Toe would want us to be skating and passing fast as we can. He would also work extra on the power play and penalty [killing] because the scores are close and there are many penalties in the play-off."

As well as drilling specialty teams, Blake made two chess moves of his own in game one—pitting Provost against Mahovlich, and reuniting Balon, Richard, and Rochefort, heroes of last spring's Cup win. The strategies worked to perfection. Midway in the first, Richard hit Rochefort with a 70-foot strike at the blueline. Sawchuk got a pad on the shot, but Balon, hustling, gathered the rebound, passing to the swooping Richard, who tapped the puck home. In the third, the line struck twice, with Henri converting another generous Sawchuk rebound, then deflecting a waist-high J.C. blast into the top corner. While Richard's line took care of the scoring, Provost and Béliveau handled the Big M and Keon. The Captain also scored, splitting Sawchuk's legs with a short backhand in the middle period. Habs were also masterful with a man advantage, as Cournoyer scored another powerplay goal (his 12th this season against Toronto) on a peek-a-boo move from behind the net that caught Sawchuk frozen in thought.

Down 5–2, Punch replaced Sawchuk with fifteen minutes left. He also pulled Stanley, Horton, Keon, and Mahovlich. "I just tried to keep my good guys off the ice in the last ten minutes," Punch explained. "I took Terry off to conserve energy." The Leaf line-up for Montreal's sixth goal included Bower, Aut Erickson (in from Victoria) and Baun on defense, with Conacher, Walton, and Shack up front. The strategy was another Imlach chess move, a way of saying to Blake: we're tired, I'll give you this one.

Toe retaliated with a little poke at Imlach in his post-game press conference. Reporters commented on how cool Vachon looked. The rookie hadn't given up a bad goal (Pappin scored the second Leaf goal on a low blazer off the post), and made the saves his team needed: the early stop on Horton, and a neat pad save on Mahovlich with the score 4–2.

"Isn't this a hell of a thing?" Blake said, shaking his head. "Vachon's got to be the only junior B goalie in history who has come up and won five straight games in Stanley Cup play-offs."

FIRST PERIOD

1. Montreal, Cournoyer 1st (Béliveau, Rousseau) 6:25
2. Toronto, Hillman 1st (Pappin) 6:40
3. Montreal, Richard 1st (Rochefort, Balon) 11:19
Penalties—Larose (high-sticking) 1:07; Mahovlich (interference) 5:56; Harris (hooking) 8:35; Harris (hooking) 11:53; Toronto (too many men on the ice, served by Aut Erickson) 12:48; Béliveau (elbowing) 14:51; Rochefort (charging) 18:27

SECOND PERIOD

4. Montreal, Cournoyer 2nd (Rousseau, Richard) 5:03
5. Montreal, Béliveau 3rd (G. Tremblay) 6:36
6. Toronto, Pappin 4th (Horton, Pulford) 12:59
Penalties—Pappin (hooking) 2:06; Conacher (elbowing) 4:28; Harper (elbowing) 12:41; Larose (slashing) 13:12; Horton (hooking) 14:35

THIRD PERIOD
7. Montreal, Richard 2nd (Balon) 4:53
8. Montreal, Richard 3rd (J.C. Tremblay) 8:21
Penalties—Conacher (charging) 9:14; Balon (tripping) 13:25;
Ferguson (hooking) 18:34

Shots on goal
Toronto   8   10   8 — 26
Montreal   12   18   14 — 44

Punch gave Dodo a call after game one, then had to step away
from the receiver when his wife jumped on the line. "She just
about came straight over the telephone at me," he told Scott
Young. "She was mad about the television coverage [after
Montreal's 6–2 win]. Even the guys from Toronto talked as if
the body was ready for burial. The next day one of the
Toronto writers called it humiliating. Another [the *Star*'s Red
Burnett] said it was like jet fighters against Sopwith Camels."

Soon Imlach was mad as Dodo. Madder. He couldn't
believe experts were predicting a Montreal sweep. "I'll get
them," he promised. But not right away. In fact, Punch was so
subdued Friday morning one newspaper headline declared
"Imlach's snarl oddly suppressed at practice." Punch was quiet
because he had some thinking to do; for one thing, he had to
decide which goalie would start game two on Saturday afternoon.

"Don't know who I'll start," Imlach said that practice,
"they will decide themselves who'll play." Bower was incredible that morning work-out, "making every save as though it
was the last period, score tied, in the last game for the championship," according to one report. After calmly assessing his
team, Punch quit the rink for the Queen Elizabeth Hotel. A
few hours later, he rang Clancy.

"Come with me," he said. "We're going to the press room
to show the flag." On the way, Imlach explained how everyone had written the Leafs off. Imagine, here they'd knocked
off the Hawks, number-one team in the world according to
experts. Now these same guys were calling for Leafs to lose
four straight to Montreal. With every "no way" and "your

darn tootin'," the men grew more agitated. Upon reaching the press room they were past ready. Britches hitched and fedoras lowered, Imlach and Clancy burst into the writers' quarters.

"Oh, they were something," remembers George Gross. "'Who's gonna win?' Punch would ask. If you said 'Montreal,' he'd shout back, 'Ah, you're nuts,' then explain Toronto was going to win four straight. Which everyone thought was crazy after the first game. Clancy, he worked the other end of the room. Both of them went from reporter to reporter, pointing and yelling, 'We're gonna win this thing, just watch us.'"

One Los Angeles reporter, in for his first taste of hockey, approached Imlach and peered in closely. After watching Punch stain the air Leaf blue for twenty minutes, the writer shook his head and asked, "Are you for real?"

After a couple of drinks, Imlach grabbed George Gross.

"C'mon, let's go."

"Where we going?"

"Never mind, you coming or not?"

Punch then lead Gross out into the bustle that was Montreal on a late spring afternoon. "A lot of people recognized me," Punch told Scott Young, "and gave me the business about the game the night before, just one long raspberry all the way along St. Catherine Street. I kept telling them not to bet their whole wad on Canadiens. Finally I wound up at a tailor shop. I told the guy, Tony, to make me a suit. 'It has to be something special, because I want to wear it on the night we win the Stanley Cup.'"

"If you want to wear the suit when you win the Stanley Cup, I think you're going to wait awhile," Tony replied.

"Look, just get the suit ready," Imlach snapped.

"I picked out a green check that I figured would look good on colour television," Punch told Young. "Then I picked out accessories, including an Oleg Cassini tie. On the way back I straightened out a taxi driver and a bellhop about who was going to win the Stanley Cup."

While Punch was off on a clothes-buying spree, his players held another team meeting. Unlike their coach, the Leafs were very impressed with Montreal in game one.

"Montreal were the only team that I found myself watching on the bench, going, 'Boy, are they good,'" Stanley remembers. "They had five guys in your end racing around, and if you were lucky enough to get the puck in their end, they had the same five guys back, checking you into the ice.

"At the meeting that night we talked about how fast they were getting into our end. We weren't getting back in time. We decided we had to do something to slow 'em down at centre. Finally, Dave Keon said, 'Listen, we kept one [forward] back against the Black Hawks, how about we keep two back against Canadiens.'"

Keon's plan was simple:

"You know how Green Bay Packers'* big defensive ends force the other team's ball carrier into the middle," Keon said. "That's what your wings can do in hockey if they're skating. If our wings come back, their wings are tied up at our blueline. That means their centre comes to our blueline with no one to deal the puck to. If you backcheck, their forwards can't break across your line in full flight. That way, your defensemen can stand up outside and kill off all the traffic before it gets in your zone."

"That was Davey, always thinking defense," Stanley says. "Leaf defensemen used to go out together after practice or on the road. No forwards. But sometimes we'd invite Davey. Horton would say, 'Ah, he's almost a defenseman anyway.'"

On Saturday afternoon, the Leafs, with Bower in nets, demonstrated right away there would be no repeat of game one. At eight seconds, Stemkowski beat Vachon with a low shot that clanked off the post.

"Ohhh."

Seconds later, Pulford and Stemkowski joined together to lowbridge Larose.

"Unnhhh."

When the Habs finally fought their way into Leafs' end,

---

* Vince Lombardi's Green Bay Packers won five NFL titles in the 60s. On January 15, 1967, Green Bay beat Kansas City, 35–15, to take the first ever Superbowl.

Horton spilled Larose, depositing the winger head first onto the ice.

"Ehhhhhh."

Ellis was sent off. Keon and Conacher, skating hard, kept Hab marksmen off balance and outside the circles. But Cournoyer slipped through on a Béliveau set-up. Yvan had a corner. Shot. But Bower, sprawling, kicked the puck wide.

"Ahh. Ohhhh."

Then the Leafs got a power play chance. Walton, from the right boards, sent a blind backhand to Pulford between the circles. Number 20 missed the pass, but chased the rebound up boards. J.C. had time to clear, but overskated the play. Pulford turned with the puck, spotted a blue-and-white shirt free, then threw a pass into the slot that Stemkowski deflected past Vachon. Suddenly, the only sound in the Forum was Blake yelling at the time clock.

Down 1–0, first intermission, Toe implored his men to quicken the tempo, and to for God's sake stay away from penalties. Canadiens had given up six power play goals against New York in the semis, now two in eighty minutes to Toronto.

But in the second period, the Habs had even less luck penetrating the forest of mid-ice Leaf checkers. Conacher, playing with Kelly and Ellis, along with the reunited Mahovlich-Keon-Armstrong unit, kept the Richard and Béliveau lines quiet. And Stemkowski's line was winning the war against Ferguson, Backstrom, and Larose. Worse still for the Canadiens, the Leafs seemed to have finally figured out Rogie.

"After playing against Vachon a while we noticed that he stayed way back in the net," says Conacher. "Also, he had this little habit of kicking out instead of kicking wide on low shots to the corner. So that's where we shot for every chance we got. Low, inside the post." (Hearing this, Stanley chuckles. "Boy, if I thought our guys could bang a shot low in off the post any time they wanted, I would've slept a lot better back then.")

At seven minutes, Cournoyer took a bad slashing penalty. With Toe fuming at the Hab bench, Mahovlich took off

behind his net and raced down the left boards. Provost captured Frank's centring pass, but made a poor clear. Pappin
nabbed the puck and dished to Walton in the middle. The
rookie stepped into a low slapshot from fifty feet that rang in
off the left post.

Montreal played its best hockey after Walton's goal.
Backstrom's line pressed. Ferguson banged a pass-out low to
the corner that Bower fell to kick wide. Pronovost, then
Conacher took penalties (for twenty-five seconds both were
off). Cournoyer, Béliveau, Gilles Tremblay, and Rousseau
swarmed…had chances. But Bower jumped, flopped, and
threw himself sideways to keep the puck out. After every save,
he jumped to his skates, his ancient black trapper dangling,
and did his signature backwards shuffle, kicking his feet as if a
carpet had been given a tug beneath him.

Back at full strength, Leafs zeroed in on what they considered Vachon's weakness. Conacher banged a Hab off the
puck. Stemkowski (the "magnetic Pole," the papers were calling him) then passed back to Horton, who rammed a low
fifty-five-footer wide of Vachon's left boot to make it 3–0.

With Horton's goal, Montreal grew frustrated. Harris skew-
ered Stemkowski, leaving the centre with a ten-inch welt on
his abdomen. Pete spent second intermission on all fours,
barking like a dog trying to bring up a chicken bone. A
minute into the third, Ferguson crashed the Leaf crease and
jerked his stick under Bower's nose, lifting the goalie off the
ice. When Bower scrambled to his feet, Ferguson swung by
and clipped him with another high stick. Bower flopped to
the ice, bleeding from his nose and lip.

When Bobby Haggart got to the fallen goalie, Bower was
white and shaking. "Wanna come to the bench?" the trainer
asked. Bower, a modest but intensely competitive individual,
had already spent too much time on the bench this season.
"I'm hot!" he yelled, skating away. "Just leave me alone!
Don't bother me!"

"Cool it, John," a teammate suggested.

Boy, did he. For the remainder of the period, the forty-two-
year-old veteran attacked Canadien shooters with a cold,
implacable fury. In the game's last minute, Backstrom's line

put on a final charge. Larose shot. Fergy poked for a rebound
that wasn't there, lancing Bower in the shoulder. When
Bower climbed to his knees, he spat the puck back at the
Canadiens, removing his blocker and hurling the puck down
the ice with his bare hand.

"I was mad. I wanted to win that game bad," Bower commented the next day. What Bower or any other Leaf had to say
immediately following the team's big win is not known. Punch
barred reporters from the dressing-room. The players had to
catch a train in an hour, he said. Just as he had after the second-game upset in Chicago, Punch positioned himself outside
the dressing-room. Minutes later, Clancy joined him for a
reprise of their performance in the press room the day before.

"Don't forget to remind them how we couldn't skate with
Montreal, Punchy," Clancy said, winking.

"Listen, the only way to beat the Canadiens is to ram it
down their throats," Punch crowed.

Someone asked about Ferguson's rough handling of Bower.

"Three times Ferguson charges Bower," Imlach roared.
"Once, he cracks open Bower's nose and now he's bleeding for
the rest of the game. What Bower should do is hold his stick
straight out whenever Ferguson runs at him. Bower should
whack at him so hard we'd be picking splinters out of
Ferguson's ass."

Then this:

"Ferguson's lucky I'm not Bower."

FIRST PERIOD
1. Toronto, Stemkowski 4th (Pulford, Walton) 12:14
Penalties—Ellis (holding) 1:29; Harper (roughing) 10:59; Stanley
(tripping) 14:56; Harris (hooking) 17:17; Conacher (high-sticking)
19:41

SECOND PERIOD
2. Toronto, Walton 3rd (Pappin, Mahovlich) 9:12
3. Toronto, Horton 2nd (Stemkowski, Conacher) 16:57
Penalties—Horton (hooking) 5:23; Cournoyer (slashing) 7:18;
Pronovost (tripping) 10:23; Conacher (charging) 11:58; Ferguson
(interference) 14:26

THIRD PERIOD
No scoring
Penalties—Conacher (hooking) 7:48; Béliveau (slashing) 14:21;
Stemkowski (tripping) 16:02

Shots on goal
Toronto   14   10   19 — 43
Montreal   13   9   9 — 31

"Toronto shocked us second game," Harper says today.
"Everything had fallen into place nicely up until then. We go
on a long winning streak to end the season. Finish off New
York four straight. Then Leafs beat Chicago, the team we
were really worried about. We couldn't believe our luck. Man,
this is great, we thought. Then we win the first game easily.
And don't forget we'd handled Toronto the year before in the
play-offs. Expo was coming up in Montreal. It seemed like our
year. We thought it was going to be easy."

"Going into the series we might've thought we were playing the old Leafs," Ferguson says. "But a few games in we realized we weren't playing the same team we beat in the [1966]
play-offs. That line of Stemkowski and Pappin [and Pulford]
was new. And they were giving us problems."

Then there was an old Canadien problem: Johnny Bower.

"We knew [Sawchuk] played well against Chicago, but we
wanted him, not Bower, in the finals," Ferguson says. "We felt
we could handle him better."

"Plante was the best goalie I ever saw. Sawchuk was the
best I ever played against," Béliveau says, "but for some reason, don't ask me why, I always had more trouble with Bower,
especially in the play-offs."

"In my rookie year, Bower stopped me on a breakaway and
after that I was never comfortable against him," mentions
Cournoyer.

"They were both very good," J.C. says, "but Sawchuk, he
could have a bad game. Sometime, I don't know, he seemed to
lose strength. Like I remember once I beat him on a flip shot
and after that he was shaky. Bower, he was different. Once in
the play-offs [the fourth game of the 1964 semi-finals], I beat

Bower on a long flip shot. He just got mad and never let in another goal."

To speed Montreal's attack game three, Toe went to four lines, changing frequently. The plan yielded immediate results. On Tuesday in Toronto, the Canadiens broke out with twenty first-period shots, more than they managed the last forty minutes of game two. At first it seemed Blake's team might run Leafs right out of the rink. The Habs forced an early penalty. Rousseau moved in from the point, wound up, drawing Bower, Stanley, and Baun, then threaded a pass to Béliveau, alone in the crease, for a fast 1–0 lead.

For the next five minutes, Bower kept his team in the game, giving the defense time to settle. By the middle of the period, a blue wall had descended around the Leaf net. This was the team's special talent, says Emile Francis. Nobody could turn turtle when in danger better than Toronto.

"Cripes, they'd get those big defensemen in front," Francis recalls, "and Armstrong and some of the old guys would get in the way of the shooters. You'd think you were winnin', you'd have the puck in their end all the time. But at the end of the game, you'd ask yourself, 'Why didn't we get more than two goals?' Then you'd look at the film and see that there was never a Leaf out of position. And if they ever got a late lead, oh brother, you could fire away until July, you weren't gettin' that goal back."

Toronto rallied to collect the period's only other goal. The ingredients were by now familiar: Stemkowski, on a power play, won the draw to Pappin, who passed to Hillman. The defenseman's low shot was deflected by Stemkowski wide of Vachon's left leg (and yes, Rogie kicked out, not at the skimming puck).

Leafs found their form in the second period, controlling neutral ice and forcing play in the offensive zone. Mahovlich, in front of Vachon, banked a shot off the diving Rousseau that bounded in a crazy arc just off the post. Laperrière, playing brilliantly, smothered chances by Pulford and Stemkowski. And Vachon blithely turned aside close-in tries by Pappin and Keon. Although he had let in two long shots the game previous and had a bad stretch in the first game against New York, Rogie had been effective this post-season. Everyone commented on how cool the gum-snapping rookie looked in the Cup spotlight.

"One day just before a play-off game in Montreal, when we were coming back from the [team hide-away in the] Laurentians, I fell asleep on the bus," Vachon recalls. "The other guys couldn't believe it. I didn't know what to say—it's just the way I am."

Although Vachon was dauntless in the second period, allowing a single goal, a short Pappin backhand that trickled between his pads, he made one seemingly insignificant play that points to the problem of having an inexperienced goal-tender in a close series. On a power play, Hillman lobbed a shot from centre. The puck struck J.C. inside the blueline and rolled to the net. Rogie came out to clear, then looked up to find his defense as he swiped at the puck. He missed, causing an instant panic. Forwards Provost and Talbot hustled back to erase the mistake, so the fumble didn't cost Montreal, but these little misplays, which Rogie would commit every other period, took the edge off the Habs' attack.

"With a veteran goaltender," Béliveau comments, "you get comfortable. You know he won't make any mistake. He gives you the big save. You can think about offense more. You're more aggressive. A rookie, he can make the big save, too. But you're not as sure of him. He makes you a little nervous. You protect him more in a close game. You start coming back to your net all the time. Soon, every time you get the puck you have the whole rink to skate. It's hard to score like that."

The next mistake, however, was made by a forty-nine-year-old Leaf veteran. Toronto had enjoyed a face-off edge so far this series. "Stemkowski was stealing the puck from Canadiens' centremen all [through game three]," according to Red Fisher. Yet with seconds to go in the middle period, Imlach had Pronovost take a draw against Béliveau in the Leaf end. Stemkowski, meanwhile, stood back in the corner. This was old-fashioned hockey. In the 40s and 50s, defense-men routinely bowled centres over in draws. A face-off inter-ference rule in the mid-60s eliminated that manoeuvre; now coaches used centres at both ends. Except Imlach, who employed Horton and Pronovost on the odd draw.

With the drop of the puck, a confused Stemkowski rushed the circle. Pronovost won the draw, then turned and fired a pass back to his centre in the corner. Only big Pete was now six feet away. The hard pass sprang off Stemkowski's stick to Ferguson, who swiped a quick backhand past Bower.

Blake got hold of his team in the dressing-room. As always, his instructions were direct. "Win this period, and we kill Toronto," he said. "Skate hard for twenty minutes."

The Canadiens came out playing with that special passion that was theirs alone. Béliveau's line finally shook free of Keon and Armstrong. Ferguson, Backstrom, and Larose lost their checks. The entire club was on fire. Skating. Digging in corners. Rushing Bower. The Leafs responded with gallant hockey. Hillman and Stanley had been throwing murderous checks all night. In the second period, Conacher clubbed Larose to the ice with a looping right, splitting his head for seven stitches. Now that referee John Ashley swallowed his whistle (an ancient third-period play-off custom), the Leafs were free to swing shoulders and hips with impunity.

The first ten minutes of the period saw a classic clash of styles and purpose. Both teams were at their best. Gradually, however, Montreal asserted itself. At eleven minutes, J.C. set up Cournoyer between the circles. Then Béliveau found Gilles Tremblay with plenty of room down the left side. A shift later, Ferguson was alone with the puck in the slot. The Leafs found themselves outmanoeuvred, stranded and lost at the wrong end of the ice floe. Bower, though, was always in position, crouched and ready for more work. He'd lost forty-five games this season to injuries. Missed all but a period in the semi-finals with a split finger. Now he was determined to make up for lost time, lunging hungrily at everything flung his way.

The third period ended as it began, a two-all tie.

If anything, the Canadiens were faster and stronger in overtime. Blake deserves credit here. The Montreal coach employed four lines and seventeen skaters most of the night. Imlach, meanwhile, kept Baun, Shack, Walton, and call-up Milan Marcetta on the bench, going with fourteen skaters after the second period. In the first six minutes of overtime, the drooping Leafs failed to get a shot on Vachon. The Habs, meanwhile, rolled in on the Leaf goal in waves.

At four minutes, Rochefort was in alone, but Bower steered him wide. A minute later, Béliveau sent Cournoyer around Pronovost. Bower kept with the shifty forward's every move, forcing him into a bad shot. Duff was right in with one shot...then another. J.C., pinching, had a clear try from the circle. Laperrière, Ferguson, and Rousseau had chances. Béliveau seemed to have an open net, but Bower got a fat pad in the way. Backstrom and Gilles Tremblay had a two-on-one. Backstrom made a good pass. Tremblay picked his corner. Fired. But the shot rang off the post. Then Béliveau found Cournoyer at the Leaf blueline. Hillman stumbled. The winger cut in free, but when he looked up, Bower was sliding sideways on top of him, with his stick stretched out forever.

"I knew he was going to stop me," Cournoyer said later, "and there was not a thing I could do about it."

"[Bower] was fantastic in overtime," Vachon says. "Sometime looking down the ice I could feel myself about to celebrate, I was sure we were going to score, but he always made the save."

Vachon made fine saves, too. After Cournoyer's miss, Stemkowski had Gardens fans up and screaming when he walked in alone on Vachon. But breakaways were the little goalie's specialty. Big Pete shifted, fired. The puck ticked off Rogie's pad then clanked off the post. Later, Mahovlich moved in from the left side, but Vachon got a foot on his low screamer. Keon banged one at a free corner that Rogie kicked into the glass. The Canadiens also enjoyed late chances, with Gilles Tremblay and Duff testing Bower. The game was so close, so tense, some couldn't watch. Leaf owner Stafford Smythe left the Gardens for a stroll to ease his jangled nerves. He walked up and down Church Street, ear cocked to the wind. But no conclusive cry was forthcoming. The first overtime ended with teams still deadlocked.

"You know, I never minded all the practice Punch gave us," Stanley says today. "I figured I needed it. The harder I worked, the readier I felt. I felt stronger, too. It makes sense.

You're just building up endurance and muscle."

Stanley, at forty, would've put in fifty minutes of hard sledding by second overtime. But he was still hungry for action. In the game's eighty-third minute, he caught Henri looking backwards for a pass at mid-ice. Sam wasn't fast (Rex MacLeod once wrote of Stanley "snow-shoeing in from the blueline"), but always in position. The defenseman lowered his shoulder and caught Henri the instant the puck arrived on his stick. Richard flew backwards as if hit by a car. There was a bubble of blood in his nostril when physiotherapist Yvon Belanger lifted his head and broke a capsule of smelling salts under his nose.

The Stanley check energized Toronto. Soon the team was skating and hitting harder, taking the game to the Canadiens. "We got our fourth wind," Stemkowski would explain later.

With Richard gone, Blake lost his best face-off man this evening. Rousseau now centred Duff and Provost. Eight minutes into second overtime, Rousseau took a draw to the right of Vachon. Stemkowski pulled the puck back to Stanley. His slapshot deflected off a charging Rousseau to the right boards. Laperrière, Pulford, Stemkowski, and Duff converged. The Leaf centre arrived first and swung into the corner. Laperrière rode him into the glass. Stemkowski managed a desperate backhand just as Harper escorted Pulford through the crease. The shot went off Harper, bouncing toward Pappin at the circle. Feeling the puck on his skate, Harper turned, allowing Pulford to roll free and slip back into the slot. When Pappin reached the puck he hurried a backhand wide of the net that Pulford, reaching quickly, flicked into the open side of the goal.

A great roar ripped the Gardens. Even Stafford Smythe, strolling outside on Church Street, could hear right away that it was all over. By the time Milan Marcetta joined the happy Leaf pile-up at centre, Canadiens were in the runway back to the dressing-room. Minutes later, the grieving was underway.

"So many clear chances we had on Bower," Béliveau moaned. "Gilles Tremblay two or three times, myself a couple and, best of all, Cournoyer." He shook his head. "I put Cournoyer in twice, alone, and we can't score. How can you beat it?"

Someone asked Richard about the Stanley check.

"I don't remember," he said.

How about the game? the reporter continued.

"I don't remember the game," Henri mumbled.

Blake paced the training table, eyes to the floor, and talked about Bower and spilt milk. One you could cry over, the other you couldn't. Larose complained about how the linesman had held him down when Conacher delivered his knockout blow. No one spoke above a whisper. "Great game," someone mentioned to Ferguson. "Sure, great game—for them," he hissed.

"We were very disappointed after that game," Harper remembers. "We lost the second game because we played badly. But we played about as well as we could that [third] game and still we lost. Bower—Bower just beat us that night."

"I still don't know how he stopped me on one shot." Béliveau says almost thirty years later. "I had the whole net and he stopped me."

FIRST PERIOD

1. Montreal, Béliveau 4th (Rousseau, Duff) 2:27
2. Toronto, Stemkowski 5th (Hillman, Pappin) 8:30
Penalties—Horton (interference) 1:13; Ferguson (interference) 8:04; Bower (tripping, served by Walton) 9:27; Larose (slashing) 13:52; Mahovlich (tripping) 15:57

SECOND PERIOD

3. Toronto, Pappin 5th (Horton, Pulford) 10:34
4. Montreal, Ferguson 4th (Béliveau) 19:10
Penalties—Stanley (tripping) 2:31; Conacher and Larose (majors, fighting) 6:10; Cournoyer and Shack (high-sticking) 6:38; Mahovlich (cross-checking) 19:32, Béliveau (charging) 19:32

THIRD PERIOD
No scoring
Penalties—Ferguson (hooking) 3:23

FIRST OVERTIME
No scoring
No penalties

SECOND OVERTIME
5. Toronto, Pulford 1st (Stemkowski, Pappin) 8:26
Penalties—none

Shots on goal
Montreal   20   8   14   13   7 — 62
Toronto   12   12   10   11   9 — 54

Imlach was a poor winner the morning after the glorious
struggle that was game three. He and Clancy were in the
Gardens coffee shop, nursing their second cup of tea, when a
Montreal reporter happened by.

"How's your team?" the Leaf coach inquired, stirring his
drink. "Ask them if they want to be humiliated any more?"

Clancy cringed. "For crying out loud, will you cut that
out," he shouted.

"There's no way we can lose to the Canadiens if this team
plays the way it has," Imlach continued, enjoying himself.
"That game last night should have tipped you off."

Punch also had a message for Toe Blake.

"Vachon's up to Junior A now. He's graduated from Junior
B to Junior A."

That afternoon, Blake's mouth tightened when reporters
asked about his rookie goaltender. "Vachon didn't lose the
game for us the other night," he said. "If we win, he's the hero."

Before Wednesday's work-out, Imlach told his club to take
it easy on the goalies. "There's a $25 fine for anybody who
gets one [a shot] up," he told players. (In Tuesday's practice,
Mahovlich had ripped a puck off Bower's chin, nicking him
for three stitches, and Shack had whacked Sawchuk's wrist
trying to dislodge a puck, sending the goalie to the clinic.)

Both goalies made it alive through Wednesday's practice.
Thursday's, too. But five minutes before game time that night,
Bower stretched for a shot in warm-up and felt a stab in his
groin. When referee Art Skov called the teams to centre ice,
Sawchuk was in goal for Toronto.

For the first five minutes, it didn't matter who was in Leafs'
net. Stemkowski won the opening draw. Pulford dumped the

puck in Montreal's end. Then Vachon made a rookie mistake, stopping the puck behind the net instead of letting it curl the boards to Harper. Stemkowski got there first, forcing Laperrière into a penalty. On the power play, Pulford fed Stemkowski in front, but Vachon kicked the puck wide. Then Walton cruised in free between the circles, snapping a shot wide of Vachon's glove. Rogie showed a fast hand to snare the puck, then lifted his trophy high, calling attention to his save with a Plante-like flourish. Seconds later, he made a big stop on Walton. Then he stole a goal from Keon.

After that, the Habs settled down and the game fell into a tight-checking battle, with the teams playing careful play-off hockey. Midway into the period, Gilles Tremblay made a fine sweep check on Stanley, sending the puck to Backstrom. With Horton rushing in, the centre hurried a blind backhand. Sawchuk fell in anticipation of a low shot. It was high. Canadiens had a 1–0 lead. A minute later, Rousseau took aim from the point. Again, Sawchuk was on his hands and knees. The puck went off Horton wide. The goalie lurched to his feet and fell to the net, arms extended to catch the post. Béliveau's pass from the corner struck him on the skate, trickling past the goal line.

Up two, Habs played with the pluck and assurance they displayed in game one, outshooting Toronto 8–1 the rest of the period. First intermission, Punch attempted a quick repair job, replacing Armstrong and Stanley with Shack and Baun in hope of giving his club more speed and grit. The moves worked. Shack excited the crowd and almost forced a backhand past Vachon. A minute later, Rogie lost his moorings, and had Walton's corner pass go in off his skate to close the gap to 2–1.

As the Gardens glee club joined together in its first "Go Leafs Go!" of the evening, Richard bobbed down the right side and let go a floater from the circle. Sawchuk grabbed at the puck, but missed. Three-one, Montreal.

Leafs continued to play hard. Hitting. Skating with purpose. Pressing Vachon. Their diligence was rewarded when Horton smacked a long, low slapshot past Rogie at twelve minutes. It was 3–2, a game again. But only until the next

Hab rush. The following shift, Béliveau and Cournoyer traded passes down the right side, working the puck inside the blue-line. The Captain's quick, low forty-footer restored the Canadiens' two-goal bulge. Two minutes later, Backstrom tore down the right side at a bad angle, faked a pass to Gilles Tremblay, then sped around Sawchuk, who stumbled forward like a man probing for a light switch in the dark. Backstrom's backhand tally killed whatever interest the Leafs had left in the game. In the third period, Baun and Shack took four penalties, and Roberts beat Sawchuk on a long shot to make the final 6–2 Montreal.

Although Montreal's centres clearly dominated the match, scoring five goals and controlling play in both ends, Blake hailed Vachon in his post-game press conference. "If there's any such thing as a turning point I'd have to say it came on the first two stops Vachon made [on Stemkowski and Walton]," he said.

"Toe didn't like goalies, I don't think," J.C. says. "They made him nervous. Once Plante wanted to talk to him about goaltending and Toe said, 'I don't care what you do, just stop the damn puck.' But that spring with Vachon, he was different. That Imlach stuff about Vachon was a big story, eh? All the reporters wanted to know about that. Toe, every game he would say how good Vachon is to support him."

Imlach had no comments to make about Vachon this evening. Nor did he defend Sawchuk or barbecue referee Art Skov. Punch was so depressed after the final whistle that he walked right out the Gardens and let Clancy handle the press.

King made a few gracious comments—"Canadiens were just too good"; "Vachon was fantastic," then got out the pom poms: "What is this? You'd think it was a wake. It's not the end of the world, for God's sake," he told players. Then he turned to reporters and made a face, "We just didn't play good, that's all, and you reporters should like that—it's a short story."

Clancy was even optimistic about Sawchuk.

"We hope Bower is OK for Saturday, but if he's not ready, what the hell, we'll go with Sawchuk, and why not? He was dandy against Chicago. Why won't he be coming up with the biscuits?"

The Habs' trip home after game four was a happy one.

"We were in the driver's seat again," Harper says. "We had home ice advantage. We were two and two, and as far as we were concerned, Bower had beat us those two games as much as anything else. Now we had Sawchuk again and he'd looked pretty shaky. There wasn't a guy on that team who wasn't sure, absolutely sure, we were going to beat the Leafs at that point."

Well, there were maybe two worriers on the flight back to Montreal: Blake and Pollock.

"I remember flying home after game four and we were all feeling pretty good about the series again," Pollock says. "Then I remembered we were playing Saturday afternoon and I had a little twinge. I remember thinking, 'Geez, I hope we have time to get ready.' I don't know there was just something that bugged me about having to play on Saturday afternoon. No, it wasn't a premonition. I just would've felt better about playing Saturday night."

FIRST PERIOD
1. Montreal, Backstrom 4th (Larose) 12:25
2. Montreal, Béliveau 5th (Rousseau, Cournoyer) 13:08
Penalties—Laperrière (interference) 0:18; Armstrong (interference) 6:19; Pronovost (tripping) 12:36

SECOND PERIOD
3. Toronto, Walton 4th (Pulford, Stemkowski) 2:09
4. Montreal, Richard 4th 2:26
5. Toronto, Horton 3rd 12:16
6. Montreal, Béliveau 6th (Ferguson, Cournoyer) 13:41
7. Montreal, Backstrom 5th (J.C. Tremblay) 15:58
Penalties—Béliveau (boarding) 1:46; Armstrong (hooking) 4:35

THIRD PERIOD
8. Montreal, Roberts 1st (Richard) 15:17
Penalties—Harris (tripping) 2:32; Shack (charging) 8:21; Larose (slashing) 16:34; Baun (hooking) 16:34; Harris and Shack (slashing) 17:09; Ferguson and Shack (roughing) 19:29

Shots on goal
Montreal   19   10   11 — 40
Toronto   11   16   10 — 37

So far this series no team had been able to build any momentum. Montreal stormed to a one-game lead only to suffer a letdown. Leafs were superb in game two, but needed a magical performance by Bower to take game three. Then Toronto fell apart. "The next game is important for us," Blake said. "We'll see how much we want [the Cup]. We're playing well. The game's in our rink. If we win that would make it hard on Toronto, they'd have to win two in a row." Did Toe think it'd go seven? "I didn't say that." Prophesizing, Blake once noted, was for gypsies.

On Saturday afternoon, the Canadiens got the firewagon out of the station early. On the first shift, Backstrom swung around Hillman and danced in. The centre deked, picked an empty corner, but Sawchuk flashed a right leg to kick the puck wide.

During his brilliant play-off tour against Chicago, Sawchuk received a telegram of congratulations from a Newfoundland fan. After game four of this series, the same fan sent a less friendly note. "How much [of a bribe] did you get?" he asked. The telegram stung Terry, but only for a while. Goalies were used to suffering. It came with the pads. Sawchuk, at age ten, received his first pair of pads from a brother who died of a heart attack.

"Terry was upset after a game if he didn't perform," remembers Kelly. "But all goalies are like that. Next day though, well, it was another day, you know. He was an old goalie. They all get philosophical. Sometimes a puck hits you when you're not looking and you look great. Next day [a long shot] hits something and goes between the legs. What can you do?"

"When I go into the nets, I take a sideways peek at the goal posts," Sawchuk once said. "If they look close I know I'm gonna have a good night. Some nights those damn posts look a mile away."

This afternoon, Terry must've looked back and found the net looked no wider than a doorway. After two bad games, the veteran goalie was on top of his game again. As good as he'd been against Chicago. That was good news for Toronto because the team started game five in a wild panic.

A minute after Backstrom's chance, Béliveau fed Cournoyer in the high slot. In the instant it took the winger to gather the puck, the goalie stole out ten feet. When Cournoyer looked up there was no more net, just Sawchuk. Then Pappin took a penalty and the Hab power play carousel was underway—J.C., Rousseau, Duff, and Béliveau sped the puck around the periphery, stopping three times for shots by Courneyer, Béliveau, and J.C. Defenseman Tremblay's try was the best, a snap shot from the circle that Sawchuk, crouched and weaving behind a shifting forest of legs, managed to deflect wide with a straining blocker.

The Canadiens didn't let up when the Leafs returned to full strength. Finally, inevitably, Montreal squeezed one past Sawchuk. Stanley was chased into the corner by Duff. When the defenseman turned to clear, the puck rolled off his stick. Duff wheeled and found Rochefort sailing into the left circle, stick waving frantically. The pass was too far ahead. Rochefort poked instead of fired. The puck carried under Horton through Sawchuk's legs, exciting a thunderous roar from the home crowd.

Then something curious happened. An important goal in a big game at the Forum was normally the splitting of an atom. Feeding on the crowd's fury, the Canadiens would recklessly apply themselves to further destruction. Another goal would come, bringing more noise. Team effort would again multiply. Inevitably, the opposition was swallowed in the ensuing explosion. It happened in the first game of this series, and, more memorably, in Canadiens' 6–4 third-period comeback against New York in the opening round. This afternoon, however, the big eruption never came. If anything, the Habs sagged after Rochefort's marker. Oh, Montreal controlled the game—Sawchuk made splendid saves on Laperrière and Backstrom, and Béliveau hit the post from a scramble—but the team did not force the issue with the passion of other Canadien teams.

Late in the first period, Larose took a boarding penalty and

Leafs made their first organized trip into Montreal's end. Keon swung inside the Hab blueline at the left boards and slipped a pass to Pappin at the opposite circle. With Laperrière charging, the winger hurried a wrist shot from forty feet out. Vachon kicked, but he was too deep in the crease. The skimming puck wrapped around inside the post. Suddenly the game was tied.

Blake saw what was happening. Through this series the chess master had deployed his pieces brilliantly. In the first game, Richard had picked up a hat trick on a new line. After game two, Gilles Tremblay was switched to Backstrom's line, and Cournoyer placed on Béliveau's right. Any of the four would've won game three if not for Bower. Béliveau and Backstrom then counted two goals each in game four. Roberts, in for Provost, also scored that night. This afternoon, with his team lagging, Toe made another move. At the first intermission he switched Larose back to Backstrom's line. In the opening minute of the second period, Larose burst past Hillman, and found Backstrom in front. The centre shot before Sawchuk turned, but the Leaf goalie was so sharp today he sensed what he couldn't see. Shifting instinctively to the middle of the crease, Sawchuk had the puck rip off his arm just wide.

Two minutes later, the Leafs got a break. Béliveau was wheeling out of his end when Kelly got a stick between his legs. The Captain fell, then looked up. Referee Bill Friday shook his head. While the Forum crowd shouted its disapproval, Kelly tapped the puck back to Hillman. Vachon got a pad on the defenseman's long, low shot, but left a delectable rebound. Conacher, swooping in, ripped the puck into the short side and Leafs had their first lead in two games.

Teams were fidgety for the next ten minutes, scrambling and working hard without getting anywhere. Passes hopped sticks. Wingers broke offside. With every shift, the anxious crowd was pulled further into the contest. The next goal, everyone knew, was the game. Maybe the series. Just past the midway mark, Kelly bumped Béliveau at the boards, impeding his progress. It was a routine move in a tight-checking play-off game, but the aggrieved crowd responded with a great injured roar. Up went Bill Friday's arm, and out came the Canadien power play.

The next minute was excruciating for Forum fans. The Canadiens controlled play, but Pronovost and Hillman clogged the crease, and the darting Keon kept Montreal's pointmen off-balance. Worse still, Béliveau, the team's best shooter this play-off, and a vital power play cog, was having trouble on face-offs. With a minute left in the man advantage, Blake made an adjustment, bringing Rousseau in from the point to take a face off to the right of Sawchuk, and dropping Béliveau back several yards to the right, in the deep slot. Rousseau pulled the puck back to Big Jean, who blasted a short slapshot on a line to the far corner that Sawchuk, falling, managed to kick wide.

"Ohhhh."

Seconds later, Pronovost broke up a play and floated down the left boards, killing time. J.C. finally forced him wide. Marcel then flicked a harmless-looking forty-footer that sailed past Vachon's left boot just inside the far post. When the rookie hopped from his crouch, his eyes and mouth were three wide Os.

With that, the Habs grew as frustrated as their fans. The game turned chippy. Harris, then Ellis and Duff together, were sent off within a four-minute stretch. Béliveau, pressing deep in the Leaf end in the final minute, threw a pass back to the blueline to J.C. The defenseman had retreated to centre, however, and was greeted with a chorus of boos when he retrieved the puck. When he turned, the indefatigable Keon was on him immediately. The puck squirted loose. Keon bolted into Montreal's zone, circled, then slipped a pass to Horton. His shot bounced off Laperrière to Keon, who deked the staggering Vachon and pushed the puck into the empty net.

Down 4–1, Toe put Worsley in to begin the third period. Leafs never bothered trying to score—just skated, bumped, and checked. Keon in particular was magnificent. The Leaf centre was a perfectionist who often displayed a wicked temper off the ice.* Once on skates, however, Keon assumed a

---

* During the team golf tournament at training camp, Keon carded a 90, well back of Pappin (78) and Shack (79); upset with his play, Davey fired an iron into the trees one hole.

near religious discipline. The league's best checker collected one two-minute penalty all season.

Against the Canadiens, number 14 always played his best. "When I think back to the Leaf team of the 60s, their games against us in the play-offs, I think of Keon," Béliveau says. "They had many fine players, but to me, he was outstanding." Bugsy Watson was traded back to Montreal for the 1967–68 season. "First thing I asked guys when we went out for a drink was what happened with Toronto in the play-offs?" he remembers. "'Keon,' they said. 'He was everywhere at the end, he wouldn't let us move.'"

The Canadiens struggled to get back in the game in the third period. The centres toiled hard. Ferguson and Harris took their men out forcefully. But they couldn't get anything going. After two months of exceptional play, the Canadiens returned for one period to their rudderless mid-season form. The Forum was three-quarters empty in the last minutes, and the remaining fans were so quiet you could hear the scratch of the players' skates on the ice.

After the game, the Canadien dressing-room was funereal. Players undressed quietly. Blake paced. The only sound in a room of thirty men was the far-off hissing of the showers. Reporters stared at their notepads, hoping someone else would ask Blake the first question. Finally, the Canadien coach turned to his guests.

"Did I say you could come into our dressing-room?" he asked, his voice hoarse with emotion. "I shouldn't let you in here. Punch doesn't let you guys into the dressing-room when he loses. I'll let you take a shot at me for barring you from our dressing-room."

When the questions finally came, Blake stared off. He interrupted a Toronto reporter's question with a humourless smile. "There should've been a penalty on the Leafs' second goal [by Conacher]. Go and tell Punch that. Tell Punch to get the films of the second goal and show them to the referee. Ask them about the Lady Bynger's [Red Kelly] trip."

With that, Ferguson lifted his head.

"A Lady Bynger's trip, that's what it is," he hollered. "You bet your life that if it was me it would have been a penalty."

Only once during the press conference did Blake display the enormity of his famous temper. When someone asked about the move to Worsley, Toe's eyes lit up as if he'd swallowed a candle. When reporters approached Vachon for comments, he exploded again. "Leave him alone. He's just a kid. Leave him alone," the Montreal coach roared. Red Fisher reported sportswriters then "scattered like kids who have just broken a neighbour's window."

"As far as I'm concerned Toe Blake was the best hockey coach in the world," Harper says today. "He always had the answers for any problem the team had. And he had this unbelievable ability to figure out how to fit players together. Well, I just think he was a genius. I never saw him outsmarted once in my whole career. Except that Toronto series. Man, Imlach got to him with all that Junior B stuff with Vachon. All the taunting. Toe, I think he wanted to cram Vachon down Imlach's throat."

Harper skates backwards a minute to clarify himself.

"Listen, no knock against Rogie. He played real well for us at the end of the year. He helped us get to the finals. And he didn't play bad in the finals, either. And I know he became a real good goaltender in the NHL. But there he was a kid playing against Toronto in the finals, against Sawchuk and Bower and all those old pros. I couldn't agree more with what Jean Béliveau said about a rookie goaltender in tight games. A team can get tight and not play as well. Yeah, in that series, the way Toronto was playing, a real old-fashioned play-off war, I think we would've played better with an old pro like Worsley."

"That game I let the team down," Vachon recalls. "Sawchuk played real well. I didn't, and that's why we lost." He clucks his tongue. "I thought I played pretty well that series, except for that game. I know for sure that if I had've stopped a couple of those shots—say we were only losing 2–1 going into the third period, the guys could've come back. Yeah, like we did against the Rangers."

But Leafs weren't the Rangers. The series was going back to Toronto with the Canadiens down three games to two.

FIRST PERIOD
1. Montreal, Rochefort 1st (Duff, Richard) 6:03
2. Toronto, Pappin 6th (Keon, Mahovlich) 15:06
Penalties—Pappin (charging) 3:09; Larose (boarding) 13:30;
Horton (interference) 18:29

SECOND PERIOD
3. Toronto, Conacher 3rd (Kelly, Hillman) 3:07
4. Toronto, Pronovost 1st 12:02
5. Toronto, Keon 3rd (Horton) 19:27
Penalties—Ferguson (charging) 6:54; Kelly (interference) 10:40;
Harris (elbowing) 14:55; Ellis and Duff (roughing) 17:55

THIRD PERIOD
No scoring
Penalties—Mahovlich (tripping) 6:17

Shots on goal
Toronto   7   12   10 — 29
Montreal   13   13   12 — 38

Rain started building in Toronto on Tuesday, May 2 early in
the morning. By the time John Ferguson stepped out of the
Royal York to grab a cab for Maple Leaf Gardens and practice,
the rain snaked in heavy diagonals up and down Front Street.
"Lousy weather, damn," Fergy grumbled, then headed off to
work.

Both teams were grim that afternoon. A Toronto reporter
shouted hello to aquaintances on the Leafs as they stepped on
the ice for a pre-game work-out. They stared past as if he was-
n't there. Even Imlach had nothing to say. On Monday, he
proclaimed, "I'm talked out. I'll let my team do the talking for
me tomorrow night." Then he asked Montreal reporters if
they'd heard who was starting in nets for Canadiens. Not to
torment Blake. He just wanted to know.

The reporters couldn't tell Imlach much about the
Montreal goaltending situation. Neither could the players. As
was his custom, Blake kept his decision secret until just before
the opening face-off, when he advised the trainer, who in turn

handed Worsley the puck. Minutes before the sixth game, Blake was composed. "Give your best," he told players. "I know you can beat Toronto."

The Leaf dressing-room was equally calm. Earlier that day, a smiling Horton suggested the game was in the hands of God—and Terry Sawchuk. "Know what they say," the defenseman laughed, "goalkeeping is like pitching. If Sawchuk is like Koufax tonight, we win. If he isn't, well, as they say in Montreal, c'est la guerre."

The most outwardly nervous man in the home team's quarters was Imlach.

"We have to win this game tonight. If we go back to Montreal for a seventh game, all bets are off," he told players. The superstitious Imlach was terrified at the prospect of having to play another Thursday match. So far, the Leafs had played four games that day in the play-offs, losing 5–2 and 4–3 to Chicago, and 6–2 the first and fourth games of the Montreal series.

Imlach then had a few words for his young players:

"Bill Gadsby played twenty-one seasons in this league and never won a Stanley Cup," he said. "You're sixty minutes away."

Finally, he turned to his veterans:

"Some of you have been with me for nine years. It's been said that I stuck with the old ones so long we couldn't possibly win the Stanley Cup. For some of you it's a farewell. Go out there and ram that puck down their goddamn throats."

The first twenty minutes of game six defined what was unique and wonderful about these great teams. The Canadiens were bold—continuously in motion, hurtling themselves at the crowded Leaf blueline. And yet, for all that passion, the team exhibited even greater style. More precision. One rush, Béliveau, Rousseau, and J.C. made four short, blind passes in a swooping, swirling centre-ice ballet, exciting hoots of pleasure from the Toronto crowd.

In the face of all that grace and fury, Leafs were imperturbable, cautious. This supremely coordinated defensive team always felt it was ahead in a tie game. The first period was spent almost entirely inside Toronto's blueline. It was apparent how badly Montreal wanted this game from Béliveau's play. On his second shift, the Captain bulled past a check and scorched a low shot off Sawchuk's glove. In the corners, he used all of his 210 pounds to pry the puck from defenders. Big Jean's effort was contagious. Soon every Canadien was hitting. And skating. The result was continuous activity around Sawchuk.

In response, Leafs employed what was basically a five-man defense, with forwards Keon, Pulford, Ellis, Conacher, Armstrong and Kelly joining Horton-Stanley and Pronovost-Hillman in the heroic stand of the Leaf net. Still, the Habs broke through. Cournoyer, on a power play, ripped a close-in shot off the advancing Sawchuk's left leg. Backstrom had an open side, but the Leaf goalie threw the shot high with his blocker. Béliveau, after coming out of the penalty box, had the best chance. He was open and fired quickly, but Sawchuk, diving sideways, kicked the puck to safety. Then Henri put Rochefort in alone. The forward deked, went to a backhand, only to have Sawchuk take away an empty corner with a stabbing pad.

Not often, but enough times to keep Montreal nervous, the Leafs counterattacked. Keon, dipping at mid-ice, found Mahovlich free. Midway through the period, Stemkowski set Pappin up nicely. Worsley, shaking off three months of rust, made several fine saves on Toronto's big lines. The one shot he missed, a Walton snap shot from the circle, rang off the post. The first period ended with the teams in a scoreless deadlock. As Dick Beddoes would say, "the game was so tense you could've grated carrots on fans' goosebumps."

With the second period face-off, the Habs rushed the Leaf net. Rousseau, with time in close, threw one low that Sawchuk sprawled to turn aside. Worsley made a fine save on Pappin during a Leaf power play. Returning to full strength, Canadiens again pressed their advantage. Then came the game's first break. Laperrière grabbed a loose puck at Toronto's blueline with three Leafs—Stanley, Kelly, and Ellis—stranded motionless seventy feet from the net. As Richard's line broke toward Sawchuk, the big defenseman wound for a slapshot. Stanley, hopelessly out of position, fifteen feet away, flashed out a leg. The shot hit his shin, rocketting the other way. Suddenly Kelly and Ellis had a two-on-one on Harper.

"Red took the puck down ice," Ellis remembers. "Until he hit the blueline I just watched, making sure I didn't go offside. When Red crossed the line, I skated as fast as I could to the net, with my head turned so I could see what was going on. Red, he was such a smart hockey player, he knew to wait until I was in position before firing. That way he might score, and if Worsley made the save he knew I might get a rebound. Which is what happened. The puck came right to my stick and I saw all that net and threw the puck upstairs."

The goal unnerved Montreal. Toronto was back quickly for more. First Pulford, digging down his wrong wing, let a hard backhand go that Worsley got a glove on. Seconds later, Harris's slapshot bounded off Stemkowski, and Pappin and Pulford had another two-on-one, with Laperrière back. Pappin made a perfect pass. Pulford's shot was targetted for the corner but Gump let his left leg trail to steer the puck wide.

This was Leaf hockey. Thirty minutes of careful defense, and then, with the opposition overextended, a stinging series of counterpunches.

After Worsley's big saves, the Habs collected themselves and resumed their steady, driving assault on Sawchuk. Stemkowski was in the penalty box when Cournoyer tried to swing around Stanley and Horton, with Keon and Duff trailing. Stanley steered the winger wide, but Keon, sliding, knocked out the legs of both defense partners. The puck came off the boards to Duff and Backstrom alone in front. Sawchuk stopped Duff's first shot. The second try, with the goalie down and out, hit the post. When Hockey Night in Canada cut to Béliveau on the bench afterwards, you could see the Captain grimace and spit out a single word:

"Damn."

The next five minutes were spent around Sawchuk. Richard put a short pass on Balon's stick in the slot. Sawchuk, falling, lifted his top leg to knock it wide. Ferguson, in close, had a free poke from the left side. So did Béliveau, from just off to the right. Béliveau then set up Ferguson again. Every time the Canadiens got the shot they wanted. But never the result.

"I don't know about the three stars," CBC colour commentator Brian McFarlane told fans across the country, "but if someone asked me right now, I think I'd have to give Sawchuk all three stars."

But the players around him were brilliant, too. Keon, at his speedy, determined best, managed to keep the Canadiens' power play a manageable headache. Hillman played astonishingly well. As in the sixth game in the Chicago series, he turned the game around with a play early in the second period. During a furious scramble in the Toronto crease, Sawchuk found himself turned the wrong way. Cournoyer, his eyes big as saucers, swung the puck around to the open side, but a fraction before he could stuff in the equalizer, Hillman slid through the crease, blocking his shot.

A clever play ended Montreal's furious second-period siege. Ellis broke up a Hab power play and spotted Conacher in the clear down the left boards. He hurried his pass, however, putting his teammate offside. Instead of touching the puck and killing play, Conacher stood guard over the loose puck. With valuable power play time running, Rousseau poked to get at the puck, but couldn't penetrate Conacher's shielding legs. Exasperated, he finally gave the winger a hook. Up went referee John Ashley's arm.

There was three minutes left in the period when Rousseau emerged from the penalty box. Again Montreal returned to the attack. The Leafs stalled, delayed, flipping the puck into the neutral zone when possible. With forty-five seconds left, Stemkowski and Pappin ragged the puck up ice. Laperrière and Harper were back for Montreal. The Leaf forwards slowed, then criss-crossed at the Hab line, fooling no one. Laperrière chased Pappin into the boards. Harper had a hold of Stemkowski's left arm in front of the net. Pappin fired a forty-foot pass-shot in the direction of the crease. It ricocheted from Stemkowski's skate off the left goalpost, curling into the back of the Montreal net.

After joining his teammates in a modest celebration, Stemkowski skated to Ashley. Hollering to be heard over the cacophonous din that was Maple Leaf Gardens, he told the referee, "Puck hit off Harper." It hadn't, but Stemkowski figured another goal might give Jim the zippy convertible *Sport Magazine* was handing out for series MVP.

At the Hab bench, Blake just stared at the clock. We bust our rear ends for two hours and they score on a fluke, he must've thought. What are you gonna do? Still, intermission was coming up. His team was down two. The Montreal coach had to think of something.

"When we were down in a game, Toe was very smart," Béliveau recalls. "If we were losing by a lot going into the third period, he wouldn't yell, 'Score five goal!' He would say, 'All I want you to do is win the period.' Well, that we could try to do. And sometime," he chuckles, "we won the period enough to win the game."

"If we were down two goals," J.C. says, "he wouldn't say, 'I want you to score three goals.' Maybe you were playing against a hot goalie; how could you expect that? He would say, 'Score the first goal. See what happens if you score the first goal.'"

The Canadiens opened the third period with another surge. As always, the centres led the way. For five minutes, Béliveau, Backstrom and Richard, players who had been with Blake since the 50s and had shared in seven Stanley Cups, dug deeper, found a little more of themselves—kept skating. So then, too, did the rest of the team.

When it finally happened, the goal Blake was looking for came with breathtaking swiftness. At six minutes, Duff idled down the left boards, one-on-three. He did a sideways double-stutter to get by Horton, weaved past Stanley, slipping a short backhand through Sawchuk's legs before skidding to the ice.

Now Blake started pacing in earnest. Lines were scrambled. Ferguson was sent out with Béliveau. Rousseau moved to centre. Roberts popped up on right wing. Laperrière rejoined J.C. on defense. But this night there was no furious gust of energy. No ten o'clock galoshes. Here the mystery of this Montreal season deepens again. For the second time in as many games, the atom was split, but there was no explosion.

Up by a single marker, the Leaf defensemen became stern-er, the forwards more energetic. Midway through the period, Kelly, playing his best game this series, skated the length of the ice, turned Harper inside out, then tested Worsley with a tricky backhand. Suddenly, the Leafs were in control. With two wingers and as many defensemen back along the boards, the Montreal forwards had nowhere to go. The Hab centres flew up the middle only to run out of room and ideas at the blueline.

At eleven minutes, the Canadiens were given an opening when Pappin was tossed for slashing. Blake turned out Duff, Béliveau and Cournoyer, with J.C. and Rousseau back. Imlach countered with Armstrong and Keon, along with Pronovost and Hillman on defense. The Habs worked hard, but every time a puck carrier turned around, Keon was there. For the first time this series, Canadiens failed to generate pressure with a man advantage. As the power play wound down, Leaf fans joined in an urgent "Go Leafs Go, Go Leafs Go." For the first time this game, the cowbells in the Montreal section failed to respond.

Still, the fragility of Toronto's lead became evident with six minutes remaining when an exhausted Richard laboured up centre, stalled in front of Stanley and Horton, then lobbed a shot over their heads. The puck bounced ten feet in front of Sawchuk. Six months earlier exactly, on November 2, J.C. pulled the Habs to a 2–2 tie with the same shot. That bounc-er had kicked ten inches to the right just past Sawchuk. Richard's flip shot bounced nine-and-a-half inches right, struck the edge of Sawchuk's arm, and dribbled a fraction wide.

The next four minutes were fought along the walls of the rink. This was where Toronto liked to play hockey, with old warriors like Armstrong shuffling the puck across every slow inch of the boards. The new Leafs showed how well they could play this game when Conacher, with the skill of a Saskatchewan curler, threw a rock the length of the ice that came to rest inches before the red line (and, of course, an icing call).

During a break with two minutes left, Gump looked to the bench. Blake, head down, sucking his lip, refused to acknowledge him. Another tense minute passed at centre. Montreal was skating uphill now, fighting to even get the puck in the Toronto end. Finally, Cournoyer squeezed inside the Leaf blueline. Hillman found the puck in the corner and whistled it down the ice for icing.

Fifty-eight seconds left. Blake finally glanced at Worsley, who skated to the bench.

The rival coaches made their last chess moves. The face-off was to to the left of Sawchuk. Blake had Ferguson, Roberts, Béliveau, and Cournoyer up front, with Laperrière and Henri back. Then he changed his mind and put Backstrom in Richard's place. There was some confusion. Both Béliveau and Backstrom were out. Who took the face-off? Blake, looking frantic, waved four fingers. Béliveau.

Watching on TV, Canada caught Imlach at the bench, barking orders. As promised, he was wearing his green check victory suit. He looked to be enjoying himself, and why not? This was his moment. He could with justification proclaim that he'd been right, dead fucking right, he'd say, in all the major hockey decisions made this long season—keeping Stemkowski instead of Kurtenbach; resisting trades for Pulford and Pappin when the team was slumping; sticking Pulford on left wing; bringing up Hillman and Walton. And he'd played Sawchuk like a ten-pound fish on a five-pound line all year. The unhappy goaltender had tugged, threatened to break away a dozen times, but Punch kept with him. More than anything, Imlach had been right in believing in all the veterans everyone else felt were too old. To pay tribute to them (and to give the world the finger), Punch composed an appropriate last-minute defensive configuration:

"Horton and Stanley," he hollered. "Pulford, Kelly, and Armstrong."

All were veterans. Except for Pulford, all were Imlach loyalists. Lord knows Punch had his troubles with number 20 this season, but Pulford had come through when it counted. He belonged out there, too. In fact, there was nothing really out of the ordinary in the Leaf line-up. Being who he was,

Punch couldn't resist one last showy move.

"Stanley, you take the face-off," he snapped.

"I kind of looked around at him and went, 'Whaaa…',"
Stanley recalls.

"Yeah, you heard me, get the hell out there."

"Thing was," Stanley says, "I hadn't taken a big face-off in,
I don't know, years. I used to take them all the time before
they made that new rule about face-off interference. Boy,
what a time for him to put me back doing face-offs, right?
Anyway, there I was skating into the circle. Sure I was worried. I had so much respect for the Canadiens. One break, one
little opening, and I knew they could win the game. Then I
look up, and oh geez, there's big Béliveau. The best. Well,
right away I start to panic. What am I gonna do? Anyways, I
finally decide to do what I used to do on face-offs. When the
referee dropped the puck, I just made up my mind to run that
big son-of-a-b right out of the rink."

When Ashley dropped the puck, Stanley lowered his
shoulder and charged, surprising Béliveau. The puck rolled to
Kelly, who nudged it up to Pulford. Pulford took three steps,
then lateralled a careful pass to Armstrong. The Leaf captain
skated past centre to avoid icing, then took an old-fashioned
wrist shot, which travelled like an arrow 100 feet into the
centre of the Montreal net, carrying right through into the
heart of the Canadiens' team.

"I didn't see the score," Stanley says. "I just followed a little behind Béliveau, listening to him yell at the referee, 'Face-
off interference, ref! Face-off interference!'"

Ashley shrugged, shook his head. What could he do? What
could anyone do? The Toronto Maple Leafs were the 1967
Stanley Cup champions.

With the final siren, Blake left the bench and crossed the
ice. He found Imlach in a happy scrum and thrust out his
hand. Punch waved Toe off, figuring he was a fan. Blake
dropped his head for an instant then tapped Punch twice on
the arm. Finally, Imlach turned and recognized his old adver-
sary.

"Congratulations," Toe offered.

"Helluva series," Punch replied.

Blake nodded, then hurried over to Bower, shaking his hand, before shuffling back to the visitors' clubhouse. He ordered the doors closed, then moved from player to player, shaking their hands. "I'm proud of you, you played well. Tonight Sawchuk was too much," he said. After giving his team ten minutes to compose themselves, Blake allowed reporters and well-wishers into the room. "This is the toughest series I ever lost," the Montreal coach told newsmen, "but I'm very proud of all my players." He stopped, then forced himself to go on. "Leafs played well," he said. "Very well." He didn't say much else. There wasn't much else to say.

Imlach had lots to say, of course. But as was often the case, he had trouble getting players to listen. When Imlach left Blake and joined his team for the ritual centre-ice hug, Stemkowski grabbed Punch's fedora and tossed it sailing to the blueline. Someone else stepped on the hat before Imlach retrieved it. In the dressing-room, Punch was loudly praising his veterans when youngsters Pappin and Walton yanked him away and dunked him in the showers. A minute later, Clancy, yelping and screaming, also took a sudsing.

There was laughter in the Leaf dressing-room. "But I think there was maybe less antics than the [three] previous times we won," Stanley recalls. "More than anything else we were just so satisfied. Especially the old guys. Everybody had told us it was over for us. Hockey was changing and we were too old. But we proved them wrong. We'd won the thing one more time. And in Centennial year to boot, when everyone figured Montreal was going to take it. Well, that was just icing on the cake. I never got more satisfaction out of anything in my hockey career. I still think about those games today."

So do the Canadiens. "My biggest disappointment in hockey," Henri has said more than once. There were tears in Ferguson's eyes that rainy night in Toronto. He wasn't alone. "I felt sick for a month afterwards," Harper says. "To lose the Stanley Cup, that was horrible, but to lose to Toronto, and have to live in Canada afterwards, oh man, everywhere you'd go you'd run into Leaf fans, well, that was like losing twice."

Yes, Harper would receive some kidding if he went back to his home town, Regina. The city was a Canadien stronghold, with a Montreal junior team. But there were Leaf fans in Saskatchewan, too. After all, Bower was from Prince Albert, and Baun hailed from Lanigan. What about Vancouver? Fergy's home, yes, but the Leafs had a junior club in Victoria. Harris was from Winnipeg, but so was Sawchuk. Then there was Kirkland Lake? Two Habs (Backstrom and Duff), and one Maple Leaf (Hillman) came from that small Ontario town. Toe still had childhood friends back in Ontario mining country, just as Punch had well-wishers in Quebec City from his coaching days with the Aces.

Every Leaf and Canadien was from somewhere in the country. And every part of the country was somewhere in both teams. In hockey, if nothing else, Canada was truly bicultural. On this May evening in 1967, seventeen million people went to bed thinking about the same thing. Half went to sleep happy, the other half depressed. (The halves switched every year back then.)

One Canadian didn't go to sleep at all.

After getting his photo taken with the Stanley Cup, Imlach and a few cronies retired to the Gardens Hot Stove Lounge, then back to Punch's home in Scarborough. A little past dawn, Dodo chased the last hanger-on out the door. Punch went to bed, but couldn't sleep. He kept going over the game, the season—all the seasons. By ten o'clock, Friday morning, he'd had enough. With nowhere else to go, he headed back to the Gardens. No one was there except Bobby Haggert, who was busy stowing equipment.

"What you doing here?" the trainer asked.

"Couldn't sleep," Imlach said. "I knew I shouldn't have had that bottle of champagne at five o'clock." Just then Pronovost walked in. He and Imlach compared hangovers. Imlach complained about his stomach. "Go and get some honey from Joey in the Hot Stove," Marcel suggested. Punch left in search of medicine. On the way back, he decided to drop down and have a look at his rink. Standing by the boards with a cup of honey in hand, he looked out at the blue-white expanse that was home to a million dreams. He should've been happy. He'd won. The whole country had seen him do it, wearing his spiffy new jacket. But he wasn't

satisfied. Something was wrong. What was it? Finally, he figured it out. There was no one in the stands, cheering. Blake
wasn't across the way, glowering. And where were the
Canadiens and Leafs? They should be here. They should
always be here. Punch hurried back into the dressing-room for
Haggert and Pronovost.

"How come everybody isn't on the ice?" he asked.

FIRST PERIOD
No scoring
Penalties—Conacher (interference) 2:30; Backstrom (holding)
5:36; Béliveau (cross-checking) 10:21; Conacher (boarding)
13:25; Ferguson (elbowing) 18:50

SECOND PERIOD
1. Toronto, Ellis 2nd (Kelly, Stanley) 6:25
2. Toronto, Pappin 7th (Stemkowski, Pulford) 19:24
Penalties—Harper (holding) 3:05; Stemkowski (cross-checking)
7:14; Stanley (hooking) 13:23; Rousseau (tripping) 14:44

THIRD PERIOD
3. Montreal, Duff 2nd (Harris) 5:28
4. Toronto, Armstrong 2nd (Pulford, Kelly) 19:13
Penalties—Pappin (slashing) 11:44

Shots on goal
Montreal   17   14   10 — 41
Toronto   11   16   9 — 36

Crowd noise

"Losing to Toronto like that was a horrible
feeling, but I think it helped the team
maybe. To learn how to win, sometime you
have to know what it feels like to lose.
When we lost to the Leafs it was awful, eh?
Me, I would remember that feeling in every
Stanley Cup I played after that. Same with
the other players on the Canadiens, I think.
Next year we won. Year after that we won.
We kept on winning because we didn't ever
want that losing feeling again."

—Yvan Cournoyer

18
Unhappy Endings

After surrendering the Stanley Cup to Toronto, the Canadiens flew back to Montreal. None of the players felt like getting up the next morning, but there was one more bit of business to attend to.

"The day after the season ended, if we win or lose, Toe would invite the team to his tavern [on Ste. Catherine just west of Guy]," remembers Cournoyer. "That was the best time. All year Toe was tense, thinking of what he had to do to make the team win, but that day was different. It was all over. He could relax. He would serve hamburgers and beer to us with a big smile on his face. He was happy. You could see then how much he loved the players."

"It was terrific seeing him like that," Harper recalls. "Loose and telling jokes. Say someone bragged about a play he made that season, Toe would crack, 'Yeah, some skater, remember that night in Boston when you fell and couldn't get up. First time I ever saw a player swim to the bench.' And everyone would break up. We'd talk over the season. All the funny moments. The camaraderie, the closeness that day…well, it was just terrific."

Bryan Watson, who would rejoin the Canadien organization the following season, remembers Doug Harvey talking about those late spring get-togethers at Blake's Tavern. "'It's not the games or the Stanley Cups I miss,' Harvey said, 'it's those parties at Toe's after the season was over. The feeling in that room, that was the best part about being a Canadien. I wouldn't have missed those days for all the world.'"

After their downtown Stanley Cup parade, Friday May 4, the Leafs also enjoyed a team party at Stafford Smythe's mansion in Etobicoke. After a few too many beers, Horton started throwing guests in the pool. Later, Shack cross-checked Gary Smith's date. "Eddie came up to her. Next thing I knew her boobs were hanging out of her dress," Suitcase remembers.

But the wild, happy times were over for Imlach's Leafs. The Stanley Cup champions were a white dwarf—an exploded star that is still visible in the heavens long after it has disappeared. Even as the Leafs rejoiced that warm spring evening, the organization was dying. Government investigators would soon prove that Smythe's house had been renovated with funds appropriated for the reconstruction of Maple Leaf Gardens. Soon, Ballard and Smythe would be headed for jail.* Before leaving, the Leaf owners auctioned off Toronto's top farm teams, Rochester and Victoria, for $900,000. After Gerry Cheevers, Brad Park and Garry Unger were allowed to escape, the long-ignored junior league system finally collapsed.

Imlach himself was an extinct species. "With expansion came unions, new teams, agents...coaches couldn't run players' lives any more," Milt Dunnell says. "Times were changing. If a player didn't like it in Toronto, there was another team he could go to. Guys like Imlach couldn't run roughshod over people any more."

Lord knows he tried. Imlach fought the birth of Eagleson's union tooth and claw, driving player representatives Pulford and Conacher from the club. He even tried to sneak Sawchuk by expansion teams, listing him as a skater ("well, he can skate can't he?"). Despite, or perhaps because of Imlach's

---

* Smythe never made it. He died of a bleeding ulcer a few weeks before his trial date, in early October, 1971.

efforts, the team fell apart. Kelly retired. Mahovlich had another breakdown, then was traded to Detroit along with Stemkowski. Pappin was foolishly dealt to Chicago for a spent Pierre Pilote. Hillman was sent packing after a feud over a $500 raise. Finally, at the end of the 1968-69 season, Imlach himself was fired by Smythe. He expected Clancy to go with him as a matter of course. He didn't. When the two next met, at a league function months later, King approached his old friend and smiled hello. "Fuck you," Punch snarled, speeding past.

There were other unhappy endings:

Six seasons later, Horton visited Maple Leaf Gardens for the last time as a member of Imlach's Buffalo Sabres. He played brilliantly for two periods (was named third star in fact), then broke his jaw, left the game, took some painkillers, left the rink, said goodbye to Imlach and old teammate Dave Keon on Church Street, left Toronto, stopped in at the head office of his donut chain in Oakville, had a couple of drinks and a few more painkillers, then left this world, driving his sports car off a highway in the middle of the night.

Three years after his heroic stand against Chicago and Montreal, Sawchuk was a part-time goalie for the New York Rangers. That spring he returned to his house in Long Island after an unsuccessful reconciliation with his wife in Detroit. Morose and increasingly despondent, one night he took a drunken swing at roomate, Ron Stewart, missed and fell, impaling himself on a backyard barbecue pit.

"They rushed him to the hospital," Emile Francis said later. "And the next day we had the doctors lined up at Cornell in Manhattan. The tests showed he was bleeding internally, and he was fading in and out. They had to operate. We got a priest. I'll never forget this: They were wheeling him to the operating room. He took his Red Wings Stanley Cup ring off. He turned to me and said, 'Make sure my son gets this. And make sure my son [a goalie] gets a chance.' I said, 'You'll come out of it, don't worry.' They operated for six hours. He died at six the next morning. I had to go the morgue. It was the Memorial Day weekend, and about 30 people got knocked off in New York. This guy came up to me with breath that could blow you over. He goes, 'Francis, follow me.' We go down winding steps. [Terry] was laid out on the cement floor, in one of those big body bags we carry our hockey sticks in. He had a tag around his neck. There he was, the greatest goalie I ever seen."

Blake coached the Canadiens one more season, bringing the team another championship, his eighth as a coach. Then he retired, leaving the Canadiens with grace and dignity. But he couldn't let go of the game. Those who knew him best say that he was restless in retirement. An unhappy ghost that occupied the Forum. He lost his temper more often. Yelled at people he didn't know. Soon he stopped knowing anyone. In the late 80s the indomitable Blake fell victim to Alzheimer's. He died quietly in the spring of 1995.

Toe gathered countless accolades over the years. Peers acknowledged that he was the greatest coach of his era. Blake also received another rare distinction: an apology (of sorts) from Imlach. Punch once surprised Dickie Moore, a friend of Toe's, by saying, "I know Toe doesn't like me much, but he's one helluva guy." The story got back to Blake the day Imlach passed away, from his fourth heart attack, December 1, 1987. Toe smiled and said, "Punch was a good coach and Toronto left their mark on us a few times. When he was there, he made all our lives a lot more interesting."

Blake and Imlach's teams won nine of ten Stanley Cups in the 60s. In doing so they made all our lives more interesting. For many Canadian fans the game has never been the same. In 1966, there were six major league hockey teams in the world. By 1972, with expansion and the WHA, there were 27. No one even noticed when Montreal and Toronto were put in separate divisions in 1974. The rivalry was dead.

Except in memories. The first person I interviewed for this book was J.C. Tremblay. I had no idea at the time J.C. was ill. (He would die a year later, succumbing to a long battle with cancer.) I got his number in Switzerland and started dialing. He wasn't there, but I was given another number. Then another number. Finally, I got hold of him. It was late in the evening over there and he had no idea why I was phoning. I told him I wanted to talk about his flip shot. "Who are you?"

he asked. Finally, we hit a conversational rhythm and he began speaking freely. Soon he was enjoying himself. Near the end of our conversation, I asked how he figured the old Canadiens would do today.

"Oh, I don't know. We were pretty good, but today everyone is bigger and faster and stronger."

"Toe would find a way to win," I said.

He laughed. "I remember an old Canadien from the 40s came to visit Toe at the Forum one day at practice. He started giving Toe the business about the team. We weren't playing too good, maybe. He was saying how great the old Canadiens were. Like they could beat us. Toe, he just laughed. 'Sure, sure,' he said. Then later someone asked him how good that guy was. Toe said, 'Not as good as he thinks he is. The only thing that gets better with age are memories.'"

Acknowledgments

In the spring of 1967, my grade seven Centennial project was to keep a scrapbook of the NHL playoffs. I clipped articles out of the Ottawa *Citizen*. Dad sometimes brought home copies of Montreal papers. And a kid next door, Raymond Gagne, the Globe delivery boy, dropped extras my way. Back then I thought the Montreal *Star*'s Red Fisher and the *Globe and Mail*'s Dick Beddoes were absolutely terrific. Reading them 29 years later, I'm even more impressed. Fisher was (and is) the best hockey beat reporter around. You'd have to wear skates to get any closer to the action. I got much of the dialogue involving Blake from his columns, including the story about Toe's house painter losing number six. Beddoes was a delightful clubhouse snoop who captured the nutty flavour of the Imlach era. "You're not asposed to write that stuff!" Punch once shouted at him. I'm glad he did. Much of Beddoes "stuff" is sprinkled throughout this book.

Indeed, this history is as much about the work of hockey writers as it is the players they covered, and I'm very much indebted to countless beat reporters and sportswriters from the period. In particular, I'd like to thank Pat Curran (Montreal *Gazette*), Jacques Beauchamp (Montréal *Matin*), Louis Cauz, Scott Young and Rex MacLeod (Toronto *Globe and Mail*), Red Burnett and Milt Dunnell (Toronto *Star*), George Gross (Toronto *Telegram*), Gerald Eskenazi (New York *Times*), and Ted Damata (Chicago *Tribune*) for the wealth of material they left behind. I also found magazine articles (in *MacLean's*, *Weekend Magazine*, *Sports Illustrated*, and *Hockey Illustrated*) by Trent Frayne, Paul Rimstead, Peter Gzowski, Pete Axthelm, Stan Fischler, and Jim Hunt illuminating and useful.

Books consulted include: *Hockey is a Battle* and *Heaven and Hell in the NHL*, by Punch Imlach and Scott Young; Scott Young's *The Leafs I Knew*; Billy Harris's *The Glory Years*; William Houston's *Inside Maple Leaf Gardens*; Brian Conacher's *Hockey In Canada: The Way it Is*; Doug Hunter's *Open Ice: The Tim Horton Story*; Trent Frayne's *The Mad Men of Hockey*; Jean Béliveau's *My Life in Hockey*; Red Fisher's *Hockey, Heroes, and Me*; John Ferguson's *Thunder and Lightning*; Paul Henderson's *Shooting For Glory*, and Stan Fischler's *The Rivalry*.

I'd also like to thank all the hockey people who took time to share their thoughts with me, including John Halligan, Emile Francis, Harry Sinden, Glenn Hall, Bryan Watson, Eddie Giacomin, Sam Pollock, Rogatien Vachon, J.C. Tremblay, Terry Harper, Jean Béliveau, John Ferguson, Yvan Cournoyer, Allan Stanley, Red Kelly, Brian Conacher, Ron Ellis, Gary Smith, Brian Kilrea, Art Skov, Red Fisher, George Gross, Milt Dunnell, Louis Cauz and Stan Fischler. Thanks also to private citizens, Larry Black, Chris Murray, Pierre Godbout, Alain Richard, Therese Seguin, Eric Johnson, Ken Rockburn, Sheila Bird, Bill Kretzel and Frank and Bill Cole for helping reel in the years. Little bows as well to Doug Hunter and Bill Arnold for lending me hockey broadcast tapes from the 60s. And special thanks to Curtis Field at the Canadian Consulate in New York; I still owe you about $12.00 in newspaper photocopying.

Most of all, I'd like to thank the players...all the players from the last years of the six-team league. From 1961-1967, I don't think I missed a Saturday or Wednesday night game on TV. The players from that era defined hockey for me. Even today, if I see a number 14 for the Leafs, I'm surprised to dis-cover someone other than Dave Keon inside the jersey.

Number 21 has to be Bob Baun. For Montreal, numero trois will always be J.C. Tremblay. Number 22? John Ferguson, of course. The clubs never retired their sweaters, but I did years ago. Finally, this book is for and about all the great players on the Blake-Imlach era Canadiens and Leafs.

Assists: A million thanks to my wife, Jacquie McNish, for all her comfort and support. I owe you one. Maybe more than one. Thanks also to Meg Masters and Dean Cooke for tea and sympathy.

Index

341